Thank you for
at the Saugatuck-Douglas
Rotary Club!
Laree

Raising the Roof

A History of the Buildings and Architecture in the Saugatuck and Douglas Area

REVISED EDITION

James Schmiechen

with photographs by
Vicky Stull *&* Bill Werme

The Saugatuck-Douglas Historical Society
2006

The publication of this book was funded by
the Saugatuck-Douglas Historical Society Publication Fund,
which was established in 1996 through the generous
donations of members and friends to document the history of the
Saugatuck-Douglas area. Other titles include:

*Painting the Town: A Century of Art
in the Saugatuck Area,* 1997

Heroes, Rogues, & Just Plain Folks, 1998

*Raising the Roof: A History of the Buildings and Architecture
in the Saugatuck-Douglas Area,* 1999

Lost & Found: Ghost Towns of the Saugatuck Area, 2000

*Storm, Fire, & Ice: Shipwrecks of the
Saugatuck Area,* 2001

Off the Record: The Photographs of Bill Simmons, 2002

Snapshots: A Saugatuck Album, 2003

*Lincoln's Ready-Made Soldiers: Saugatuck Area
Men in the Civil War,* 2005

BOOK DESIGN: Ken Carls

Distributed by
Wayne State University Press
Detroit, Michigan 48201

COPYRIGHT 2006
Saugatuck-Douglas Historical Society
Post Office Box 617 | Douglas, Michigan 49406

ISBN: 0-9657042-0-3

INTRODUCTION

. . . *to the* FIRST EDITION | "What architecture? What buildings?" | This book tells a story about the collection of buildings that make up the Saugatuck and Douglas area. Generally quite common both in size and style and some of architectural and historic merit, these buildings act as a mirror of area history. Admittedly the area does not possess a large number of extraordinary specimens of "Architecture" (with a capital "A"), but the two villages and the lakeshore can boast of a good plenty of common honest buildings from many layers of the American past and of every architectural style. As separate structures, many deserve preservation and/or some sort of "restoration." But what makes this story worth telling is what these buildings, as a group, say to us. Streets and structures are woven together into a unique visual and social fabric, into the threads of which are enmeshed our historical memory. This patchwork quilt of our past tells us where—and who—we are.

The character of our villagescapes is derived as much from the spaces in between built structures as it is from the individual buildings themselves. Thus, it is in the conglomerate that these buildings contain their power to define this place as "home."

So, the purpose of this book is first to define and describe what is good about Saugatuck and Douglas area architecture and second, to show how "reading" buildings is a way of connecting with our past. *If we listen, our built environment will tell us its fascinating story.*

. . . *to the* REVISED EDITION | "Cracks in the Looking Glass" | This revised and expanded edition continues the adventure of using the buildings and architecture of the Lake Michigan port villages of Saugatuck, Douglas, and Pier Cove as a mirror of the life and times of people who lived there and how they interacted with each other, their environment, and the outside world. From this mirror of the past we derive a sense of place—learning where and who we are—but always urging the question: how well does the Saugatuck and Douglas townscape/landscape reflect its history?

The answer is partly upbeat—but only partly. In 2004 both Saugatuck and Douglas received the prestigious national "Preserve America" designation; Saugatuck was named a Michigan "Cool City," and the Saugatuck-Douglas Historical Society received the Michigan Heritage Guardian award. These distinctions grow out of the efforts of people within the communities and the Historical Society to protect the traditional townscape/landscape in a manner that gives meaning to contemporary life. The benefits are many—not the least being economic.

But the mirror also reflects a darker side of the picture: a view of our fragile "traditional" small towns overwhelmed by intense pressures to grow, succumbing to the forces of sprawl that threaten to render them anonymous. Big houses crowd out small homes and cottages, historic structures and farmland give way to subdivisions, streets are widened, trees and even hills are mowed down, and the surrounding countryside is built over. History and nature are uprooted, and the substance of place—in all its quirkiness and patina—is in danger of being lost. Quick profits are taken and with them the town's soul.

This book argues that good architecture is simply that which expresses the many layers of the remarkable, sometimes common, often unique history of these legendary Michigan villages collectively called "Saugatuck."

TIMOTHY COATES HOUSE

1852

521 Butler Street | Saugatuck

Coates was one of Saugatuck's early lighthouse keepers and merchants. He and his wife Mary had 6 sons—several of whom became well-known ship captains. The house is a classic example of a rather common Greek Revival house—gable to the front, white clapboard, with a boldly projecting roof and corner recessed columns. The porch was added later. "Greek Revival" was the most "American" and "democratic" architecture ever invented—and hence an important part of America's early identity.

CHAPTER ONE

Pioneer Builders and Buildings: From Log House to Greek Revival, 1830 – 1865

THE CONTEXT | Who were the people who built the first buildings? Saugatuck, Douglas and surrounding early communities such as Pier Cove, Ganges, Goshorn, Wallinville and Plummerville—later often awarded the collective air of magic called "Saugatuck"—grew out of the woods and water as rather typical Lake Michigan mill-harbor towns to which rugged people came in search of work and fortune—largely by exploiting spectacular natural resources. The Butlers came to speculate in real estate, the Morrisons and the Gerbers to use local hemlock trees to process hides into leather, the Wades, Johnsons, Stockbridges, Plummers, and Dutchers to cut the trees and mill logs into lumber and shingles—and so on. A few of this generation or the next became senators or congressmen, some Civil War heroes, some became very rich, some failed, and many, simply through hard work, succeeded in carving out their own niche. Most of the pioneer settlers were from eastern states—particularly New York, Connecticut, and Pennsylvania, and some were European immigrants. Although some arrived on foot or by wagon from points south, this frontier history is integrally connected to the growth of Lake Michigan transportation routes and, most important, the growth of its great metropolis, Chicago. In a real sense, it was Chicago which was the gateway to Saugatuck—the place from which poured people, capital and, most of all, an insatiable demand for lumber, leather, grain, and fruit, and, later, summer resorting spots. Chicago was, as the historian William Cronon recently called it, "nature's metropolis"—binding the city and the country into an expanding and integrated economy. The lakeshore port villages of western Michigan became outposts of the metropolitan market.[1]

More important, perhaps, is the fact that over time the villages that make up "Saugatuck" became important cultural outposts of Chicago as well—providing the natural settings for sport, spiritual enrichment, and the arts.

Saugatuck's first white settlers were William and Mary Butler who set to shore where the Kalamazoo River meets Lake Michigan, arriving by the schooner "Madison" in 1830. They eventually rafted the several miles upriver to build their crude house and trading post at what is now the corner of Saugatuck's Butler and Mason Streets. For the next fifteen or so years Saugatuck (first known as Kalamazoo, then as Newark) was nothing but a few dozen people crowded into a half dozen log or rough-plank shacks—local "plank" houses being made of large milled boards laid side-by-side (vertically), possibly in the manner of the native Ojibwa people who lived nearby. The area's economy, which stretched east to Wallinville (now Clearbrook) and south along the Lake Shore Road (laid out in the early 1840s) to Pier Cove and Ganges, was based on a good number of small leather tanneries and sawmills. Even though Butler had his village platted (memorializing some of his family in the naming of the streets), his new town and his own fortune were disappointing even by pioneer standards—so much so that some early arrivals even left town to head on out west.

Saugatuck's laggard growth was given an economic (and technological) push when

LUMBER YARDS & SAUGATUCK LUMBER
1883
Chicago

Chicago was the major market for Michigan lumber. From the 1840s onward, Saugatuck-Douglas boats carried millions of feet of lumber and shingles up the South Branch of the Chicago River to be stacked in these yards, some of it to build Chicago and then rebuild it after the Great Fire of 1871—but some of it was re-exported to the cities and the prairies to the great west. By 1883 the great lumber boom in both Saugatuck and Chicago was essentially over.

RAISING THE ROOF

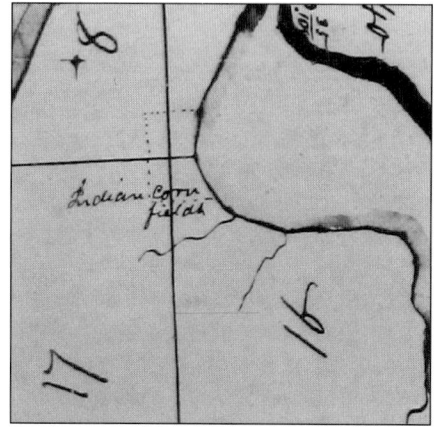

INDIAN CORN FIELDS
ca. 1835
Douglas
Ferry Street at Campbell Road

A rare "white-man's" documentation acknowledging Native American land use. It is known that William G. Butler, the first settler, negotiated "treaties" with the Indians but about what is not clear. In addition to this, a second sort of acknowledgement of Indian land use was a burial ground on the area that became the Saugatuck village fire house (today the village hall). [Commercial Record, May 9, 1890.] Early settlers, it appears, recognized this Indian right for sometime after white settlement in 1830. In the eyes of white colonists, only cornfields and burying grounds could be regarded as real property of Indians because it was the only property they held that had definable boundaries or were "improved" sufficiently (such as a planted field) to call their own. [Corn Field Map: Detail from a larger map drawn by Butler, SDHS Archives]

a new lumber mill settlement opened close to the very spot the Butlers had landed only a few years earlier. Called Singapore, it was here in 1837 that seven boilers were installed in a mill to furnish steam power for a huge lumbering operation which, in turn, attracted further investors to the area, one of whom was Stephen A. Morrison who began to put new capital into Saugatuck's first real factory, its tannery. Within ten years, and with a staggering demand for lumber in the rapidly growing Chicago, three new lumber mills, three shingle mills, and an enlarged tannery interrupted nature's riverfront with smokestacks and sail masts. Like most of Michigan in the 1850s, Saugatuck (with Singapore) flourished. Entrepreneurs made their fortunes in the pine lumber trade: Daniel Gerber, O. R. Johnson, H. D. Moore, F. B. Stockbridge, H. B. Moore, among others. Unfortunately, some of these local profits simply provided capital for enterprises elsewhere.

THE VILLAGES | Saugatuck proper became a village clustered along the river and along a half dozen carefully laid out streets: new houses, warehouses to hold flour and other goods brought from up river for shipment across the lake, a few shops, various mills and mill-ponds, lodging houses for mill "hands" and, in time, several boat building yards. On the periphery of this rearrangement of former Native American space were a number of lumber camps—thriving, but temporary, colonies of lumbermen, often complete with general store, post office, mess hall and sleeping quarters.[2] We don't know much of anything about how the lumbermen got on with the local Indians, except that Butler had some treaties with them—and they marked out certain plots of land for growing food. Saugatuck and Douglas boomed for a decade until a nationwide depression in 1857 threw the local economy on the skids.

Across Lake Kalamazoo to the south, "pioneer" Douglas evolved slightly later but with a similar building pattern. It came by its first sawmill, founded in 1851 by Jonathan Wade one of the first of the Singapore mill owners, and thereafter was settled by people from Saugatuck and Singapore, and then by large families from Canada, Pennsylvania, and elsewhere—some coming by way of Chicago. As a tannery and lumber mill town (Wade's mill later became Michigan's largest basket factory), many of its earliest dwellings were "workers cottages" and boarding houses for the mill workers. Between 1851 and the beginning of the Civil War in 1861, about 25 structures were built along the Douglas riverfront and its newly platted streets. In fact, the village was platted as two separate clan-dominated rival villages: Dudleyville of the Wades, and Douglas of the Dutchers. The Douglas economy also slowed with the coming of the Civil War, the only new structure of note a large residence-hotel, called Wade's Tavern (also known at times as the Douglas House and the Eagle Hotel) built by the Wades.

Meanwhile another village was in the making along the lakeshore to the south. The first pier was built at Pier Cove in 1849, and the first permanent settler built a one-room house in 1852. As the little village's economy thrived, the villagers built more, larger piers out into Lake Michigan to serve as the export point for lumber from nearby mills, including those in Ganges. In 1858 Pier Cove had a population of 140.[3] By the 1860s the village consisted of several dozen buildings, including several mills, four stores, a hotel, a schoolhouse, a post office, and more than a dozen houses. The

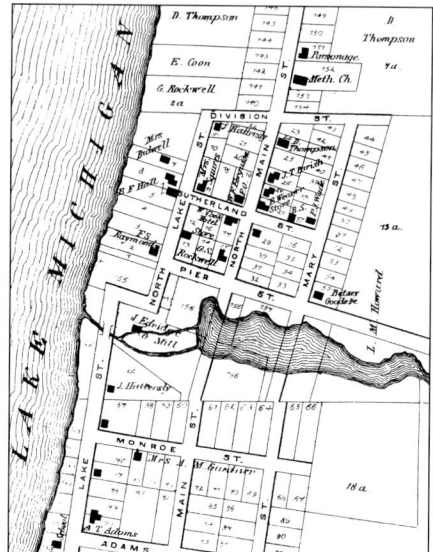

PIER COVE
1873

A major shipping point for lumber and other products of the woods and farms, shown here about twenty years after the first settlers arrived. North Main and South Lake Streets are now Lakeshore Drive. In the 1860s there were 34 buildings in the town—and three lawyers! Most of the structures were abandoned as the village declined in the later 1870s—but the Adams (now Simonds) and Raymond (now Curtis) Houses still stand, as does the parsonage. The Methodist Church was moved to Ganges and later burned; other structures were moved to Fennville. The hotel stayed open until 1875. On one night in 1871, 101 couples danced in the hotel hall. [Roberta Simonds, "Notes on Pier Cove," SDHS Archives. See also, *Lost and Found: Ghost Towns of the Saugatuck Area*. Saugatuck-Douglas Historical Society (2000).]

village prospered with the growth of the fruit industry, at least until the freezes of 1899 destroyed much of the local traffic in peaches. Today the mills, the piers, and the fleet of schooners that moved goods back and forth across the lake are gone; but the Methodist Parsonage, the Nikols House (Orchard House), and the Adams-

A History of the Buildings and Architecture in the Saugatuck and Douglas Area

LAST MILL AT PIER COVE
1873 (photo ca. 1898)

Looking west. The mill, with its giant waterwheel, at Pier Cove was built in 1853 by Charles Richards and functioned as a grist (flour) mill on the second floor and a wood turning mill for a small furniture factory on the lower floor. The mill ceased operation in 1882—and it collapsed about 1915. Another mill, a steam saw mill, was nearby.

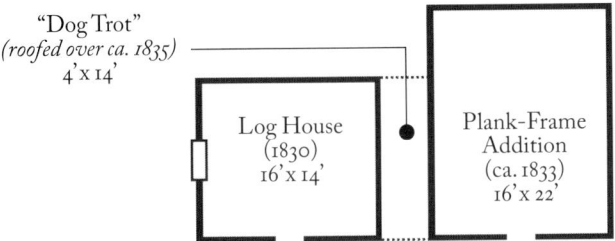

THE FIRST HOUSE
Butler's Floor Plan
1830
Saugatuck

William and Mary Butler constructed a one-room house of hand-hewn square logs (with a fireplace) at the northwest corner of Butler and Mason Streets in 1830, and in about 1833 added a a plank-framed house of cut boards a few feet away—most probably with a fenced, roofed center passage in between for protecting the Butlers' cows and pigs. This open space (called a "dog trot") was later walled in to join the two houses. In 1834 this structure housed 15 people and was also a general store.

Curtis house, all on Lakeshore Drive, still stand.

THE FIRST HOUSES: CROWDED, DISPOSABLE, AND DARK | William and Mary Butler had no choice in housing but that which was temporary and disposable. Their one-room log house (14 x 16 feet) was typical of the time: logs hewn square and laid one atop the other to make a solid wall and then attached at the corners by interlocking or notching. It was safe, probably warm, but small and dark. There is no recorded image of this house, but it was probably similar to the log house built a few years later by James McCormick near Fennville, although McCormick used sawn (or "milled") planks for the floors and roof while the Butlers had to make do with dirt floor and split log roof. The Butler house was solid but difficult to add on to and was enormously labor intensive to build. By the time the Butlers were ready to enlarge the original house in 1833, milled planks (or "board" lumber) had become available from upriver mills. Their new plank house appears to have been set a few feet away from the log house in order to create a protected yard (known as a "dog-trot")—which, in turn, was eventually roofed over to join the two into one structure. By 1840 this plank house, or "shanty," form was the norm, as evidenced by Mr. Butler's brother-law's house, the Levi Loomis House, in nearby Ganges, and Jonathan Wade's plank house that still stands at 149 Washington Street, Douglas.

The Butler's little house was also a trading post (including the sale of liquor to local Native Americans), and practically a hotel. For the Butlers and other early families, work, leisure, and family life took place side-by-side in virtually the same spaces. This too was the case with Stephen and Mary Morrison, ultimately the most important of Saugatuck's founders—who, incidentally, regarded the Natives in a more affirmative manner. Morrison, who purchased Saugatuck's small leather tanning factory in 1836, built a two-story plank wood house for himself and his family close by the tannery along Culver Street at the bottom of the Allegan Street hill (probably Lot No.199). It was 18 x 20 feet, with a "living" room in the front and a small bedroom and pantry in the rear with "unfinished and unplastered" rooms, probably for lodgers, above. Not only was the Morrison's living room a workspace—they operated a general store there and the village Post Office—but also served as what amounted to a hotel, often offering a free refuge for local Indians who sometimes slept by the Morrison fire.

As in many similar places in America, these frontier houses, be they log houses or plank wood shanties, were treated as temporary and strictly functional shelters to be disposed of or altered as soon as the land or lumber lottery paid off. Protection was the key—as later generations were reminded with stories of the early days of wolves, snakes, and even

PIONEER CHILD
Julia E. Morrison Francis
1846-1924

Born in her parents' plank cabin along what is now Lake Street in Saugatuck in 1846, one day little Julia was lost in the woods. After much searching, her parents asked their Indian neighbors for help—and soon thereafter the Indians found her picking flowers on top of the nearby hill. The Morrison's tanning factory brought them considerable wealth and little Julia eventually attended a private school for girls in Allegan. She died in Saugatuck in 1924.

LOG HOUSE
James McCormick's House
1837
Fennville Area

A typical area log house, probably similar to the first Saugatuck dwelling of William and Mary Butler—although McCormick's house had the luxury of a sawn plank roof and floors.

PLANK HOUSE
Levi Loomis's House
1840
Ganges

With the sawn planks running vertically (probably with "battens" to cover the cracks), this was an advance over the hand-hewn log house of Butler—and is probably close to the typical local dwelling between 1833 and 1850, including Wade's plank house in Douglas.

3

WHAT IS A "DOG TROT"?

The protected space between two sections of early houses used for sheltering animals

THE EARLIEST REARRANGEMENT OF LAND USE: THE CONQUEST OF NATURE

Because the Kalamazoo River did not have enough water discharge to scour a clear channel through the tremendous sandbars and dunes created by the winds and waves of Lake Michigan, the river backed up to create Kalamazoo Lake as well as marsh flats many miles inland. Being impounded on its way to the Lake, the river formed a great twisting of water resembling an oxbow. It was out of this natural tension between wind, sand, water—and human industry— that earliest white-man's architecture arose: the government lighthouse and pier, docks and warehouses to store goods coming from and going to the outside world, the first commercial fishing settlements, and the first mill to process the great white pine trees that were hauled out of the nearby forests. All connected by paths or water routes, the organizing principle of this enterprise was access to resources, and, consequently, the conquest of nature.

OLD LIGHTHOUSE, HARBOR, & FISHTOWN
ca. 1906
Saugatuck

Few structures were as important in the early life of western Allegan County as that of the Saugatuck Lighthouse. As most "lighthouses," the Saugatuck structure (originally listed as the "Kalamazoo Lighthouse") housed the keeper and his family as well as the light—and as a result the lighthouse held the memories and history of travelers, shipwrecks, fishermen, and the many stories of the lake. Built to replace the earlier 1838 stone lighthouse, the 1859 structure shown here sat on the tallest dune at the mouth of the Kalamazoo River and was considered built to last for hundreds of years. It was 30 x 32 feet in dimension, two floors (a total of 3,033 sq. feet), with 2 wings to the rear and a 15-foot tower atop the roof at the front. It sat on 10" x 10" timber beams and iron plates which, in turn, were connected to 1" diameter iron bars attached to stone foundations. The walls were nearly 9" thick. It had eleven rooms. An addition, including a porch, was added in 1898. The wide board siding was replaced with sawn shingles in 1898. The last lighthouse keeper ended his service in 1913. Within this "Lighthouse Reservation" were, over the years, Mr. Nichols' warehouse compound, a tool house, boathouse, barn, and an area for raising livestock. It was destroyed by a tornado on April 3, 1956, after which its owner, Arthur F. Deam, used salvaged materials as parts of a new "lighthouse cottage" on the site. It remains as a private cottage.

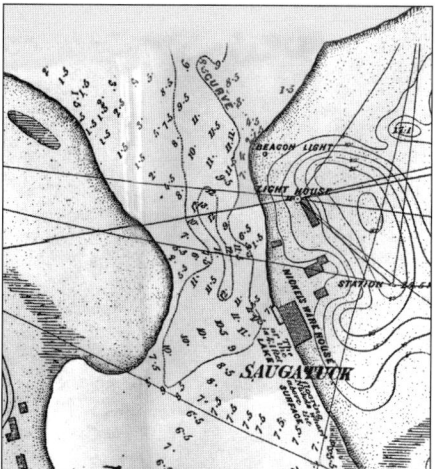

THE LIGHTHOUSE AREA
1857
Saugatuck

The original harbor entrance (now covered over with sand) had, over time, two lighthouses (although there appears to be an earlier "light" and the house of a keeper of the light). This government survey map of 1857 shows the site of the 1838 stone lighthouse, which collapsed in March 1859. (A second lighthouse was built in 1859, shown in the 1906 photo to the right.) The later piers are not shown. The trail to Saugatuck via the chain ferry is shown at lower right. [United States Department of the Interior, National Park Service, *National Register of Historic Places*, "Saugatuck Harbor," (2001) p. 2.]

The map also shows the warehouse, boarding house and wharf established by Steven D. Nichols beginning in 1834. Nichols was a merchant and first lighthouse keeper (1839-1844). One of the structures was probably Saugatuck's first saloon—kept by Moses Nichols (no relation) who was described as "a tavern keeper and vendor of ardent spirits." On the south side of the harbor was a warehouse operated by William Butler, the first settler, and a two story warehouse owned by H. H. Comstock. [James Sheridan, *Saugatuck Through the Years*, Chapter 3; *Allegan County History*, "1834."]

4

A History of the Buildings and Architecture in the Saugatuck and Douglas Area

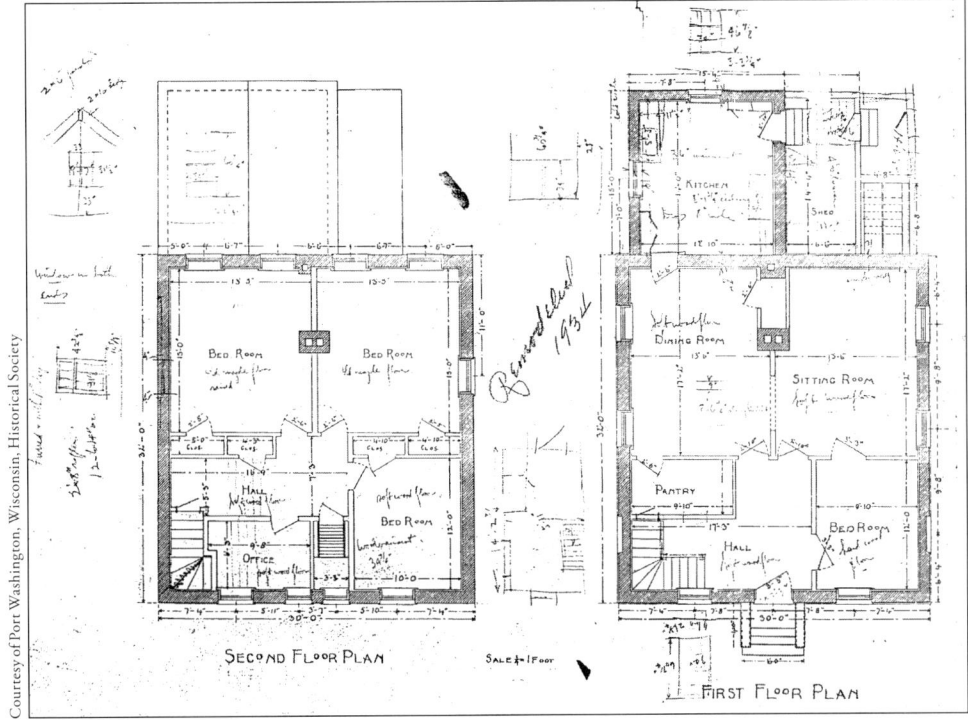

Courtesy of Port Washington, Wisconsin, Historical Society

† LIGHTHOUSE FLOOR PLAN
1859
Saugatuck

The U. S. Government issued a number of standard plans for their lighthouses. The Port Washington, Wisconsin, lighthouse plan of 1860 (shown) was nearly exact to that of the Saugatuck lighthouse. The primary differences were the exterior material (the Port Washington house was of brick whereas the Saugatuck house was of wood), the location and the levels of the rear additions, windows, chimney, and substructure.

† LIGHTHOUSE COTTAGE
20th c.
Saugatuck

After the government closed the lighthouse in 1914 it was leased to Frederic Fursman, the director of the Ox-Bow School of Painting, for $10 per year. The Ox-Bow School was located at the bend of what became (after 1906) the Ox-Bow Lagoon. He used the lighthouse as a cottage-studio for several people connected to the school. The last was Arthur Deam, a professor of Architecture at the University of Illinois. Deam later purchased the property from the government and restored the lighthouse for use as a family cottage until it was destroyed by the tornado of 1956. Portions of the old lighthouse properties remain as an important archeological/historical site.

Norm & Connie Deam Family Collection

THE FIRST LIGHTHOUSE KEEPER'S SON TELLS A STORY

"My father, Stephen D. Nichols, . . .

. . . came West to Chicago from Hampstead, New Hampshire in 1830 (and then to) the mouth of the Kalamazoo river in- 1834 where he built a store, warehouse, and docks and became keeper of the stone Light house ; [nearby was]) a barn where my father stabled his horse (that) . . . gradually covered with sand. I well remember just the roof showing above the surface of the ground . . . he also had a store in Singapore about 1858 and just opposite a long shed built of slabs. One end was used for drying slabs and the other for a school-house. An old circular saw was used for a Bell and this called me for my first days in school. We lived in Singapore for several years, there were then two saw mills, known as the upper and the lower . . . . In about 1860 my father had a store in Saugatuck [where East of Sun sits]. At one time father had two vessels which sailed from the mouth of the river to Chicago; he bought furs from the Indians; and also many fancy things they made as (well as) baskets made from willow and colored with wild roots. (I) can remember many squaws coming to our house on the farm [Nichols Homestead—from about 1855] with Papooses strapped to their backs and big bundles of baskets of all different colors in their arms."

— FRANK NICHOLS
son of Stephen D. Nichols
Feb 16, 1920, Chicago
[Handwritten letter, SDHS Archives.]

panthers![14] So, like the Ottawa Indians who constructed bark dwellings along the banks of the Kalamazoo River as their seasonal shelters, the dwellings of early settlers were without a conscious "style." They were small and crude and strictly defensive structures to protect people from the dangers of the outside. In their day they were viewed as nothing but vulgar and utilitarian and by no means the romantic symbols of a simple and virtuous life that society would later come to associate with "log cabins." As a matter of fact, the streets of Saugatuck were not graced with a painted house until 1846 when Elias Dibble put up a "grand mansion," painted white, on the southeast corner of Butler and Hoffman Streets.

SEGREGATION AND SEPARATION | To be sure, both the Butlers and the Morrisons knew what "style" was and they expected that such would come with fortune—and they all expected that fortune was just around the corner. Unfortunately, the Butlers were able to realize neither their aspiration to fortune nor to "style," but the Morrisons managed to achieve both.

"Architecture" means more than assigning a "look" to a building. In the nineteenth century it evolved as the

MORRISON'S HOUSE
1857 *(photo ca. 1940)*
Butler & Culver Streets | Saugatuck

More so than any other house in Saugatuck, this fashionable Greek Revival house was the symbol of pioneer achievement. Stephen and Mary Morrison were among the first settlers in Saugatuck and this was their third house (the first being a nearby "shanty" which served as home, shop, and village post office). The front porch and the rear wing were added later. The house was later inherited by Lee Leland, a ship captain's son, and named Leland Lodge—a boarding house for tourists. Destroyed by fire February 1978.

SAUGATUCK HOUSE HOTEL
1852 *(photo from 1880s)*
201 Butler Street | Saugatuck

The staff lines up for public inspection—from the cleaning lady on the right to the hotel barber (or barman) on the left. Is that Mrs. Cordelia Keltner, the proprietress seated near the entrance? The village's first hotel, stage stop, and virtual village center, was built on land donated by a local resident who wished to relieve village residents of the burden of boarding visitors. Its motto was "feed the hungry and rest the weary." Saugatuck House was often a beehive of political and social activity and controversy—including some heated exchanges over the merits of serving whiskey. In 1884 it was the location of a battle between supporters and opponents of the newly elected Democratic presidential candidate, Grover Cleveland, resulting in the hotel's landlady chopping down a flag which had been hung on the hotel roof in Cleveland's honor. "Not for Cleveland in this house" she said. [Commercial Record, November 14, 1884.] *It had a ballroom and "sample" rooms where traveling salesmen displayed their goods. The builder was George Hames, a ship carpenter. Later called the "Hotel Hamilton," was used until it was razed in 1913 to make room for a new drug store. Now the site of Saugatuck Drug Store.*

method by which to reorganize space in order to separate and segregate daily life into designated compartments. Another way to think about this is to consider the architecture of the time as a way of becoming "modern." In the 1850s the Morrisons separated work and home by moving to a more commodious house on Butler Street and moving their general store to the lower floor of their large new building, called "Morrison's Hall," on the southwest corner of Culver and Butler Streets. The new Morrison home (of 1857 and known later as Leland Lodge) was in the fashionable "Greek Revival" manner. It was a model home of sorts, even being pictured in the 1880 *History of Allegan and Barry Counties*. The Morrisons had arrived. Separation and segregation of space, indeed! There would be no more Indians at their fireside or villagers at the door to ask for their mail. Even daughter Julia was protected from coarse shanty-town habits by being sent off to attend a private girls' school in Allegan. But in the early villages of Saugatuck and Douglas, the Morrisons were the exception not the rule; like a true frontier town, most people in early Saugatuck and Douglas crowded into someone else's house. Indeed, the traffic in homeless people was rampant. The villages were migratory havens—full

† EAGLE HOTEL – DOUGLAS HOUSE – WADE'S TAVERN
ca. 1863 *(photo, ca. 1873)*
47 Center Street | Douglas

Built during the Civil War by local carpenter Christopher Schultz, this hotel, tavern, and stage coach stop was variously known as the "Douglas House" or "Wade's Tavern," having been established by Jonathan Wade, one of the founders of Douglas/Dudleyville." The entire main floor was a dining room, described as "a beautiful room from which one could see both the village and the lake." A tavern was in the basement and a hall for dancing "fitted up for dramatic entertainments" was on the second floor. At one time the sleeping rooms accommodated 40 to 50 persons. [*Commercial Record*, November 1, 1878; and conversation with Irma Schultz Fuller, May 2004.] *Largely destroyed by fire in 1934.*

† JUDSON–HEATH HOUSE
1858
607 Butler Street | Saugatuck

Elnathan Judson came to Saugatuck from Woodbury, Connecticut in 1857 and built this elegant Greek Revival house, with its recessed door surrounded by square columns, which was perhaps as much a reflection of his east-coast heritage as it was current fashion. This was one of the largest houses in town at the time and served as both the Judson home and a boarding house for mill workers. The house provides us with an example of "pre-modern" construction techniques. By combining machine sawn lumber with hand hewn posts and cross timbers, local carpenters adopted a system of post and frame, or "braced frame," construction whereby the house is supported by both corner braces—but also with some weight transferred to load-bearing walls. This replaced the earlier log house construction methods and allowed local carpenters to bypass the traditional east-coast (and European) "post-and-girt" system in which the strength of the structure is drawn exclusively from interlocking massive corner posts and cross timbers.

RAISING THE ROOF

JIMMIE HAILE'S TAVERN & STAGE COACH STOP
1840
Lakeshore Drive
Saugatuck Township

This farmhouse-tavern of Jimmie and Martha Haile is remarkable not just for its function but for the fact that it was so stylish for this era—when crude logs and unpainted planks were about all that greeted the guests to almost every household. Haile was a sawmill operator who probably cut the lumber for this house which served as family home and a tavern and coach stop. This is the oldest known surviving house in the Saugatuck and Douglas area—and famous for miles around for its Saturday night suppers and dances.

of sailors, ships' captains, loggers, sawmill workers, and others who came and went with the seasons and the ups and downs of the woods-and-metropolis economy. In Saugatuck in the 1850s, for example, more than a quarter of the population lived in other peoples' homes, boarding houses, or hotels. And like a true frontier town, the most auspicious and fashionable "houses" were really boarding houses. Both the Dutcher and Judson-Heath houses were, in reality, combined family dwellings and boarding houses for mill workers. Unfortunately we know very little about daily life—including household and kinship relations—in these miniature communities of expanded and temporary families.

The area's first boarding house was fondly known as Jimmie Haile's Tavern (1840) and served also as the Haile homestead, situated on the lakeshore south of Douglas. A decade later, Saugatuck's first real hotel was also its first "public" building. This was the Saugatuck House (1852) and served as a travelers' hotel as well as a boarding house for sailors, mill hands, and perhaps even off-season loggers who worked as farmhands or on the docks. From a social point of view, this was an important building because it was the intent of one of its financiers, Mr. Morrison, that the building minimize the practice of housing sailors and mill hands in family homes. These were plain and simple everyday buildings of wood with stone foundations—but they were also big, gleaming white, and aspired to architectural fashion. They could not have failed to achieve their intent to impress.

EVERYDAY VERNACULAR BUILDINGS AND NATIONAL IDENTITY | By the 1850s the villages and countryside began to take on a cultivated look. Money was pouring in, and paint and lumber were cheap. However, as much as this villagescape began to mirror the nostalgic back-east memories of a generation of pioneers from Pennsylvania, New York, Vermont, Connecticut, and other eastern states, it also reflected local, or "vernacular," style as well. A survey of Saugatuck and Douglas buildings suggests that the first consciously "designed" structure was a very plain wooden Greek Revival building, most

T. F. KLEEMAN'S RESIDENCE & TAVERN
ca. 1860
321 Water Street
Saugatuck

Built as a combination residence and tavern in the years just prior to the Civil War, this structure served the nearby docks and warehouses which were growing up in the neighborhood. Now a retail business. Restored.

probably the aforementioned James Haile's Tavern, with a pediment, columns, and fashionable upper balcony-porch. It was painted white and it most likely had shutters at the windows.

Haile's Tavern marked the beginning of a local Greek Revival craze which lasted until immediately after the Civil War. It was, in effect, an outgrowth of not only a "stylistic" revolution, but a social-cultural revolution which was taking place all over America in the 1840s and 1850s which happened here a little later. Simply stated, Greek Revival architecture can be regarded as the "American" style of architecture. It has a little to do with the Greeks *per se* and a lot to do with "being American." That is, the American Revolution against the British overlords (which really did not end until the War of 1812) brought on a somewhat delayed revolution in architecture and building: the birth of the revolutionary idea of an affordable and "architecturally styled" house for all, not just for the well-heeled and educated. Never before in history had common people gained access to not only affordable but fashionable housing.

From an intellectual-cultural perspective, all of this far exceeds mere fashion and represents the fact that America was following in the footsteps of the Greeks and Romans who first conceptualized democracy: a government without a king. Many early Americans, including Thomas Jefferson, believed that America was a happier and more virtuous place than Europe because each American family could aspire to owning their

PEDIMENT

Triangular or segmental upright front end of a roof, of moderate pitch, derived from the gable end of a Greek Temple.

TEMPLE OF ERECTHEUS

VERNACULAR

In the language of building and architecture, "construction and stylization common to a region." This includes use of local materials and following local or regional traditions, as well as incorporating local-regional interpretation of architectural style and questions of maintenance. Vernacular design seeks rooflines and room layout which fit into the functional needs of a region and involves the least effort and cost in construction.

THE FIRST HOUSE IN DOUGLAS
1851
149 South Washington Street | Douglas

Built by Jonathan Wade, one of the founders of Douglas, for his family, the house was originally a plank house—being built of rough hewn planks (from his mill) laid vertically and later given its simple Greek Revival form with clapboard siding. It still stands, with its two rooms up and two rooms down—with the addition of a lean-to kitchen and eating room to the rear.

RAISING THE ROOF

own freestanding house—independent of landlord and neighbors—where the family was protected by the rural landscape and insulated from the urban riots and dirty factories that hindered the well-being of their European cousins. The home, above all else, dictated and shaped the American character of individualism and moral virtue. Greek Revival architecture became an important part of this national identity.

It was perfect. Encouraged by cheap land, cheap lumber, and cheap technology, everyday Greek Revival structures were understood by several generations of people to represent as well as implant "American ideals." Never before in the history of the world had national identity and "belonging" become so linked to ownership of one's "home-sweet-home." Fashion, style—and virtue—were now the domain of the common people. No wonder Thomas Jefferson loved it.

The Greek Revival structure, be it house or commercial building, was a simple rectangular box derived from the form of a Greek temple. In shape it was a quite simple "gable front and wing" house, sometimes known simply as a "Gable-L," which came to Michigan from the east coast, particularly New York and Pennsylvania. A local side-gable version is not uncommon. Both the front- and side-gable forms are similar in that they have relatively low-pitched roofs, are narrow in proportion to their height, and allow for an upper Greek inspired triangular "pediment". Very often the wing portion of the "L" was a one-story later addition.

A History of the Buildings and Architecture in the Saugatuck and Douglas Area

The "Greek Revival" nomenclature derives from the fact that the gable was a reference to a Greek temple pediment while a wide plain cornice trim banding (or "frieze board") at the cornice of the roof parodied the decorated entablature of the Greek temple. In Michigan Greek Revival structures were almost always made of white pine or tulipwood planks and moldings, generally painted white, with columns or, more commonly, rather flat façades with inset side and cornice panels making reference to columns, and some sort of pediment. The earliest local Greek Revival houses appear to have been constructed in some variation of the corner post-and-girt or the braced frame manner in which heavy timbers supported the weight of the structure.

GREEK REVIVAL IN THE SAUGATUCK AND DOUGLAS AREA | Michigan's pre-Civil War architectural landscape is a testimony to the democratization of architectural style. When Greek Revival swept Michigan, it was applied to the homes of the rich and poor alike—as well as to commercial structures. It appeared in Detroit as early as the 1820s and then became the dominant building style in Marshall and elsewhere, and can be seen today in heroic splendor in nearby Holland's Pillar Church of 1856—which replaced an earlier crude log church.

Much—but not all—of the Saugatuck and Douglas area's Greek Revival townscape is now gone, the largest of the "lost" structures being the old Saugatuck House of 1852, the old Lighthouse of 1859, and the original Dutcher mansion

| WILLIAM DUTCHER HOUSE
1855 *(photo, ca. 1898)*
200 Block of South Washington Street
Douglas

Near the Dutcher's mill (later the Douglas Basket Factory), this Greek Revival house (with the lower portion of the columns altered to meet later "Victorian" fashion served as a family home and boarding house. By the 1920s it was converted for use as a resort called "Oak Manor." Razed, 1983.

| WADE-BRADLEY HOUSE
1853
26 Wall Street
Douglas

Originally a two-room house, built by Nelson Wade, a member of one of the founding families of Douglas, and where Douglas's first child was born (1854). The family had 9 children—one of whom became a member of the United States House of Representatives. The wing to the right is a later addition. The original section of the house is of "plank" (not balloon frame) construction.

| THE PARSONAGE
1860-61
2347 Lakeshore Drive
Pier Cove

The Methodist Church is gone, but its Greek Revival parsonage still stands as a reminder of the early energy and industry of Pier Cove.

| ADAMS-CURTIS HOUSE
ca. 1865
Lakeshore Drive
Pier Cove

A. T. Adams was a farmer who participated in the reforestation of Pier Cove under the direction of O. C. Simonds. The farmhouse was purchased by William and Hope Curtis in 1904, and is still used as the family cottage. William Curtis was the Dean of the Law School at Washington University in St. Louis.

HOW TO IDENTIFY
A Greek Revival Building
1840-1865 (locally)

1
clapboard siding, usually painted white

2
wide frieze (or entablature or cornice) board

3
corner pilasters (often none in common versions)

4
gabled roof of low pitch (local version is usually front gable) and often with corner "eave returns," (no dormers)

5
five (sometimes only four) divided-light windows on gable front; door to side or center—to fit into narrow lot

6
square columns (sometimes round) [absent in this example]

7
usually plain gable front (this example) or pediment front with colonnade

11

which was destroyed as recently as 1983. In virtually "buying a village" in 1855, the William F. Dutcher clan needed a house which would adequately position them as lords of Douglas—which they platted (in 1860) and named. Being from Pennsylvania, the Dutchers knew the current fashion in architecture. Their new house, with square wooden columns and a two story entry porch crowned with a classical pediment was set among a grove of trees just a short distance from the Dutcher mill (and later basket factory). On the opposite side of Douglas's Center Street the rival Wade clan built Douglas's first house in 1851, a small and modest structure in the Greek Revival manner, and then in about 1863 a fine Greek Revival structure, a hotel and tavern called the Eagle House (later the "Douglas House"), which served as hotel, tavern, and business exchange.

Other pre-Civil War Greek Revival structures remain in the area relatively untouched, including the Adams-Curtis and Nikols-Simmons farmhouses at Pier Cove, the Judson-Heath house, at the corner of Butler and Francis Streets, with its tall first floor windows; and the gleaming white "Park House" on Holland Street, home of lumber baron H. D. Moore. The current Park House porches which wrap around the building are replacements, the original porches having been at one time removed and burned as fire wood. Now a B&B, the Park House is best remembered as the home in which Susan B. Anthony stayed during a pass through Saugatuck on one of her famous temperance campaigns. Small but well-designed in the Greek Revival manner, are the T. F. Kleeman Saloon on Water Street, Saugatuck (ca. 1860), with its graceful porch colonnade; the Union Hotel building, Butler Street (1863), with its fine upper floor windows (but alteration in roof); and Marsh's General Store building, still standing on Center Street, Douglas (ca. 1862)—all of the pre-Civil War era. These structures allow us to gaze directly into the face of the past—and act as artifacts that speak to us about everyday life in times past.

Uncle James Haile's farmhouse hotel and tavern still stands on Lakeshore Drive south of Douglas, a Greek temple in wood. Haile possessed not only taste and wealth—over 1,200 acres of land—but also the rightful credentials to participate fully in his particular architectural epoch. He had fought against the British in the War of 1812 and most certainly found this national style of architecture a way to demonstrate his allegiance to his nation. Haile is long gone, but his legacy, Haile's Tavern, remains behind to tell his story.

THE LEGEND OF SINGAPORE'S BOARDING HOUSE: THE ASTOR HOUSE | One of the oldest gatherings of legends about a particular local building center on the very commonplace boarding house at Singapore, often referred to as the "Astor House." All the early chroniclers of the

MARSH'S GENERAL STORE
ca. 1862
50 Center Street
Douglas

The first of many general stores on Center Street, it was built by Hollister F. Marsh, Jr., about 1862, largely to supply the needs of the local mill hands and their families. It went through a succession of owners and functions. Restored 1998.

UNION HOTEL
pre-1861
202 Butler Street | Saugatuck

Built for Thomas Dole, this was one of the earliest hotels in Saugatuck and described by The Commercial Record *as "a quiet home with peace and plenty." However, the neighborhood was anything but quiet, and by the 1870s it was a popular saloon, specializing in fresh oysters and billiards. In 1889 it became a drug store, and then later a series of grocery stores—one called Washington Market. Additions were made in the 1880s (including a new stone foundation and the plate glass windows) and the roof line was changed to mirror the more fashionable Italianate style of the times—hence eliminating the Greek Revival gable to the south.* [Commercial Record, *May 15, 1869; May 7, 1880.*] *Considerably altered (roof); ATM structure attached to south side. Now Pumpernickels Restaurant.*

A History of the Buildings and Architecture in the Saugatuck and Douglas Area

THE BOARDING HOUSE AT SINGAPORE
1837-1869
Singapore, Saugatuck Harbor

As described by one former resident, "this great human beehive" was a gray and unpainted house (60' x 40'), three stories high and had a bar room, dance floor (the kitchen), and an "immense" cooking stove. Over its lifetime it housed hundreds of mill workers as well as travelers/immigrants seeking land and jobs.

Drawing by Margaret McDermott, based on recollections of Laura C. Hutchins, cited in H. H. Hutchins, *Western Allegan Pioneer Days* (1919, reprint, 1995).

RAISING THE ROOF

JENKINS – MULDER HOUSE
1868
333 Lucy Street
Saugatuck

A. E. Jenkins was born in Singapore in 1863 and, after spending most of his life in Chicago, he moved to Saugatuck where he purchased this Singapore house—which had been moved to 333 Lucy Street in 1868. Its "Italianate cottage" form (now somewhat disguised by the application of synthetic siding and a rearrangement of the porch) shows that some Singapore houses were built in a fashionable style. Jenkins added several rooms to the rear, shortened the porch, added a fireplace, and the artificial siding was applied in 1940. The house is now owned by Mr. Jenkin's granddaughter.

THE MILL AT SINGAPORE
1869
Singapore

Looking toward Lake Michigan at the site of the present Saugatuck channel, this is the Johnson and Stockbridge sawmill. The schooner in full view was built in Saugatuck to transport lumber to Chicago. The platted town of "Singapore" is outside the photo, to the right. The brick wall in the foreground remains from an earlier mill. Another mill is seen in the background.

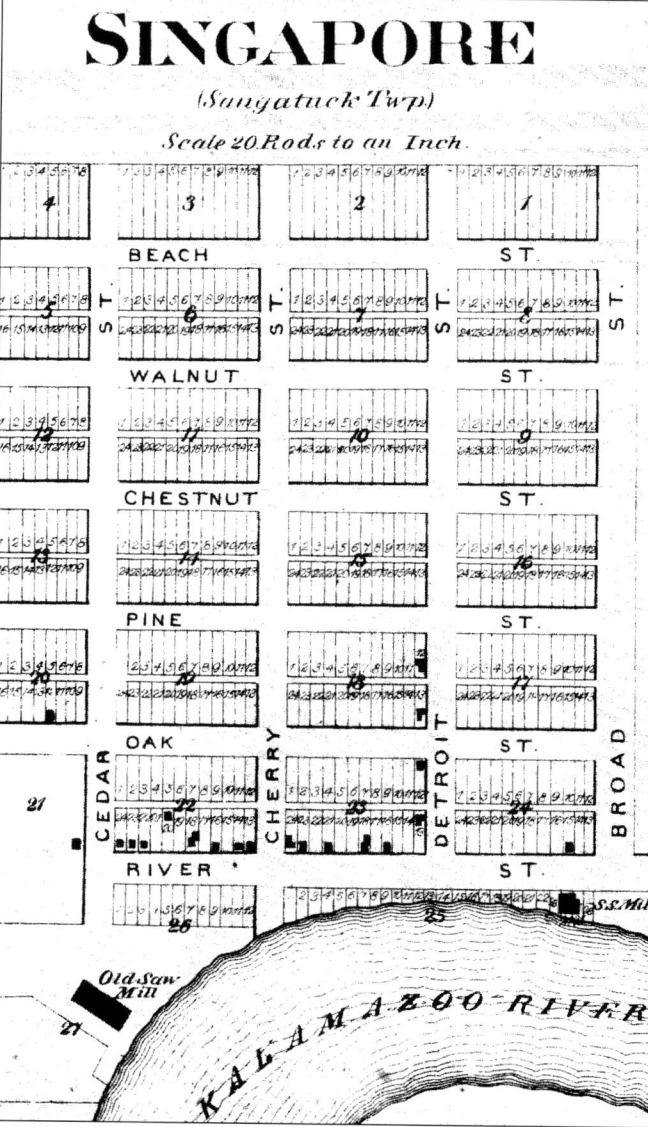

MAP OF SINGAPORE
1873

Singapore was the famous "Wild Cat" mill-town founded in 1837 near the mouth of the Kalamazoo River at Lake Michigan. As a thriving lumber producing center, it exported millions of board feet of lumber to Chicago and elsewhere during the heyday of the lumber boom era in the 1860s, but disappeared as fast as the nearby forests of white pine were clear-cut. This map from 1873 shows Singapore on its last legs. From this time the town was slowly abandoned. The mill was packed up and sent to St. Ignace. Some houses were moved to new sites upriver in Saugatuck, while the remaining structures were left to be buried beneath the moving sand dunes. The plat suggests a much larger town was planned, but in reality few of the lots ever had structures built upon them.

Saugatuck area wrote about it—partly because so many of the pioneers had romanticized it in their later years. The house stood from about 1837 to about 1869 between the two Singapore lumber mills and faced south to the Kalamazoo River. The oft told story, now discredited, is that the house was one of the finest hotels in Michigan, whereas in reality, the name was a bit of a joke at the time—a play on the New York hotel which was then the epitome of luxury. A second legend, also contested in its veracity is that James Fennimore Cooper lived at the boarding house when he was studying local Indian culture for his story "Oak Openings." What is certain, however, is that the house was usually packed to the rooftop with boarders—some of them mill hands, but many of them simply people dropped off by schooners—people on their way to someplace else, looking for fortune or just a temporary shelter. In one month of 1848, for example, the house (with 13 sleeping rooms) was filled with individuals, couples, and families, from Maine, the Netherlands, Norway, Vermont, French Canada, Prince Edward's Isle, Germany, and Ireland—and a regular contingent of Native-Americans showing up for dinner. And its dining room was large enough for a big Saturday night dance. It appears that the original house was destroyed by a fire and then replaced by another structure.

BRINGING SINGAPORE TO SAUGATUCK | Despite the wealth accumulated by some "locals," for many people of modest means the act of house building was undertaken in a decidedly more utilitarian manner, some even "recycling" older houses—such as the "shoe box" house on Francis Street, Saugatuck. Rising practically to the status of legendary have been those buildings relocated upriver in Saugatuck from their original sites in the old mill community of Singapore. We have already spoken of the old boarding house from the first years of the settlement, but in 1864 the mill's investors platted out a village—with hundreds of building lots, only a few of which saw houses on them before the sands began to bury them. Two Singapore houses—the north half of the Van Leeuwen-Randolph house on Holland Street; and the Jenkins-Mulder house on Lucy Street—were drawn by horse teams over the frozen river and set onto new foundations in Saugatuck. The Lucy Street house is of particular importance because its Italianate form suggests that Singapore builders, even on a modest scale, had a desire to mimic architectural fashion. Other houses with the claim to have been moved from Singapore are the Utton House at North and Holland Streets, the Marshall House at 1020 Holland Street, and a part of the coffee shop located at 127 Hoffman Street. More than anything, the "Singapore Houses," having been dragged across the ice from a failed village to give shelter once again, stand today as testimony to hard work, Yankee ingenuity, and "historic preservation" in its most praiseworthy form—and make for good stories.

VAN LEEUWEN-RANDOLPH HOUSE
1868
996 Holland Street
Saugatuck

The northern (two-story) portion of the house was built at Singapore by Martinis Van Leeuwen, the head sawyer at the Singapore lumber mill, for his wife Margarita Bos and their eventual nine children, two of whom were born at Singapore. The house was moved by horse team across the frozen Kalamazoo River in Saugatuck in 1868 to a low ground at Riverside Drive and then placed on this site and a new one-story wing was added. The original "living room" of the Singapore house then became the "parlor," with a small room behind which was called the "birthing room"—where Margarita gave birth to the remaining seven of her children. The old Singapore kitchen became a bathroom, and a new kitchen was placed in the new wing of the house which also included three bedrooms, a "buttery" which functioned as a pantry, and a new living room. Martinis became a fruit farmer and thus had a barn built to the rear of the house (now gone). Margarita and Martinis's descendants continue to occupy the house.

Drawing by Sylvia Bekken Randolph.

UTTON HOUSE
ca. 1898 *(photo, ca. 1907)*
North Street at Holland Street
Saugatuck

The two-story portion of the house was moved to its present site by a horse team across the frozen river from Singapore by Henry Utton in about 1898. A daughter, Florence, was born in 1896 when the house was still in Singapore, and lived in the house in Saugatuck until her death. The identity of the people in this photograph is unknown, though they are most likely the Utton family.

THE INDUSTRIAL VILLAGES
1874
View from Mt. Baldhead

Only the steam gives signs of life. Twenty years after the Civil War the Saugatuck and Douglas economies boomed as the riverfront ("the flats") became industrialized, producing flour, leather, shingles, steamboats and milled lumber. A bridge connecting Saugatuck and Douglas had been constructed in 1869—with a lift-bridge section to allow schooners and steamships to enter the lumber, flour, and leather tanning docks along the Douglas shore. The "flats" area is treeless—and by this time Saugatuck's churches and school had located on "the hill" to escape the noise, smoke, and many saloons of the waterfront.

CHAPTER TWO

Building with Style in Boom Times, 1865–1885

The twenty-year period following the Civil War was the golden age of building in Saugatuck and Douglas. From 1860 to 1870 the population of the two villages increased threefold (Allegan County's population doubled during the same period). The number of buildings in Saugatuck and Douglas increased from about 100 to over 350 between 1864 and 1873. From early 1869 to the mid-1870s Douglas alone grew by 36 buildings. Building expansion took the form of a number of nicely platted "additions" (i.e., Spencer's, Mixer's, Helmer's and Finley's Additions) which obeyed the grid-plan logic of the original village layouts. The economy was booming. Steamboat service between Saugatuck and Chicago began in 1867 and, along with the giant schooners still in service, the combined local "fleet" carried more and more cargo across the lake. By 1869 the Saugatuck lumber mills were breaking local production records. Millions of feet of lumber and shingles filled local docks and riverside yards—looking to profit from growing urban demands, not the least of which was Chicago's needs after the devastating fire of 1871. In 1873 the schooner O. R. Johnson carried over 6 million feet of lumber across the lake in 57 trips. New structures along the riverside also pointed to an expanding economy:

George P. Heath built a four-story wooden flour mill along the river between Hoffman and Main Streets in 1866. Two years later Crawford McDonald built a large flour mill on the riverfront at the base of Douglas's Center Street, and half a dozen lumber-related manufacturing enterprises started up in the two villages. By the 1870s, Douglas could boast of a flour mill, two furniture builders, several drug stores, a brick works,[1] two lumber mills, three blacksmith shops, a basket factory, a two-story wagon maker's shop, and two shingle yards, along with two general stores, two meat markets, and a shoe shop. Daniel Gerber's leather tanning factory at the corner of South and Water Streets was four stories high.

HERMAN BEKKEN'S BLACKSMITH SHOP
1897 (photo ca. 1950)
Washington & Wall Streets
Douglas

The last of the Douglas blacksmiths.

Bekken's blacksmith-shop structure still stands today, reminding us that in the days before the automobile the villages were kept on the move by the blacksmith who repaired and built carriages and wagons and shod the horses.[2]

HOW PUBLIC SPACES DEFINED "COMMUNITY" | In this post-Civil War world a better-educated and wealthier population demanded specialized spaces in which to conduct intellectual, spiritual, and social activities. After all, most communities define themselves by their public spaces. Other than a few taverns and tiny school buildings, the pre-Civil War farm and village folk had no public gathering places. In 1855 the schools

GRIFFIN & HENRY MILL
1897
Culver Street
Saugatuck

Formerly the O.R. Johnson Sawmill, this photograph, with mill hands present, shows a portion of the mill. The quantity of lumber products exported from Saugatuck and Douglas area mills was staggering in the decade following the Civil War. By the mid-1870s the boom was over, although some products, such as wood shingles, continued to be produced at an impressive level.

consisted of a little "miserable building" in a pine grove on Mary Street[3] and two little school houses in Douglas, the first of which stood on the village square (now Beery Field) and then a second, now a residence, at the southeast corner of Center and Union Streets.[4]

The first two major building projects after the Civil War were nearly identical: the architecturally imposing two-story wooden "Union" schools in Douglas and Saugatuck, built in 1866, each with a fashionable Italianate cupola/bell tower, and each situated on a commanding site overlooking its respective village. These were revolutionary buildings. Here was a new approach to education—as children were grouped into "graded classrooms" (as opposed to the traditional one-room schoolhouse), and the schools were headed by a "professor" or head teacher who trained the teachers. The message was clear: the villages were serious about education. Majestic for their time, the buildings were regarded as a "credit to their place."[5] The Douglas school (commonly known as "The Old School House"), was built by local carpenter Jonas Crouse and served as a community social center until a village hall was built a decade later.[6] It still stands.

DOUGLAS UNION SCHOOL
1866
130 Center Street
Douglas

Known as "The Old School House," this noble Italianate structure with its bell cupola, wide roof overhang with fancy brackets, classical corner pilasters on its four corners, elongated windows, and classical entryway, is regarded by some as the finest architectural specimen in Douglas. Douglas's third public school house, it was built by Jonas Crouse at a cost of $5,000 on land donated by Michael and Matilda Spencer. The building was divided into multiple classrooms—a progressive "graded school" system of its time. In the early years four teachers taught 104 children. The building was also used for public meetings and concerts. The local Congregational Church was founded here as was the Lakeshore Agricultural Society. School was discontinued in 1957. It is the oldest surviving "Union" school building in Michigan.

A History of the Buildings and Architecture in the Saugatuck and Douglas Area

The Saugatuck school was destroyed by fire in 1897 and then rebuilt as a brick two-story structure with a fine Italianate tower (a gymnasium was added in 1927). It too, was destroyed by fire in 1950, and yet another structure was built on the site which served as the village school until a modern school was built on a new site on Elizabeth Street in 1973.

SAUGATUCK'S NEW SCHOOL
1897
Elizabeth & Mason Streets
"Allegan Hill" | Saugatuck

DOUGLAS UNION SCHOOL
TEACHER & PUPILS
n.d.
Teacher Mary Hans with students Johnson Fox, Gordon Durham, and the Eckdahl twins.

SAUGATUCK UNION SCHOOL
1866 *(photo from the 1870s)*
Elizabeth & Mason Streets
"Allegan Hill" | Saugatuck

This photo is inscribed on the back "The old building as I left it in the late 1870s—signed E. "Ellie" Houtcamp. Built on "the hill" overlooking Lake Kalamazoo, this imposing structure served as Saugatuck's public school until it was destroyed by a tornado and fire in 1896. It is similar in form to the Douglas school—the cupola being largely hidden by the projecting wing to the front. Most likely it had separate "Girls" and "Boys" entrances.

DOUGLAS SCHOOL
1850s

Now one of the oldest existing structures in Douglas, at one time called "the little old school." it was the village school (with later additions) prior to the construction of the new school in 1866. An even earlier schoolhouse was located on the present village park.

19

RAISING THE ROOF

GATHERING PLACES OF THOSE WHO GOVERNED AND THOSE WHO WERE GOVERNED | Throughout history certain spaces serve to delineate and define gender and power roles in society as well as indicate the levels of social and intellectual activity. As in most towns across nineteenth-century America, fraternal orders, or "lodges were the most important gathering places for men. These were, in effect, not only male power centers but also the social mechanism by which the male citizenry monitored its own behavior (including that of drinking) and provided for its members in time of need. The Dutcher (Masonic) Lodge was formed in Douglas immediately following the Civil War and named for one of the Lodge's founders, Thomas Benton Dutcher. It moved into its new hall on Center Street in 1875. This plain Shaker-like Italianate building with its simple classical entrance originally had a hipped roof and cupola. In 1902 the building was doubled in size to accommodate a Village Hall to be used for village business and social activities.

At that time the roof was changed to the current shed type and a twin entrance was added. This new double building had a stage at one end which served as a bandstand. Thus, in serving the fraternal elite and village governors—who were mostly the same good fellows—and as the venue for community business, lectures, concerts, and the weekly Saturday-night dance, the Dutcher Hall became Douglas's most important building, the very hub of village life.

Then, not to be outdone by any of this, Saugatuck's own lodgemen produced that village's most impressive and modern structure to date: the Odd Fellow's Lodge, the three-story "Landmark Building" (1878). The structure still stands at the southwest corner of Butler and Mason Streets, though some of its former Italianate splendor has been lost. Claimed at the time to be "the crowning glory of Saugatuck" and "an ornament to the village, the ground floor housed retail premises, including Saugatuck's first bank; a public hall and Masonic Lodge occupied the second floor while the Odd Fellows met on the third floor.[7] With the two leading fraternal organizations on the upper floors, it became overcrowded as a male preserve and a music and dance hall.

Like Douglas, early Saugatuck did not have a "village hall" built for official village affairs. Indeed, the community's first purpose-built "public hall" was a two-story structure privately built in 1863 by the town's principal benefactor, Stephen Morrison, at the southeast corner of Culver and Butler Streets. The upper

Vicky Stull

| DUTCHER LODGE & DOUGLAS VILLAGE HALL
1875, 1902
86 Center Street
Douglas

This was the most important building in the daily life of Douglas. Being the location of both the Masonic Lodge and the Village Council, it was the Village's male "power center" as well as being the place for the Saturday night dance, meetings, and other community "socials." The original 1875 structure was only the right half of what we see here, with a typical Italianate cupola perched at the peak of a hipped roof. The lodge was named for Thomas Benton Dutcher who was a local mill owner and the Lodge's first Worshipful Master. Recently restored.

20

A History of the Buildings and Architecture in the Saugatuck and Douglas Area

floor of "Morrison's Hall" was used for musical events and acted as a community meeting place. Civil War rallies were held here as were dramatic presentations ("The Drunkard's Child—or Father Come Home" in 1868) and meetings of the various temperance clubs. It was destroyed by fire in 1879, and soon after this (1880) the village built a "hall" nearby, but it was essentially a fire house and jail. Up "on the "hill" on Hoffman Street another "public" building emerged—an opera house. This was the creation (in 1870) of Captain Sherman Upham. Complete with kerosene floodlights, it operated helter-skelter as a public auditorium until about 1920. In 1900, for example, it offered a "St. Patrick's Ball" in March, a lecture on "monastic life" and "the Old Maids of America" meeting in July, and a "colored minstrel" in August.

No purpose-built spaces for community worship existed in the two villages or in the surrounding countryside for the first thirty years of settlement, but when they appeared it was in the respectable parts of the village, not the industrialized "flats." Saugatuck's earliest church, the First Congregational Church at Griffith and Hoffman Streets, was in progress "on the hill" when the Civil War broke out in 1861. It was, in fact, used in an unfinished state that year for the village's first rally in support of the North's

REFORMED CHURCH
1868 *(photo, ca. 1903)*
Holland Street
Saugatuck

Built on land donated by H. D. Moore, probably intended as a church for his mill workers. Interurban tracks in foreground. It was described at the time as "an ornament to the place." [The Commercial Record, August 16, 1868.]

LANDMARK BUILDING
1878 *(photo, 1880s)*
152 Butler Street
Saugatuck

The first owner's guard dog ate the store's stock of fur coats. It was Saugatuck's best-known clothing "dry goods-store" (first Taylor's, Goshorn's, then Flint's). Flint & Co. had existed elsewhere in Saugatuck and had been in the clothing business since 1857. A popular dance hall on the upper hall, its first event was a benefit dance in 1878 for yellow fever sufferers. Here as it looked in the 1880s when it housed the Arbeiter Verein orchestra and the Saugatuck Dancing Club. Some of the Italianate details have been removed. Now occupied by Kilwin's confectionery.

RAISING THE ROOF

cause. It was a simple one-room wooden building and described by one observer as a "miserable building." Later additions to the church included an 1890's "stick style" open belfry, a new chancel, and a new stucco veneer, which reflect the building fashion of the time.[8] The stucco was later replaced with brick. Also distancing itself from the "flats" was Saugatuck's second church, the Reformed Church (now gone) of 1868, built on the north ridge of the hill along which now runs Holland Street. A tall folk (or "country") gothic Methodist Church was built on the hill in 1883, complete with a central entrance tower at the corner of St. Joseph and Main Streets. Somewhere in this churching geography was a Universalist Church, but its location remains a mystery.[9] On the Episcopal side of the hill architectural fashion was certainly in mind when Reverend J. Rice Taylor, the founding pastor of Saugatuck's All Saints Church, brought the well-known Detroit architect Gordon W. Lloyd to the village to design the a new Episcopal church (1872-1874). Rice had been to the area earlier to conduct baptisms. The building, accomplished by highly skilled local carpenters, was undoubtedly inspired by Taylor's fellow New Yorker, Andrew Jackson Downing, whose architectural "plan books" did much to popularize the "Carpenter Gothic" style. This Americanized version of the English Gothic Revival was particularly popular among those of Anglican (Episcopalian) taste. Interestingly, Reverend Taylor clearly had a Downing plan in hand when he commissioned his own house in the Carpenter Gothic style, nearby on Pleasant Street. This is the second known example in Saugatuck and Douglas of a very early "plan book" house *(see the description of the "Octagon House" in Chapter 3)*.

Owing perhaps more to poverty of cash rather than spirit, Douglas citizens were not able to worship in a purpose-built structure in their own village until 1870, a full twenty years after the town was

† FIRST CONGREGATIONAL CHURCH
ca. 1890
296 Hoffman Street | Saugatuck

The church's bell-tower entrance and new wing have been added. Original eave brackets remain. A center window was added in 1896—a gift from Warner P. Sutton, one time Saugatuck School Superintendent who became a well known American diplomat.

† FIRST CONGREGATIONAL CHURCH
2006

A new chancel was added (to the right side) in 1938, along with a redesign of the belfry and entrance—and the stucco veneer was covered with brick. The architect was the local architect-painter, Carl Hoerman.

† FIRST CONGREGATIONAL CHURCH
1861
269 Hoffman Street | Saugatuck

Saugatuck's first church. By the time of the Civil War it had 80 members. The pews were rough hewn, straight back seats, painted gray with black trim. It was heated by two pot-bellied stoves. The first community Civil War rally took place here in 1861—to recruit volunteers for the Union army. At this time the American Congregational Church was a leading liberal denomination—and was establishing a large number of colleges throughout the East and Midwest.

METHODIST CHURCH
1870
Center & Mixer Streets
Douglas

The first purpose-built place of worship in the Village of Douglas was built in 1870 and was officially dedicated as a Methodist Church in 1872. It now serves as the Saugatuck-Douglas District Library and has been given a compatible addition and garden to the rear.

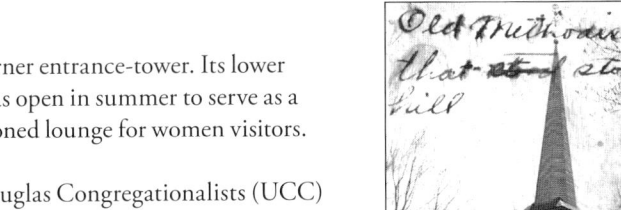

OLD ST. PETER'S CATHOLIC CHURCH
1900 *(photos ca. 1947)*
Washington & Chestnut Streets
Douglas

Sunday Morning (l) and a wedding ceremony (r). Located near the basket factory, St. Peter's Catholic Church was founded in 1894 to serve factory workers. The church was built in 1900 and became a parish in 1938. When the parish was moved to new quarters, the building was used by the newly formed Community Church and later abandoned. The structure was radically altered in 2001 to become condominiums. The original stained glass windows exist at two sites the new St. Peter's and the Community Church of Douglas.

METHODIST CHURCH
1915
Griffith & Mason Streets
Saugatuck

The earlier structure was moved down the hill to its present location and altered considerably—taking on an Arts & Crafts look that was popular at the time. It has since been altered again. The view is from Griffith Street.

settled. This church, dedicated as the Douglas Methodist Church two years later, was a variation of Midwestern folk-gothic manner: a tall and narrow clapboard-sided structure with its gable end to Center Street and a tower entrance tucked into the corner. By 1918 the congregation had merged with the Saugatuck Methodists. The Douglas church was thereafter used by several community organizations, including the Odd Fellows, the Douglas Athletic Club, and today the busy Saugatuck-Douglas District Library. The Saugatuck Methodists moved their building down the hill to its present site in 1915, and enlarged it, giving it a fashionable (but since changed) Arts & Crafts façade and new corner entrance-tower. Its lower level was open in summer to serve as a chaperoned lounge for women visitors.

The Douglas Congregationalists (UCC) built their church in 1884 in a charming countrified gothic manner with a steep-pitched roof and an open belfry atop a corner tower-entrance. Altered

METHODIST CHURCH
1883
St. Joseph & Main Streets
Saugatuck

Known for its revival services in the 1880s. The original church, with seating for 175, on "the hill" in Saugatuck was moved (and altered) to its present site at Griffith and Mason Streets.

RAISING THE ROOF

ALL SAINTS
EPISCOPAL CHURCH
1874
Hoffman & Grand Streets
Saugatuck

Transforming lumber from the local forests into a spiritual message. The architect was Gordon W. Lloyd of Detroit. The inspiration behind the design was that of the church's founding pastor, Reverend J. Rice Taylor, who was influenced by the Gothic Revival preoccupation of his Episcopal faith at that time.

Board-and-batten exterior siding, decorated vergeboards, wood buttresses placed between the pointed windows, and a large pointed bracket above the east rose window are all features of this Carpenter Gothic style. The highly skilled builders were local carpenters George E. Dunn, William Dunning, and George Hames. This is one of the finest Carpenter Gothic churches in Michigan.

only slightly over the years, it became a popular venue for community musicals and other events. The St. Peter's Catholic congregation moved from is 1900 home to a new and very modern structure on the Blue Star Highway in 1958. First established near the local basket factory, its mission was to serve the Douglas's factory workers.

GOOD BUILDINGS AND BAD BUILDINGS | House building after the Civil War reflected several changes in American culture and thinking. While pioneer life depended on a close proximity of residential and industrial space, "modern" life by 1860s standards, (what is now called "Victorian"), demanded greater and greater separation of work and home. The Butlers and other early settlers may have tolerated all sorts of mixed function spaces, such as a living room serving both as a work room and a sleeping room, but by the 1860s it became increasingly fashionable to separate the work and street environments from the home and to arrange the "home" itself as to encourage individual and family privacy. Space for individual contemplation, family life, gender separation, as well as special spaces for children, and even the segregation of housework such as sewing and cooking from home leisure became the elements of the ideal home. Few things touched America's spiritual and moral heart-strings as did the idea of the Victorian family nestled snugly into its "home sweet home"—or as one historian has put it, "a haven in a heartless world." The problem was not imaginary. In Saugatuck in August of 1871, for example, nearly 500 sailors were "in port" most of whom found their way to the many taverns of the village and in turn found shelter in the homes of the villagers—a fact which, we have seen, led one villager to donate land for the construction of the village's first hotel in order to get these strangers out of peoples' homes.

What was happening was that Victorians were reshaping social roles for men, women, and children by redefining the home. This was the age in which children were increasingly protected, wives and mothers were idealized as the guardians of domesticity, and virtuousness could be achieved by maintaining the perfect home as a moral refuge in a troubled world. "House love" was invented.

BAD WHISKEY AND GOOD WOMEN | It is difficult for us today to appreciate the urge to escape the village's river banks. The smoke, smells, noise, dirt, and overall rough character of the nineteenth-century village streets were more than enough to offend the sensibilities of a growing middle class. Contrary to the romance one might attach to the "good old days," Saugatuck, and to a lesser

"HOUSE OF THE SEVEN GABLES"
1873
758 Pleasant Street
Saugatuck

Reverend J. Rice Taylor first came to Saugatuck to baptize children at the nearby mill settlement of Singapore and later returned to establish All Saint's Episcopal Church. For his own house he turned to the Gothic Revival style he favored for the church—and appears to have used the "plan book" design for a "River Cottage." Locally, the house became known as "The House of the Seven Gables."

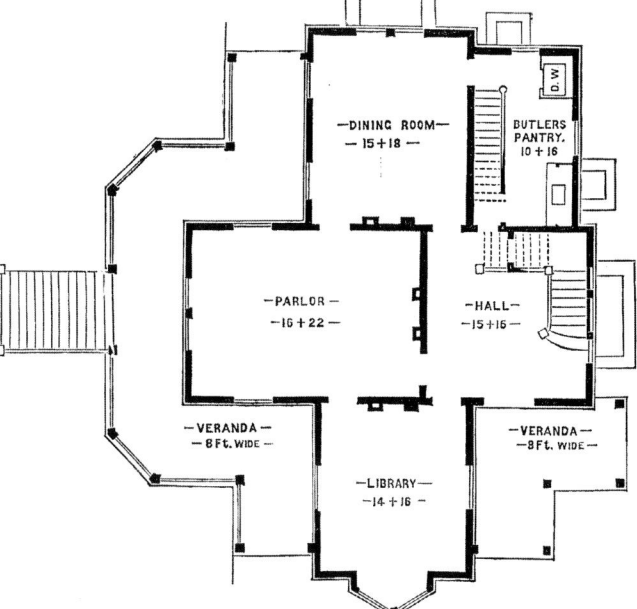

"A RIVER COTTAGE"
mid-19th century

This early house-plan-book design was the inspiration for Reverend Taylor's Pleasant Street residence in Saugatuck. "A River Cottage" by R. G. Hatfield in the Gothic Revival style, was "intended to be located upon a sharp declivity, where a fine view, either upon a river or extended valley, is to be had…" It was included in the popular house plan book, Cottage Residences, *by Andrew Jackson Downing (frequent editions from 1841 to 1873). The floor plan is similar to the Taylor House.*

RAISING THE ROOF

FIRST CONGREGATIONAL CHURCH
(UNITED CHURCH OF CHRIST)
1884
Spring & Wall Streets
Douglas

The countrified Gothic Revival design was likely by its carpenter-builder, Hugh F. Graham of Douglas. With its prominent tower and steeple the structure today looks much the way it did a century ago. The church measures 32 by 50 feet and seats 200. Ramp added. Interior has been restored.

extent Douglas and Pier Cove, were boisterous and brawling river/lumber towns filled with sailors, rivermen, shipbuilders, and millworkers—with undoubtedly a few lumberjacks and itinerant "nailers" from the basket factories thrown in for good measure at the right season.[10] Plenty of saloons, the most plentiful supply of bad whiskey in Michigan, and plenty of customers were to be had: a "roughhouse gang" as one of the early historians called it.[11] Certain buildings had assumed an illicit character. The two-block area centering at Water and Mason Streets had a good half dozen saloons in 1873, the most infamous being the "Lake House," the "Union House," "Miller's," "The Globe," as well as the Douglas House tavern in Douglas—known as "rough" places and often the scene of brawls, license violations, and even shootings. And it was not just men. Women, it was said in 1884, were seen playing pool in Saugatuck saloons![12] When Susan B. Anthony brought her temperance campaign to Saugatuck in 1879 she was successful in shutting down only six of the village's fourteen saloons.[13]

LAKE HOUSE TAVERN
1878
Culver & Water Streets
Saugatuck

Traditional port-town "leisure" was very much based on escapist outlets such as brawling and excessive drinking. Lake House was one of the most notorious for such activities and led to community temperance organizations (e.g., The Red Ribbon Club) to limit drinking. By 1900 some taverns in Saugatuck withdrew the devil whiskey all together and sold beer only—but this saloon was described as a place where "Satan seems to be holding his own. . . ." [Commercial Record, June 9, 1890.] The Lake House was located at the site of the present Singapore Yacht Club.

Following her visit a new village hall (the present hall—with a jail—at Butler and Culver Streets) was built in the midst of this tavern district, and "dedicated to temperance."[14] Saloons meant crime and disturbance, and accounts put forward by the local newspaper suggest that the local constable was a busy man indeed.

FIRE | But the raucous saloon trade did not present the only peril. Shingle mills, lumber mills, and steamboats were sources of noise—and posed a constant threat of fires. Fire was the community's greatest fear. It was common knowledge that many village fires started at the riverside, very often the consequence of hot sparks from an overheated or exploding steam boiler. As local reports attest, many fires started with sparks falling on a roof, spreading to other buildings, and in too many instances, raging out of control. It's no wonder. Like most Michigan towns of the day, neither Saugatuck nor Douglas had any effective fire fighting system to protect its buildings which were primarily wooden; in both villages the "fire fighting" could only be called "primitive," the water supply for which was nearly nonexistent, and at times even the citizenry refused to work the hand pumps. In Douglas the fire house caught fire and destroyed the fire engine, leaving the town without a fire fighting system. In 1886 nearly half the commercial buildings of Saugatuck were destroyed by a fire which swept through the village center. Considering such civic irresponsibility with regard to fire protection, it is interesting to note that when the great fires of the summer of 1871 destroyed forest and farmland of West Michigan (including nearby Holland), they were blocked by a heroic community fire-fighting effort that held the line against the fires along the top of the Allegan Hill, east to Goshorn Lake, and southwest along the Lakeshore road. Saugatuck's buildings were saved.[15]

GOOD HOUSES ON THE THE HILL | Fear of fire was matched by fear of disease. Medical advice of the day recommended moving from damp houses to those with plenty of fresh and clean air— preferably on higher ground. This Victorian obsession with fresh air was partly because medical reformers and doctors had wrongly convinced the public that disease was airborne, or, as they put it, was due to "miasma" (bad air). The absence or presence of ventilation, depending on the source of the air, became crucial, as did windows, doors, porches, and the elevation and directional placement of the house. The diagnosis was wrong, but the treatment was worthy.

So there were many reasons for our Saugatuck and Douglas ancestors to rush to higher ground and distance themselves from the water's edge. Nothing was better than living upon a hill above the dangers of the village streets and away from the stench of the river. The place to be in Saugatuck was "on the hill," and in Douglas it was the high ground to the south of Center Street—or to the west to catch the fresh lake breezes. Prior to the Civil War "the hill" in Saugatuck had less than a dozen dwellings. By 1873 that number had grown to over 50, along with the village's three churches, the school, and the opera house. By 1900 approximately half of the village's houses were located "on the hill." Not until the mills and warehouses became hotels, parks, marinas, boardwalks, and restaurants would living at the water's edge become fashionable—and that part of the story did not unfold until later.

VICTORIAN ARCHITECTURE IN SAUGATUCK AND DOUGLAS | The social and moral concerns about place and space, which historians call "Victorian sensibilities," took on an architectural aesthetic. By the time of the Civil War and increasingly in the years immediately after, the Greek Revival style of architecture disappeared from fashion because it no longer met the needs of a changing society. Out of the bloodshed of America's killing fields, the nation needed a new image. Already as early as the 1840s, a few eastern architects such as Andrew Jackson Downing carried on a relentless campaign to sway public opinion against Greek Revival houses. After the war, a host of other authors of building plan books did the same. They argued that Greek Revival was unfitting as a national style, not moral enough, and was monotonous and dull besides. They ridiculed the idea of living in a clapboard Greek temple, and, more important, taking their cue from their European counterparts, they pointed out that exteriors and interiors of buildings could be used to teach important lessons

HISTORICAL CONTEXT
Who Were the Victorians?

Victoria was the Queen of Great Britain (England, Wales & Scotland) during an age of unprecedented British-led growth and change in the European-American world; hence, it was Victoria who gave her name to this age. Britain was the world's leading power and economy, but America's growth was spectacular and, to some, shocking. The "industrial revolution" was not only transforming the landscape and townscape but was bringing forth all sorts of new products, from inexpensive cotton underwear to machine-made furniture. New forms of transportation—the railroad, canal boats, and steamships—made available seemingly unlimited supplies of natural raw materials, such as lumber. Saugatuck's pioneers saw themselves as part of this march to modernity.

QUEEN VICTORIA
1819-1901 (reigned 1837-1901)

A youthful Alexandrina Victoria ascended the throne in 1837 at the age of 18 and ruled the British Empire as Queen Victoria until her death in 1901. "Victorian" is the rubric applied not only to the era but also to a whole host of social virtues prevalent during the reign of this "bourgeois" queen—modesty, prudence, temperance, frugality, self-control, respectability, etc.—as well as to an elaborate style of architecture and interior decoration characterized by rampant historicism and eclecticism. Prince Albert, Victoria's husband, was himself an amateur architect. Together they shared an interest in buildings and "modern" processes (such as photography) among other things. One Saugatuck resident, Richard B. Newnham, gained local distinction for having been born in the same hour and within a stone's throw of the palace where the Queen was born.

FOLK VICTORIAN

"Folk Victorian" is a term given to a widespread house form that mimics the Gothic Revival or Greek Revival (or both) forms but is less elaborate. It was very popular from the 1860s through the early 1900s and often features porch detailing—such as fancy spindlework or jigsaw cutouts—and bay windows. It is often in the "gable front and wing" form, sometimes called an 'L' house with one wing being of two stories.

MORRISION-AMES-JOHNSON HOUSE
early 1850s *(photo, ca. 1890)*
344 Main | Saugatuck

One of the oldest known houses in Saugatuck. Built with a rough hewn timber frame and interior walls of 3-x-9-inch planks. Shown here as the home and family of Captain Richard Ames. Captain Ames was a sailor and captain of a number of the great schooners that sailed out of the Saugatuck harbor. He purchased this house in 1857. It was said to have begun as a trading post called the "White House" built by Stephen Morrison.

HENRY BIRD HOUSE
ca. 1868
290 Spear Street | Saugatuck

The one-story portion (about 28' x 18') of this house was built by 1868, and the two-story wing was added in the 1880s after it had became the home of Deziah and Henry Bird Jr., and since then it has been owned by their descendents. Bird was a furniture maker and owned one of the local saw mills. Deziah converted an old woodshed attached to the back of the house into a kitchen—and papered the rough wall boards with wallpaper samples from her son's drug store on Butler Street. Period barn in rear.

JOB HOUSE
1850s
256 Spear Street
Saugatuck

Built by Jacob Richards, this is one of the oldest existing houses in Saugatuck and the home to a number of families—including that of a doctor, a lighthouse keeper, and a well-known American diplomat, Frederick W. Job. Since 1938 it has been the summer cottage for six generations of the Job family.

WALLBRECHT-DUGAN FARMHOUSE
ca. 1863
42 Union Street
Douglas

Henry Wallbrecht, a sailor, purchased the entire block of open land bounded by Union, Mixer, Randolph, and Fremont Streets at about the time he moved here in 1863, turning the land into an orchard and farm enterprise which he operated for 30 years. Recently restored, with addition of new barn-studio.

LUDWIG-NELSON HOUSE
1869
346 Hoffman Street
Saugatuck

Built by Stephen Morrison, owner of the Saugatuck tanning factory, apparently as a wedding present for his daughter Julia and her husband John Francis. In about 1904 it became the home of the Ludwig family whose son Daniel Keith Ludwig grew up to become the richest man in the world—having gotten his start selling popcorn at Saugatuck's Big Pavilion. At one time the property included a small fruit farm that extended to Main Street.

WALZ-WALKER HOUSE
ca. 1882 *(photo ca. 1900)*
309 Grand Street
Saugatuck

Dr. R. J. Walker (shown in buggy), Saugatuck's principal doctor for a half century beginning in 1896, purchased this house from Fritz Walz, the local butcher. Walker was famous for his house calls, traveling by way of his buggy and later automobile—all housed in the barn that still stands to the rear of this house. His daughter wrote:

"Our house was a white frame Victorian house surrounded at first by a white picket fence. . . . and [had] the speaking end of a speaking tube next to the front door. The other end of the speaking tube hung on the wall next to my father's bed. With few telephones in town, many night calls came through the speaking tube." [*West Allegan County History*, F52, "Barr, Jeanette (Walker),"]

TISDALE HOUSE–DEER CREEK INN
1877
Ferry Street
Douglas

Built by carpenter William Graham Tisdale for his wife and six children. Tisdale built a number of the large mills in the area—including the Gerber tannery nearby and a lumber mill on Culver Street in Saugatuck. It is claimed that Tisdale was a friend of James Fenimore Cooper and that Cooper used the creek that bordered Tisdale's property as subject matter in his book, Oak Openings. *Tisdale's son George became a ship captain and then ran a local ferry service from his property here on the Kalamazoo Lake.*

about moral or historical truths. Hence, "Victorian" architecture, decoration, and furniture became ways of imparting both a national image as well as moral and social values—or what the Victorians called "respectability." Decorating a house in the "proper" manner was encouraged because it inspired and demonstrated individual virtue, taste, and intellect. "Art" in its many forms—including the embellishment of the home—became an avenue to respectability. As a widely read magazine on architecture and landscaping stated:

> We feel that the source of all improvement has its origins in the desire of individuals to rise higher in the scale of worth, to endeavor to raise his taste, and give evidence of it to his friends and the world.... We therefore cannot but approve of displaying this taste, in a preeminent manner, on houses, gardens, furniture, and every thing connected with the home.[16]

That is, "Decorate, decorate, decorate!"—and that is exactly what our village folk did for half a century. In the 1860s and 1870s the building and furnishing industries faced a barrage of populist writing encouraging the public to participate in America's new aesthetic sensibility by approaching house design with great creativity: the more "artistic" the designs the better.[17]

Thus, by the late 1850s local homeowners and builders of fashion, aided by the invention of the "balloon" or "stick" frame construction method that allowed for cheaper and more complicated design, turned to a variety of "Victorian" styles.

The first of these was the so-called Gothic Revival that imitated the English middle ages, especially its Christian emphasis, all with irregularity of form (many gables and wings) and with considerable decoration such as vergeboards, spindles, pinnacles, and pendants. Its promotion in Michigan was through house plan books for carpenters and builders, particularly those of Alexander Jackson Davis, and Andrew Jackson Downing (whom we have already met as having furnished Reverend J. Rice Taylor with house plans) and Calvert Vaux. They advocated Gothic Revival as the proper plan for villages, farmhouses, churches—and even a barn for farmer Till on Spear Street—because it was, to them, the most virtuous and the most "picturesque" of all styles. The most common translation of the Gothic Revival was the high-pitched "Gable L" house with its standard porch, variety of wood detailing—usually vergeboards and finial—and occasionally either one centered gable or a pair of gables to the front. Sometimes known as "Folk Victorian," it is actually a merger of Gothic Revival and Greek Revival in "countrified" way—and found throughout the Midwest. The style continued until the turn of the century—and is nicely preserved in the Charles Bird House (1860s) and the neighboring Wright-Job House (1850s) on lower Spear Street, and the Van Leeuwen-Randolph house at 996 Holland Street. On the other hand, the very epitome of Gothic Revival in Saugatuck stands at the corner of Hoffman and Grand Streets, the "Carpenter Gothic" All Saints Episcopal Church by Detroit architect Gordon W. Lloyd. The architectural interest of its founding pastor, Rev. Taylor, has already been noted. Small in scale but majestic with its stained glass set into its pointed windows and abundance of wood buttressed board-and-batten walls, All Saints, is a builder's masterpiece and a spiritual expression in wood for a community which lived and worked by the lumber and boat building trades. It remains one of the finest Carpenter Gothic churches in Michigan. As a footnote, it may be said that by combining the skills of his shipbuilder carpenters[18] with the robust pocketbooks of H. D. Moore and Francis B. Stockbridge, Reverend Taylor and architect Lloyd gave the "hill" exactly what it wanted: fresh air, a healthful separation from the village below, beauty, and respectability.

THE ITALIANATE STYLE IN SAUGATUCK AND DOUGLAS | Gothic Revival overlapped somewhat with a new form of "classicism"— the Italianate style. American and European trendsetters,

A HOUSE & FACTORY AT DINGLEVILLE
ca. 1860 *(photo 1870, showing the Wallin House & Wallin Tannery)*
64th Street – Clearbrook

Also known as Wallinville, Dingleville was a settlement on Goshorn Creek, now Clearbrook Country Club. It had an abundance of cows, all with bells, giving the air a constant "dingle and hence its name. It is best known for its tanning factory, operated by the Chicago firm of C. C. Wallin—with Franklin B. and Orcelia Wallin living next to the factory in this early Italianate house of 1860. The house stands. The stacks of material on the tannery ground are hemlock bark from the nearby forests—a key material in the tanning process.

The Franklin Wallin family poses on the lawn—demonstrating that the family is in that social class with considerable style, respectability, and leisure. The tranquil scene, however, has a sad ending. At Christmas time in 1873 the Wallin's oldest son, Alfred, drowned while on a skating party at nearby Goshorn Lake. His mother organized the tannery men to recover the body—but the shock was so severe that she died on New Year's morning. ["Wallin, F. B. and Orcelia," *The History of Western Allegan County Michigan* (1988)]

GRAHAM FARMHOUSE – WINDOVER FARM
1868
400 South Union Street
Douglas

A farmer and builder's house, nearly square (26' x 28'), the simplicity of the house is complemented by the elaborate porch columns and the "cresting" on both the porch and main roofs. Graham was a carpenter and builder and had a furniture and carpentry shop on Center Street. He was also a member of the local grangers organization and superintendent of the Douglas Methodist Sunday School. Like most of the villagers at that time, the Grahams were fruit farmers as well, having planted 800 peach trees on their 27 acres about the time the house was built. "Bonnie Meadows" was a name given to the house by later owners.

particularly in the Midwest, took to this Italian "renaissance classicism" and reshaped it into a wildly popular American architectural style and called it "Italianate." This style had several main elements: a square or rectangular boxlike silhouette, usually tall but with a low-pitched hipped roof (without dormers), and always with a rather wide overhang. Fancy wood work was sought after—as seen today with Captain Martel's front porch and window framing.

Windows and doors were often arched or "hooded"; cornice brackets were added to support the roof overhang; and in the up-market versions the roof peak was crowned with a cupola. Higher class Italianate houses of the "villa" type had corner towers, e.g., the now lost Wheeler House on Water Street in Saugatuck. With a near four-story tower, Captain George Dutcher's rather eccentric version of the style can be found on Douglas Union Street—but with the tower removed. It is a big house for a big man—a Civil War hero, world traveler, and ship engineer and inventor. Most local Italianate houses were of the plainer "four square" type, often with side or rear wings. An example of this type is the sizable Samuel Johnson House (now stripped of its cupola and brackets), 765 Allegan Street, Saugatuck (1867), built for Saugatuck's first customs collector. Later the house became the "Frolic Inn." Other examples include that of Hugh Graham, a local carpenter and furniture maker, as his own residence on South Union Street in Douglas; gentleman farmer Albert Nysson's farmhouse and the Whitney-Barr-Cappelletti House on Allegan Street, Saugatuck (ca. 1868); and the brick one-story Burns House across the street; the Wallin House on 135th Avenue (1860); and the Riley-Slack-Ellis House (1860 with later additions) on Ellis Street. An example of an Italianate farmhouse on a smaller scale stands at 165 Elizabeth Street, Saugatuck (ca.1870).

These big, boxy Italianate houses of the 1870s and 1880s well fulfilled "modern" demands for spaces in which to play out new ideas about the separation of private

† FLINT HOUSE
1860s
178 Union Street
Douglas

Built as the residence (possibly a wedding gift) for Noah and Catherine Flint. Asymmetrical Italianate with portico and typical Italianate door with paired windows; patterned shingles above, and very fine window frames. Unusual window sills and pendant detail extending down from central gable. Fishscale – diamond shingle pattern above. Catherine was raised by the Gerber family. Daniel, a son, was a ship engineer was killed in an accident in Chicago in 1890; another son, William, a sailor, was lost overboard in a storm on Lake Michigan. A third son became the successful operator of Flint's Store in Saugatuck.

HOW TO IDENTIFY
An Italianate Building
1840-1885 (locally)

1
low-pitched hip roof (occasionally a front gable)

2
wide eaves overhang, often supported by decorative brackets

3
tall vertical windows (single or double lights), often with decorated arched tops)

4
square central cupola at the peak of the roof (or in some cases a corner tower)

5
local examples usually box-shaped, often with side wing (wing not shown in this example)

6
classical columns, often set in to door frame

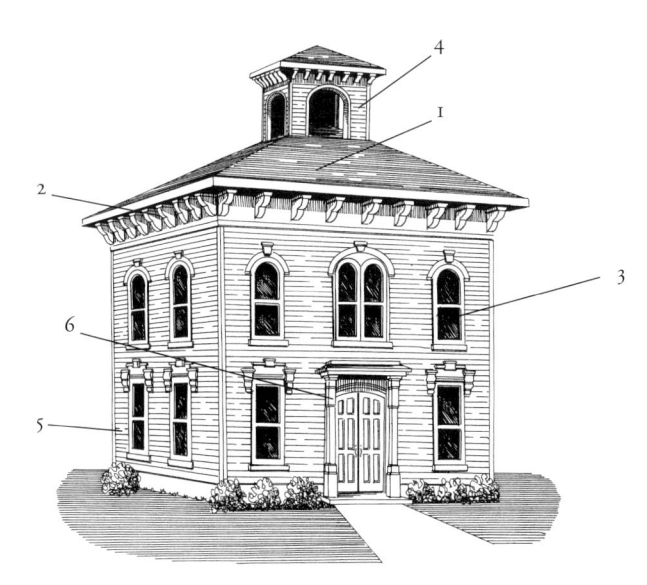

KALAMONT
1865
53 Randolph Street | Douglas

"Kalamont" was the residence of Thomas Gray, the owner of the "Great Bonanza Merchant" general store at the corner of Washington & Center Streets; in 1897 it became the home of Captain John Campbell, captain of Lake Michigan steamers; and then in 1905 the home of Civil War veteran and local fruit farmer, William White.

NYSSON-BALL HOUSE
ca. 1868
1001 Allegan Street | Saugatuck

Farm home of Saugatuck businessman and nurseryman, Albert W. Nysson, who joined the parade into fruit farming and the nursery trade. In 1886 he advertised in The Commercial Record that he had 40,000 young peach trees for sale. The barn became the studio of well-known artists, Belva and Clyde Ball.

BURNS-YAKSIC HOUSE
1881
6597 Old Allegan Road | Saugatuck

Burns was a Butler Street grocer (his building was later altered to become Maplewood Hotel) who built this square Italianate "cottage" brick home in 1881. Recently restored with compatible Italianate addition to rear.

RILEY-SLACK-ELLIS HOUSE
ca. 1860
203 Heirloom Lane and Ellis Street | Douglas

Home of Thomas A. and Fidelia Riley—he being a carpenter and joiner. He went off to the Civil War where he died in 1864. Fidelia was the great granddaughter of an English tea merchant who lost a fortune when his tea was destroyed in the Boston Tea Party. Fidelia later married Anthony Slack, a Civil War veteran who fought at Gettysburg's "Battle of the Wilderness." The house was later the home of their daughter and her husband, Claude Ellis, a lake captain. Enlarged in the later 1860s. Restored in 2004.

DR. ASA GOODRICH-SCHOENEICH HOUSE
1871
112 Center Street | Douglas

Dr. Goodrich was a member of a well-know family of pioneer doctors. He established the first drug store in Fennville and practiced medicine there prior to moving to this house in 1871. Shown in the photograph is his wife Florence, daughter of the Ganges pioneer, Levi Loomis. Now the home of "Old House Antiques."

JAMES DOLE HOUSE-THE WHITE HOUSE
1889 *(photo, ca. 1920)*
106 Mason & Water Streets | Saugatuck

Captain James Dole's House, with traditional Italianate cornice brackets and window trim. When completed in 1889, the local newspaper called this "the finest residence in the town." Built in two sections—with dormers added. Later it became known as "The White House" and served as Mr. and Mrs. Lown's hotel. It is now a gallery and specialty shop, "Good Goods."

DUTCHER–MARK HOUSE
ca. 1889
148 Union Street
Douglas

George N. Dutcher was a member of one of the families that founded Douglas and is one of the best known Michigan veterans of the Civil War—and a world traveler, engineer, and ship owner. The house appears to have been inherited by Dutcher's nephew, George L. Dutcher, after George N. and his wife Eliza passed away. The house was originally built with an octagonal tower lifting up from the middle of the house to make a fourth floor: it has an oak staircase brought over from a Chicago church. The floors were originally painted. The wood work was milled locally—and was matched during recent restoration. The house had suffered severe deterioration—and was covered with metal siding which was removed as part of an extensive restoration by current owner.

SCHUITEMA HOUSE
ca. 1865
554 St. Joseph Street
Saugatuck
Looman Construction, *builder for the restoration*

and public life and about the segregation of various household activities. Porches and much-coveted "parlors" became popular as places to receive the public, just as kitchens, living rooms, and bathrooms were popularized as private spaces for families and individuals. Even separate nursery spaces were invented for the children, and sewing rooms and pantries for domestic work—and bay windows for viewing the outdoors or collecting sunlight for potted plants. Houses tended to be larger as well because, as consumer culture developed, they were increasingly required to accommodate more furniture, appliances, and clothing—and still provide spaces for household production tasks such as sewing, canning, drying foods, etc. Plenty of cheap lumber along with the simplified "balloon frame" construction helped bring home ownership to even greater numbers of people. In Douglas a number of early Italianate houses, Dr. Asa Goodrich's House (1871), 112 Center Street, with its unusual porch-support "cutouts" (or wood filigree); Flint Farm, 178 South Union (pre-1872); and "Kalamont" at 53 Randolph Street (1865), reflect much of the area's history.

HOUSES FOR THE LUMBER BARONS | Big houses were generally the telltale sign of big wealth. As the site of one of Michigan's major lumber booms, the Saugatuck and Douglas area was the largest producer of cut lumber south of Muskegon, and its harbor ranked 7th in Michigan lumber exports. In 1870 alone Saugatuck exported 24 million shingles, 15 million laths, and 32 million board feet of lumber. But where did the lumber capitalists sleep? All over Michigan lumber barons were notorious for building grand mansions. Many can still be seen in old lumber towns such as Manistee, Saginaw, Owosso, Bay City, and Muskegon. Charles Hackley's 1889 mansion in Muskegon, for example, cost $50,000—at a time when the average Saugatuck house cost less than $1,000. But Saugatuck's lumber barons were not quite in the same league—or those who were took their money elsewhere. By 1878 the local paper was lamenting that "a certain class" of local businessmen had no interest in the prosperity of the area except to drain the land of its wealth "until the last pine tree should be cut."[19]

To be fair, the half dozen or so capitalist families of Saugatuck and Douglas who did build houses here did so modestly, at least by lumber-baron standards of the day. This was probably a result of the fact that the Saugatuck lumber "catch" never compared in scale to places such as Muskegon and that the lumber boom here was of shorter duration, resulting in much of the profit fleeing town as the would-be barons searched for new uncut timber and new places for investment. The most affluent man in town during the lumber boom was O. R. Johnson, who packed up his mill machinery and left town in 1876. He built a large Italianate house on Griffith Street to rival his brother's house on Allegan Street. Later the Griffith Street house was purchased by Captain R. C. Brittain. Francis B. Stockbridge, Singapore mill owner, lived on lower Hoffman Street in what was

H. D. & TAMAR MOORE HOUSE - THE PARK HOUSE
1857
888 Holland Street
Saugatuck

H. D. Moore, of Vermont's "Green Mountain Boys," came to Saugatuck as a young man in 1855 and succeeded in amassing a huge lumber empire, including a large mill near this house and three area lumber camps. The simple Greek Revival structure with its porches offered a variety of views, including that of Mt. Baldhead across the river. The house was considered "pretentious" in its day and its "beautiful grove" was enclosed by a white picket fence—to hold deer. In the 1870s Moore was considered the wealthiest man in Allegan County. Susan B. Anthony, the women's rights-temperance leader, stayed here in 1879, as a guest of Mrs. Moore, a local social reformer. In 1885 the house became the village's first "resort"—seeking high-class tourists. By 1888 the resort was offering a variety of entertainment, including a February masquerade dance with Goodrich's orchestra—"but none of the maskers may dance before 10 pm."
[*Commercial Record*, February 10, 1888.]

H. B. (HARRY) MOORE HOUSE
1863
312 Hoffman Street
Saugatuck

Built by a local ship's carpenter and owned by a lumber baron. The bracketed window tops on the first floor and pointed windows tucked under the gables on the second floor make for a simplified Gothic effect. Mr. Moore's fortune was made by stockpiling millions of feet of timber on upriver banks, and then floating them to his mill located at the end of Center Street in Douglas were they were cut into boards and shingles. Restored.

called the "finest house in the county."[20] Stockbridge left Saugatuck in 1873 and went on to become a U. S. Senator, eventually ending up in a mansion in Kalamazoo. His Saugatuck house burned sometime in the 1880s while in the possession of Captain L. B. Coates.

The two most notable existing lumber baron houses were built by two unrelated men by the surname of Moore. H. D. Moore made his fortune by cutting 200 million feet of white pine timber, which was then processed into milled lumber at his mill at "Mooreville" on Holland Street where his house still stands. This house, called "Park House" because it stood within Mr. Moore's huge fenced deer park, is a fine, large, but certainly not grand, Greek Revival house. The H. D. Moores left Saugatuck for nearby Allegan in 1879, and soon thereafter the "estate" became Saugatuck's first resort hotel—as it remains today.

The other of the two, Harry B. Moore, who owned huge tracts of pine and hemlock timber upriver and a shingle and lumber mill in Douglas, lived in a large Gothic Revival house (with Greek Revival references) at 312 Hoffman Street on the hill in Saugatuck.

THE OCTAGON HOUSE: THE ULTIMATE VICTORIAN HOUSE | The Victorians were history's busiest organizers, planners, and reformers—largely because they had so much to plan and reform. Industrialization brought them both blessings and burdens. On the one hand it brought the problems of overcrowding, a decline in religious and moral standards, and new diseases related to industrialization such as cholera and tuberculosis—all of which pointed to a need for greater social control; but at the same time it prompted advances in science, technology and architecture to solve those problems and improve daily life for all members of society. No development in nineteenth century architecture and building represents the urge for improvement of living space better than Orson Fowler's invention of the Octagon House—the plan for which was published in 1853 and an example of which was built at 90 South Mixer Street in Douglas for Captain and Mrs. Charles Mixer in 1859. Fowler, who lamented that the typical small house of the day was simply a collection of rooms of "clutter, confusion and helter-skelter,"[21] was a New York State reformer who believed that a multi-story, eight-sided house was the closest to nature, the most economical, and most functional. Having used "nature's shape" to devise the structure, Fowler believed that the octagonal house, with a variety of innovations including natural air conditioning and closets, would bring about the improvement of body and soul—predating Frank Lloyd Wright who would adopt much of the same philosophy a generation later.

WINDOW SHOPPING BECOMES PART OF LIFE | Population growth, prosperity, architectural invention and improved manufacture of plate glass after the Civil War turned Butler and Center Streets into "modern" shopping streets with fancy shop fronts—making for a

A History of the Buildings and Architecture in the Saugatuck and Douglas Area

OCTAGON HOUSE
ca. 1859
90 Mixer Street
Douglas
Orson Fowler, *architect*

The most modern house of its time, the Octagon House was built for riverboat Captain Charles S. Mixer and his wife, Julia. It is perfectly typical of Fowler's houses: broad porches and large windows for its day, tin roof with drains to transfer water to cisterns for household use. The eight sides are each 12.5 feet wide—which Fowler claimed provides more square footage on each floor than a house with a larger footprint of 25 feet square! His "Octagon" anticipated the 20th-century house in that rooms were arranged to open onto one another, usually flowing from the center, rather than a sequential progression of room after room. The practical-minded Fowler was preaching to the typical servantless housewife of the 1860s when he said: "I submit this point to the special consideration of every housekeeper, and leave them to say whether they could not do TWICE THE WORK with the same ease in the octagon." He proposed that children should have their own rooms, that air circulation be addressed by way of many windows, a verandah, and a cupola, and that built-in closets replace expensive furniture. Rain water was to be filtered for drinking purposes and the kitchen placed at the heart of the house instead of the custom of placing it as an attached back room "stomach-in-the-foot shanty," as he called it. [Orson Fowler, *The Octagon House: A Home For All* (1853, reprint, 1973) p.65.] *Over a thousand octagon houses were built in the United States in the 1850s and 1860s. Restored 1993 & 2005.*

Mixer's boat provided transport between Saugatuck and Allegan. He was also a land speculator and he and his wife had the "Mixer Addition" to Douglas platted and recorded in 1867. Mixer also owned the Newark (later called Saugatuck) House hotel, in the 1860s.

Vicky Stull

striking contrast between the commercial architecture of the village and that of the surrounding countryside with its lowly and rather "folk" buildings. The age of consumerism had begun.

Indeed, Butler and Center street merchants put on a good show. The Landmark and Stimson buildings speak a rather urbane "Commercial Italianate" language and must have caused quite a stir on Butler Street. But the more common Henry Schnobel shop front farther along the same street is perhaps more representative of what most merchants could afford. Indeed, Schnobel's friendly appearing double-door front with double plate glass windows appears to be the standard architectural formula for Butler Street—as it appears to be in Douglas with the case of Dyer Putnam's General Store. By 1900 these traditional storefronts were being replaced by even grander fronts—as we see with the new Kerr building shouldering up to what now appear to be little toy-like buildings of a previous generation.

"About twice in the summer… Papa would say: 'Today I will cook a beefsteak for you!'…First we had to go down the hill to the village to Fritz Walz's Butcher Shop. Then Papa went into the cooler, where he selected just the piece that he wanted; then he supervised the cutting and trimming. And we all went back up the hill with our 'prize steak.' It took all of us to wait on Papa: one to get the 'spider' (frying pan), another to get one tool, another to bring the seasoning. It was a real production."
—from *Heroes, Rogues, & Just Plain Folks, A History of the Saugatuck Area.* Kit Lane, ed. Saugatuck-Douglas Historical Society (1998) p.26.

| MAIL ORDER SHOP FRONT
1893

Some of the lumber sent from the Saugatuck, Douglas, and Pier Cove docks may have come back as mail order decorative shop fronts. This is from the catalogue of the Mulliner Box and Planing Company of Chicago. The company also provided plate glass. "Write for prices."

| STIMSON'S BUILDING
1878

Butler Street between Culver & Mason | Saugatuck

"Prices Cut in Two. At the new store in the Stimson building, Saugatuck, Mich. It Will Pay You to come and buy Shoes, Dry Goods, Clothing, Hats, Caps, and Notions there. They are Given Away at half the usual price." [*The Commercial Record*, July 7, 1898.]

A combination drug and clothing store. The wide roof overhang and paired cornice brackets are typically "Commercial Italianate" but the first floor is unusually tall. Note the advertisement signboards—for clothing—set between the upper windows. Dr. Stimson is to the right of the door while Mrs. Stimson is to the left. Many early druggists were also doctors. Stimson lived in Saugatuck from 1858 to 1916. The Commercial Record in 1886 called it the most "elegantly furnished building in Saugatuck" (including the apartments on the second floor). It also served as the Saugatuck Post Office in the 1870s and 1880s. It was destroyed by a great fire in July 1886 that swept away nearly the entire village block—and then rebuilt to become Friedman's Discount Clothing. [*The Commercial Record*, August 1, 1898.]

A History of the Buildings and Architecture in the Saugatuck and Douglas Area

| PEACH BELT STORE
1880s
Beach Belt, M-89

When compared to Stimson's rather imposing Saugatuck store, Gordon Spencer's country store is a striking reminder of the increasing differences, at the time, between village and rural life.

| MILLER ROBINSON'S STORE
1860s *(photo, ca. 1902)*
392 Butler Street | Saugatuck

The village's mechanical genius. A photographer, watchmaker, jeweler, and the man who introduced Saugatuck to "moving pictures," Miller Robinson purchased the building in 1887. He sold musical instruments, was the village's Western Union Telegraph operator, and had the first village photograph studio—offering portraits for sale at $2.00 a dozen. In January of 1899 Mr. Robinson entertained the village with Mr. Edison's "moving picture entertainment" at the local opera house—all for 20 cents for adults and 10 cents for children. It was also reported that he took what was claimed to be "the finest [photographic] view of the village from Mt. Baldhead and he was the person who hooked up the first local telephone line between Douglas and Saugatuck, and brought to Saugatuck a seven foot antique New England clock that had cog wheels made of wood. He also sold candy. [See *Commercial Record*, 1895, 1897, 1899.]

| CHARLES E. BIRD'S DRUG STORE
ca. 1895
Butler & Hoffman Streets | Saugatuck

Charles E. Bird was a village druggist from 1875 until 1931. Building replaced by the "Heath Block." Portions of the structure were moved to become the present "Shoebox House" on Francis Street.

| FRITZ WALZ'S BUTCHER SHOP
EAST OF THE SUN
1889 *(photo, 2006)*
252 Butler Street | Saugatuck

A new building on a disreputable site. This new butcher shop replaced an old "eye sore"—the Nicolas Building—that housed a prostitution and gambling den. [Commercial Record, Jaunary 1, 1886.] *The new owners, the Walz brothers, were well known local butchers. The building's interior was praised as being modern for its 13-foot ceiling and refrigerator.* [Commercial Record, March 22, 1889; July 19, 1889; September 20, 1889; October 18, 1889.] *By the 1950s the site had regained some of its old notoriety—as a lively bar, called "The Cabin" that attracted a mixed straight-gay crowd as well as an organ that, it was said, made the place jump.*

| DYER PUTNAM'S GENRAL STORE & POST OFFICE
1865
Center Street | Douglas

Mr. Putnam operated this simple wood-sided Greek Revival fronted store from 1865 until his death in 1894. It was built by the Gerber family. With Putnam the first village postmaster, the store housed the village Post Office from 1866 to 1886, and offered everything from flour to "four dollar suits." [Commercial Record, July 6, 1879.] *On the far right was an implement sales outlet. Later, the structure also housed the village fire engine—which burned along with the rest of the building in 1902. Later the site of a Standard Oil service station.*

Drawing by William Kemperman.

THE STREET AS ARCHITECTURE & ARTIFACT: DOUGLAS CENTER STREET

The place where the action is, where deals are made, where gossip is exchanged. No one has yet written the history of the most important place for community interaction and action in America—the street. Before the automobile age most towns were "self-orientated," that is, most of the town's material goods came from local shops. The shop fronts were local corporate identities, if you will, whereby local merchants put on displays and hung their sign boards. Here too we find places where the public gathered: the post office, village hall, church, school, and village square—and those quasi-public amenities such as coffee shop, restaurant, and tavern. All of these structures

CENTER STREET – SOUTH SIDE
ca. 1910
Douglas

Hats anyone? At least six women operated millinery (women's hats and accessories) shops in various buildings on this side of Center Street between 1870 and 1881. View looking south of the block between Main and Spring Streets—the smallest of the structures being the oldest (1860s). The wagon and horseless buggy (with a load of baskets—probably from the nearby factory) stand silent while Douglas's new electric taxi cab speeds up the street. MacDonald's "Central" Store (1878) was one of four "general" stores on the street at this time—it later became Bird's Drug Store. It was the village post office from about 1919-1934. The brick Kerr building (far right) of 1907 housed a hardware store and apartments and replaced an earlier wood structure. The only original building still standing on this block is on the far left, was built as the Douglas Meat Market in 1881 with Emma and Lora's millinery shop above. The market eventually became the Douglas Soda Bar and Grill (1940s and 1950s), then the Douglas Café, and is now part of Everyday People Café.

and spaces are tied together by that unremarkable system of paths we call "the street" —which, in effect, came to symbolize degrees of prosperity, sharing, and sociability. It was often a highly contested space but also a place where social hierarchy was submerged—and for us today the most important artifact of the cultural landscape. By 1900 the scale, mass, proportion, and setback of the main commercial streets of the villages, Butler and Center Streets, were set in a manner that was to prevail into the present century. It was about this time that paving material began to be applied—first as sidewalks and then as streets. Some of the buildings shown here still exist as the original structures.

CENTER STREET – NORTH SIDE
1930s
Douglas

Corner of Spring and Center looking east toward Main Street. John Norton stands in front of his drug store and soda fountain (Norton later moved his business to an opposite corner). The Greyhound Bus Depot was also the Central Office of the telephone company, with the telephone operator's living space in the rear. Farther down the block is Weigert's Douglas Café, which became The Auction House and then Chaps Restaurant.

A. O. WOLBRINK DEPARTMENT STORE
1870s *(photo, 1920s)*
Ganges

Probably built as a general store before 1870 and became Ganges's first Post Office in 1879. For a time Lillian Eddy, the wife of the postmaster in the 1890s, used the second floor as a private school for local children after they had graduated from high school.

THE ARCHITECTURE OF THE VERY ORDINARY

One of the most neglected chapters in the history of Saugatuck buildings is that of commercial fishing structures—this is in spite of the fact that up to about 1950 fishing itself was so characteristic of the townscape. Fish shanties of various sizes lined the riverbanks, serving as fishermen's sleeping quarters, along with ice houses for fish storage, net storage sheds, and so on. Giant net drying racks accompanied all of this—like huge cloth wheels spinning at dockside, shoulder to shoulder with mackinaw fishing boats and fishing tugs. The ancient settlement called Fishtown, the Shriver docks at the mouth of the River and, later, the Water and Lake Street docks in Saugatuck, and the fishermen themselves were a constant reminder of this enterprise—adding another layer of color to what was to many outside observers an extraordinary townscape.

FISH SHANTIES & DRYING WHEELS
ca. 1950
Kalamazoo Riverfront at Water Street
Saugatuck

The architecture of commercial fishing. Until the 1950s the riverscape was dotted with reminders that fishing had been a way of life for many families. This particular site holds the last of the commercial fishing structures.

THE ARCHITECTURE OF
MATERIAL CULTURE:
SCHNOBEL'S HARDWARE STORE
1872 *(photo, 1898)*
250 Butler Street | Saugatuck

Bird cages, tin pots, and pistols. This shop front tells us something about how people learned to aspire to and chose material objects. H. Schnobel's "Hardware, Stoves, Tinware, Cutlery, &c." store (as it was advertised) was a Butler Street institution from its establishment in about 1872 until the close of the century. The local press frequently noted the store's handsome and well painted front as well as Mr. Schnobel's wide offering of household appliances—such as stoves and washing machines. The boy is Adolph Schnobel. This wood structure was replaced by a brick building in the 1930s.

JOHN BAPTISTE MARTEL HOUSE
1884
345 Grand Street
Saugatuck

Martel was a French-Canadian ship builder who lived in Saugatuck for over half a century, building Saugatuck steamers until 1897. The shipbuilding connection is evident in the carpentry work by George Hames and fancy "scrollwork" by William Finley, both ships carpenters. The window frame decoration is of an oak-leaf-and-acorn motif. The house was later purchased by a Chicago industrialist and restored by the noted Chicago interior designer Florence "Danny" Hunn in the 1940s. At that time the rear coach house was relocated and attached to the house and the bay window was added to the north side to mirror the one on the south side.

CHAPTER THREE

Home Grown Wealth: Fruit Growers, Merchants, and Ships Captains
Show Their Stuff, 1880-1900

THE HISTORIC AND ECONOMIC PICTURE | The lumber era had meant 40 years of jobs and profits, but by the later 1870s the exploitation of the forest was over. The Great Fires of 1871 in Chicago and elsewhere had actually accelerated the process of round-the-clock clear-cutting and milling, thereby finishing off what was left of Michigan's famous white pine. The Singapore mill was packed up part and parcel and carted off to be put into service in foresting operations farther north. The two Douglas mills went out of business (one evolved into a basket factory), Saugatuck's principal mill produced less and less until it was finally closed in 1914, and the shingle mills that dotted the river front dwindled. Many capitalists and workers alike went off to find jobs, investment opportunities, and invention elsewhere. It was said that the businesses of the village were "nearly prostrated."[1] To make matters worse, despite good intentions, the villages were by-passed by the main-line railroads.

NEW GOLD IS FOUND | Nevertheless, even facing the demise of local lumbering, some of the news was good. Already by the 1870s the local economy was turning to several happily interrelated sources of wealth: boat building, shipping, and fruit growing. Because ships were cheaper to run than railroads, lake steamers and tall schooners continued to keep the local harbor busy. Thus, the earlier marriage of lake transport and the dying lumber industry was reborn as a union between lake transport and locally grown fruit.

Peaches for home use had been cultivated by nearby fur traders as early as the 1820s, in the Ganges area by 1839, and then on a larger scale to the south in Berrien County by the 1850s. The first commercial orchards in the Saugatuck-Douglas-Pier Cove area were planted in the early 1860s. As the tale would go, by the mid-1870s the Berrien County peach enterprise had been decimated by disease, while the Saugatuck-Douglas countryside had blossomed into a veritable orchard with the Village of Douglas the center. In the 1860s nearly 15,000 trees grew within the Douglas village limits alone. The sailor Henry Wallbrecht on Union Street turned an entire square block of the village into a small farm and even the local hotelkeeper, minister, and numerous merchants were growing peaches. The 48 acre Riverside Farm, for example, had a total of 1,898 trees—pear, apple and cherry trees. By 1884 there were 134,812 trees under cultivation by local farmers; and nearly a quarter of all the peaches grown in west Michigan were produced in Douglas, Saugatuck, and the surrounding township. The number of containers of fruit shipped out of local ports in 1885 totaled 195,318,[2] and during the first week of September 1897, the local steamer "Douglas" carried 6,000 bushels of Saugatuck areas fruit to Chicago where Michigan peaches were known as "Michigan Gold." It was said that local bankers were astonished at the amount of cash the peach-growers were hauling into their banks.[3]

Perishable peaches and other fruits, particularly apples, had to be shipped quickly and with care, which created a bullish market for boats, boat builders, boat captains and crews. In 1871, 672 vessels entered the port of Saugatuck. In 1888 the "Douglas" alone made 88 round-trips to Chicago. Indeed, shipping was a profitable trade until the first decade of the 20th century. Between 1865 and 1915 more than 200 boats were built in Saugatuck boat yards. It was reported in the winter of 1887 that 5 steam boats were on the drawing boards for winter construction.[4] Among the most active of the local boat builders was John Baptiste Martel whose first sailing vessel, the "Napoleon," was built in 1837. Martel was joined by Captain James Elliott who built nearly two dozen boats, and the partners Reuben Rogers and Charles E. Bird who, up to about 1900, built many large steamers and owned shipping warehouses and piers as well.

SHOWING OFF | Farmers bought boats and boat builders bought farms—and ship captains bought both. Peach money and boat money went to build barns, riverside docks, and warehouses— and new houses. Martel built a modest but handsome house for his family at 345 Grand, Saugatuck (1884); Rogers built his imposing brick-and-wood Italianate dwelling which still stand on Butler Street (having had shops added in front);

J. F. TAYLOR'S LAKE RIDGE FARM
1877-80
2941 Lakeshore Drive
Douglas

J. F. Taylor had 500 peach and 300 apple trees under cultivation on his farm. House remains in altered form. Taylor exalted the peach as capable of "the healing of the nations," of providing "a better diet than drugs," and of laying "a good foundation for moral and physical health. It relieves the system of many impurities and . . . it inspires men with a love of the beautiful." [(Michigan)State Horticultural Society: 18th Annual Report, (1888), p. 126.]

43

JONAS S. CROUSE
HOUSE
ca. 1860
11 Fremont Street
Douglas

Crouse was a lumber mill foreman, carpenter, and one of the first fruit farmers in the area, planting over 100 apple and peach trees on his six village lots in 1862. The house was later known for its rose garden.

A History of the Buildings and Architecture in the Saugatuck and Douglas Area

FERNWOOD
1860-80
2488 Lakeshore Drive
Fennville

The Joshua Weed House. In 1874 Weed's farm was 124 acres, with 30 of those acres planted as fruit orchards. The Weeds also opened their home as a summer resort. One of the Weed sons, Elmer E., was manager and part owner of Saugatuck's "Big Pavilion" dance hall. The house, with its pastiche of Greek Revival and Italianate features, had two dining rooms, one of which seated 65.

Ship Captain turned-merchant George Plummer built a new house on Spring Street in Douglas, and Elliott built a showy (now altered) Italianate residence with tower at 346 Mary Street. Even ship's carpenters built impressive new houses for their families such as the one Henry Till built at 655 Spear Street, Saugatuck, a Sears Catalogue house, and ship owner and engineer George N. Dutcher on Union Street in Douglas.

MORE SHIP CAPTAINS HOUSES | If houses are symbols of wealth and social status, we might conclude that Saugatuck and Douglas of the 1880s and 1890s were in the hands of an aristocracy of ship captains. From the end of the Civil War until about 1900, over forty ship captains built new or settled in existing houses in and around the villages. As described in Chapter Two, Captain Charles Mixer built the area's most progressive house of its day in Douglas and other captains settled in Douglas as well. But the heart of the captains' building boom was on Griffith Street on "the hill" in Saugatuck.

It was natural that the captains would gravitate to the upper reaches of the village, which then more than now allowed for grand views of the harbor. Griffith Street was home to half a dozen captains, making it a "captains' row" of sorts in the later years of the nineteenth century. In fact, unlike the lumber barons who left town when the lumber boom was

HARVEY L. HOUSE FARMHOUSE
1868 *(photo, 1880s)*
Holland & Washington Streets
Saugatuck

Harvey House to far left, with family. House was one of the most successful of the early fruit farmers. Builder was carpenter Hugh L. Graham, as an addition to an older house on the site. Note Windmill to right. The house went through a number of additions and removals including a bay window and front portico added in the 1920s. It had a library on the first floor. The family was known for its interest in education and civic affairs The House family encouraged many Chicago–Oak Park people in the to purchase summer cottage property along the Saugatuck-Douglas lakeshore and helped Reverend Gray to locate his camp for poor children from Chicago along the Saugatuck lakeshore (Forward Movement Park). Harvey House began his farming business by producing honey—sending a record 3,000 lbs to Chicago in 1878. By the time of this photograph the farm had over 1,000 peach trees and 500 quince trees.

WILLIAMS–SORENSEN FARMHOUSE
ca. 1866
550 Campbell Road
Saugatuck

Originally a 40-acre orchard and vineyard called "West Fruit Farm" founded by B. S. Williams and sons, and later known as Howard Farm. The south wing is the older section of house. The family planted 600 peach trees in 1867 and by 1875 the farm was known as "one of the best farms in the state." The giant pine tree on the property was brought from the World Columbian Exposition in 1893. [Henry Clubb, *Saugatuck and Ganges Fruit Region* (pamphlet) (1875), p. 9.]

A History of the Buildings and Architecture in the Saugatuck and Douglas Area

CAPTAINS' HOUSES

The large number of relatively large and stylish captains' houses in this area suggests that ship captains ranked high on the social and economic scale. Part of this may be that they wisely diversified their interests to include fruit growing and/or boat building. Many of the houses on this map still exist and most of them were built in the Italianate manner. Many are clustered along Griffith Street and elsewhere on "the hill," which was the most popular residential district of Saugatuck.

IN SAUGATUCK

e	Richard Ames	1857	344 Main St.
e	W. B. Minter	1867	547 Butler St.
e	Wm. Tyler	1869	Old Allegan Rd.
	J. N. Upham	1869	State & Pleasant Sts.
	Henry Allet	1871	North St.
	Issac Wilson	1870s	Mason & Grand Sts.
e	Thorton Leland	1874	346 Griffith St.
	Charles Coates	1870s	Mason & Griffith Sts.
e	W. P. Wilson	ca. 1880	439 Griffith St.
e	Reuben Rogers	1881–97	247 Butler St.
	R. C. Brittain	1887	Mason & Griffith Sts.
	Wm. Edgcomb	1881	Old Allegan Rd.
e	John B. Martel	1884	359 Grand St.
e	James Dole	1886	132 Water St.
e	George Crawford	1887	404 Griffith St.
	L. B. Coates	1886	Hoffman St. (lots 9 & 10)
e	James Elliott	1890s	346 Mary St.
e	W. G. Phelps	1890	1034 State St.
	S. W. Morgan	1892	Griffith & Francis Sts.
	Fred Sears	1894	Mary St. (lot 9)
	Robert Reid	1894	Griffith & Holland Sts.
	Richard Rode	1894	149 Griffith St.
	Harry Holt	1894	Lucy & Holland Sts.
	Henry Perkins	1890s	Lake Street
	J. B. Brown	1890s	NE Corner, Elizabeth/Mason
	Joseph Lewis	1890s	Lake St.
e	Fred Miner	1890s	711 Butler St.
	Fred Partridge	1892	Mason St.
	Dennis Cummings	1893	Mason St.
	H. John Huff	1900	NE corner, Holland/Francis
e	Fred Thompson	1906	633 Pleasant St.
e	= existing		
	= Captains' Houses (Saugatuck only)		

IN DOUGLAS

e	Charles Mixer	1859	90 S. Mixer St.
	Charles McVea		Lakeshore Dr.
	Samuel McVea		Lakeshore Dr.
	B. W. Davis	1873	Ferry St.
e	George Tisdale	1877	300 Ferry St
e	George Plummer	1897	42 Spring St
e	John Campbell	1897	53 Randolph St.
e	J. Campbell		653 Campbell Rd. ("Idylease")
	Robert Reid	1872/99	Lakeshore Dr.
	William Plummer		Wiley Rd. & Blue Star Hwy.
e	William Turnbull		Wiley Rd. & Blue Star Hwy.
e			& 30 Mixer St.

CAPTAIN R. C. BRITTAIN'S HOUSE
ca. 1868 *(photo, 1950s)*
Griffith & Mason Streets | Saugatuck

Built by O. R. Johnson, owner of several lumber mills, the house is a fine example of Italianate architecture. The over-size cupola provided a full view of the river. The Commercial Record of 1873 reported that this "beautiful residence is improved in appearance by the application of paint and the addition of window and door blinds." The house later became Captain Charles Coates' residence and then that of Captain R. C. Brittain. Brittain was a sailor who settled in Saugatuck in 1873 when he was 28 years old, having purchased a local steamboat, the "George P. Heath." In 1877 he established a boat building yard with James Elliot along the riverside at what is now Wicks Park, building nearly twenty large steamboats between then and 1898. Brittain also owned two fruit farms in Saugatuck Township. Captain Brittain died in 1905. His son, Leonard, was also a Great Lakes captain and later captained the Saugatuck Chain Ferry. The house was razed in 1967 to make way for a parking lot.

e = *existing*
● = *Captain's Houses (Saugatuck only)*

over, many ship captains appear to have stayed on to invest in boat building and fruit farming. This was the case with both Captain Richard Ames, who purchased Saugatuck's oldest known house (at 334 Main Street), and Captain John B. Campbell, who built "Kalamont" in Douglas; they took up farming in nearby Laketown while still living in the villages. Captain Benjamin W. Davis built a house and operated a 22-acre orchard farm on the hill in Douglas where Tower Marina is now located. The builder of Captain Davis's house was his brother-in-law, William Tisdale, who built many area structures, including a house for Captain William Plummer, 456 Blue Star Highway, Douglas (ca.1875).[5] Captain W. P. Wilson and shipbuilder George Hames built comfortable Italianate houses on Griffith Street overlooking Saugatuck, as did steamboat Captain H. John Huff whose ten room home boasted an interior in curly birch and cypress wood. The fine wood interior in Wilson's house reflects both his career as shipbuilder and as ship captain. Griffith Street was also home to Captain George Crawford who in 1887 moved a large house from its site five blocks to the east and connected it to a smaller house already on the property, giving himself a grand view of the village

TECHNOLOGY & WOOD

The nineteenth century saw rapid changes in building technology, resulting in a variety of changes in both the form and function of most buildings. Of pivotal importance were the development of machine-made nails and improved techniques for lumber milling. These enabled the invention of the "balloon frame" construction method which replaced the traditional heavy timber bracing system which relied on pegged joints and in which structural strength came from massive corner posts. Developed in Chicago in the 1830s, "balloon frame" construction greatly simplified building. It used closely spaced 2-by-4-inch studs running continuously from floor to roof, nailed together to form a basket-like cage or "balloon" of load-bearing walls along which weight was evenly distributed; eventually each floor was treated as a separate unit (the "platform frame method"). Balloon frame construction was revolutionary, too, from the perspective of building design and layout; since it simplified the construction of corners, overhangs, extensions and porches, it encouraged irregular layout and form, giving way to much more elaborate design possibilities. Thus, cheap and lightweight sawed lumber and ready-made nails, combined with the new construction technique, paved the way for the beginning of the American dream: a home for all.

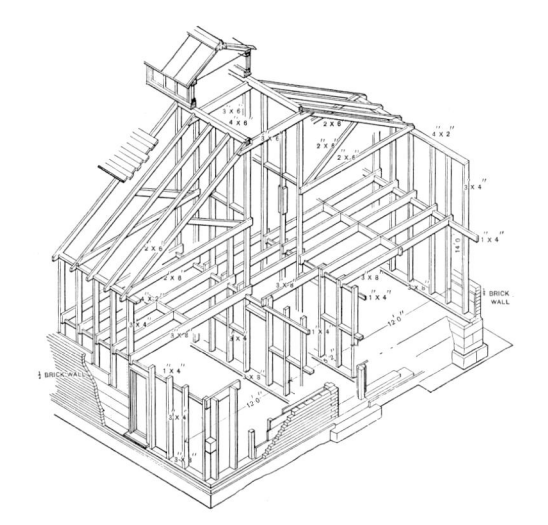

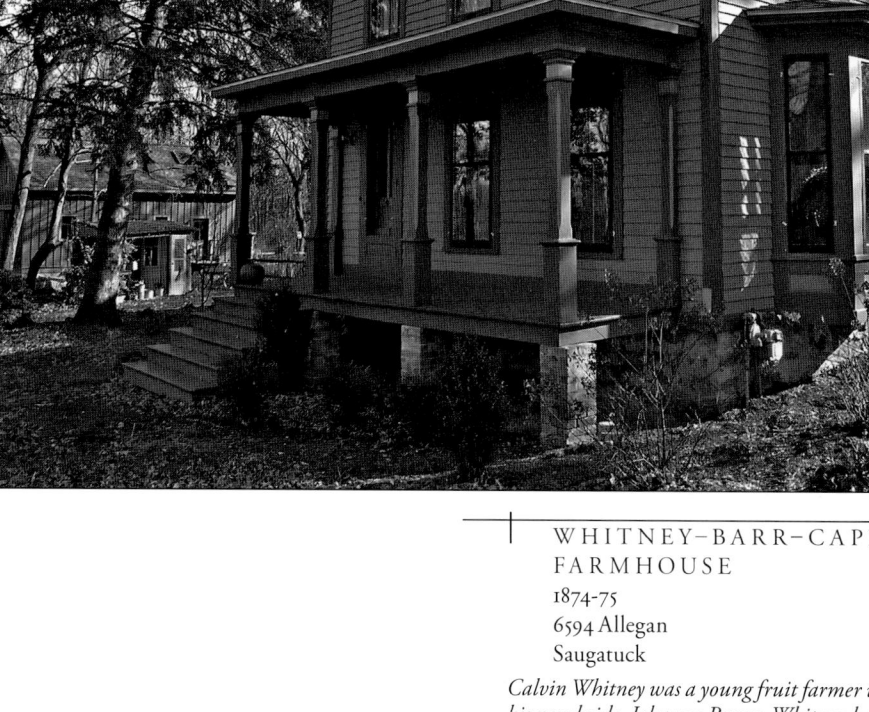

Balloon-Frame Construction

WHITNEY–BARR–CAPPELLETTI FARMHOUSE
1874-75
6594 Allegan
Saugatuck

Calvin Whitney was a young fruit farmer when this 12 room farmhouse was built for his new bride, Johanna Burns. Whitney had enlisted in the Civil War at age 17 in 1861, then came to Saugatuck after the war and had a career as hotel proprietor, grocer, fruit farmer, a partner in Saugatuck's "Iron Clad" basket factory, and a boat builder. Called a "model farmer" by the local newspaper, Whitney raised sheep and had a carp fish farm built on the property. In about 1909 the house became the home of Henry and Olga Barr. Mrs. Barr was born on a farm in Germany and preferred to live a farm-life in Saugatuck while Mr. Barr worked in Chicago. An old barn foundation is now used as garden wall. A finely preserved example of Italianate architecture. [The Commercial Record, February 17, 1882; December 3, 1886]

and the harbor. The best known of the captain's houses was the Brittain House, Griffith and Mason Streets, so-named after its longest occupant, Captain R. C. Brittain.

The fruit growers were not far behind. In fact, everyone was getting into the fruit-growing act—and putting up new houses and barns. On the "hill" in Saugatuck, the Henry Till family farmed a large orchard. The carpenter Jonas S. Crouse surrounded his lovely Greek Revival house in Douglas with peach and apple orchards, as did the carpenter Hugh F. Graham. Farmer J. F. Taylor built a splendid farm house (Lake Ridge Farm), as did Joshua and Rebecca Weed. The Weed estate, named "Fernwood," included 30 acres of peaches, apples, and grapes. B. S. Williams's Italianate farm house (West Fruit Farm—later Shorewood Farms) at 550 Campbell Road, Saugatuck overlooked the Saugatuck harbor in one direction and the family's 3,000-tree peach orchard in the other. Farmer Williams's first planting of grape vines produced one ton of Concords in 1872, and then 10 tons in 1873. Farmer House had a noble Greek Revival house settled alongside the family's orchards on Holland-

FORM & FUNCTION

The interior and exterior form of houses changed dramatically as well, reflecting changes in the middle-class family. House design responded to a different kind of family-centeredness: no longer were most Americans tied to the soil nor was the home a place for production of goods; the home was becoming a place for consuming; it served as shelter for the family against an increasingly cold and heartless world—a place for compassion, love, and attention to the raising of children. New standards of family life centered around the perfect mother—the mother who did not plow the fields or work in the mill, but who presided over the perfect home.

CRAWFORD–BLEEKER HOUSE
ca 1873-1887
404 Griffith Street | Saugatuck

This is an interesting "pieced" house, one section of which appears to have been built in the early 1870s and then connected to a larger two-story Italianate "box-like" house moved from nearby in 1887. Its owner, Captain George Crawford, was a Great Lakes captain of schooners and steamships with a long and adventurous career. The main part of the house is similar in form to its neighbor to the south at 346 Griffith Street, which was built by Captain Thornton W. Leland in 1874, and to Captain William P. Wilson's house (circa 1880) nearby at 439 Griffith Street. In 1891 the house became the residence of the local baker, John Schaberg and family. Schaberg added the porches in 1900.

WORK & WAGES
Saugatuck Fruit Exchange

"The exchange had been in operation only a few years when my father Joseph W. Prentice (1877-1961) was hired as manager, and he held this position until he retired in 1953. During this time there were many changes in the fruit industry including increased competition from western [USA] fruit as a result of improved transportation facilities. Another change was the increased vigilance of health authorities who began checking the spray residue on the fruit, necessitating the installation of fruit-washing equipment in the Exchange. The principal fruits handled by the Exchange were apples, pears, and peaches. Berries and other small fruits were not accepted. The fruit was all graded for size on mechanical graders, and wormy or otherwise defective fruit was picked out by hand as it passed down the conveyor belt. . . . . During the fruit harvest, the Exchange had perhaps 50 employees working on the packing floor. Wages—at least during the depression years of the 1930s when I worked there for a short while—were 15 cents an hour for men, 10 cents for women. One office worker was also usually on the job. Among the bookkeepers employed at various times were Minnie Williams, Edith Walz, and Clark Tillinghast."

—Willard Prentice, 1983

SAUGATUCK FRUIT EXCHANGE
ca. 1917
Culver Street | Saugatuck
Removed. Now site of Coghlin Park

TARA RESTAURANT
1861 *(photo, ca. 1937)*
Blue Star Highway | Douglas

Spencer Farmhouse, 1861, here shown in its 1930s reincarnation as a restaurant and popular jazz club. Michael B. Spencer made his start in lumbering at Singapore and then established his own mill along Culver Street at the foot of St. Joseph Street4 in Saugatuck before investing in farm land and building this house in Douglas. This farmhouse was occupied by the "Tara" restaurant from 1937 until its destruction by fire in 1975, then replaced by a new Tara. Now a condominium development.

Washington Street. The contract for this 1867 house stipulated that it have classic Greek Revival "frieze band" windows, be of "balloon frame" construction, and to be fitted with a chimney "of suitable size and dimension to accommodate 3 stoves."6 Former mill owner Michael B. Spencer, cultivated an orchard in Douglas that consisted of 500 pear trees and 200 peach trees and built a farmhouse which later became "Tara," Douglas's best-known eatery.

FRUIT EXCHANGE & BASKET FACTORIES | The Saugatuck Fruit Exchange was a large barn-like building which once stood on Saugatuck's Culver Street, a reminder of the glorious days when local fruit orchards were important enough to the local economy that the bank nearby took the name "Fruit Grower's State Bank." The Exchange was operated as a factory for sorting, grading, storing, and packing locally grown fruit. It was founded as a farmers' cooperative for the purpose of protecting local farmers from the big-city middlemen wholesalers.

Peach money was also invested in other packaging and transport facilities. New docks and warehouses accompanied two basket factories: the "Douglas Basket Factory" (also known as "E. E. Weed and Company") at the north end of Washington Street was the more famous of the two. The other one, "C. Whitney and Company," also known as "The

A History of the Buildings and Architecture in the Saugatuck and Douglas Area

DOUGLAS BASKET FACTORY
(photo ca. 1900)
North Washington Street
Douglas

E. E. Weed & Company was Douglas's largest manufacturer and the largest basket factory in Michigan for the several decades before its destruction by fire in 1927. The factory workday ended at 4:40 p.m. in order to allow its workers to get in some fishing before sunset. The tugboat to the right is loaded with baskets en route to the railroad junction at New Richmond for shipment to fruit farmers farther south.

SAUGATUCK IRON-CLAD BASKET FACTORY
Butler & Lucy Streets
Saugatuck

The C. Whitney Basket Factory, a Saugatuck competitor in the local basket trade. The company was in operation from the 1880s to 1902. It was partially covered with sheet-iron for fire protection. A section of the building was relocated a short distance up river to become part of the Tourist Home (later Mt. Baldhead) Hotel. In one week in July of 1888 the factory turned out 40,000 baskets. [*The Commercial Record*, July 6, 1888.]

Ironclad" because of its sheet-iron roof and partial sheet-iron walls, was located on the river in Saugatuck at the corner of Lucy & Butler Streets. Whitney, a farmer, moved into an impressive Italianate farmhouse on Allegan Road in 1874 *(page 48)*. Both factories apparently operated only during the summer months and in Douglas, "basket time" (clocks were set a half hour ahead of standard time) and "basket pay" dominated village life.

ARCHITECTURE WITHOUT ARCHITECTS | Farm orchards are human constructions. It is said that the first apple tree was brought as a seedling to the Saugatuck area in about 1845—carried by flatboat from Kalamazoo and planted by Herschel Seymour on his land on what is now 2941 Lakeshore Drive[7]—and the first peach tree was planted by local Indians prior to the arrival of the white people. If these were the beginnings, it was not until the 1860s, however, that the real agricultural revolution occurred—as thousands of acres of "sandland" –sheltered by dune and warmed by the lakes, were converted to orchard. A commingling of land, tree, and human structure came to replace the early pioneer's attack on the land and a new sense of place was in the making.

Extending out of these carefully laid out orchards was a multitude of barns and farmhouses, and even roadside markets—all together making a pleasant sort of architecture without architects. Today no building is a better reminder of the area's golden age of fruit agriculture than the barns that are still scattered across the villages and countryside. Often small in scale, the red structures were used for storing carts and containers as well as housing farm horses. They were recycled over the years—Dr. Walker used his for

51

RAISING THE ROOF

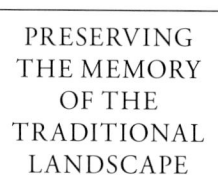

PRESERVING THE MEMORY OF THE TRADITIONAL LANDSCAPE

As technology and modern life takes us farther and farther away from the land and nature, it is the history and the preservation of historic landscapes that take us back to the age-old marriage of country and town, of nature and "village life."

[The story of this barn's reconstruction is found in Chapter 7.]

HENRY & GUSSIE TILL'S BARN
ca. 1880
Spear Street
Saugatuck

52

A History of the Buildings and Architecture in the Saugatuck and Douglas Area

SHAFER RESIDENCE
Union Street
Douglas
Jarzembowski Builders, *builders*
Reconstruction, 2004

BURR TILLSTROM'S
BARN-HOUSE
Spear Street
Saugatuck

Converted into a residence by Jim Webster, founder of the Red Barn summer theater and then home of Burr Tillstrom, America's best known television puppeteer.

MRS. KELLER'S BARN
1870s
Randolph & Spring Streets
Douglas

BARNS & ORCHARD
AT PIER COVE
(photo, ca. 1895)

WALKER–
BOROUGHS BARN
1890s
309 Grand Street
Saugatuck

MR. BIRD'S BARN
ca. 1880
Holland Street at Spear Street
Saugatuck
Now a studio.

DANIEL GERBER
BARN
ca. 1870
Union Street
Douglas
Demolished, 1998

MR. ERLANDSON'S
BARN
1870s
Randolph & Spring Streets
Douglas

A History of the Buildings and Architecture in the Saugatuck and Douglas Area

STREAMLAND FARM–QUIET CREEK
Lakeshore Drive at 126th Street
Ganges Township

How to preserve the memory of the land? Providing a fine vista from the public road, these restored farm structures that were once a part of the Streamland Farm Estate, summer home of a well-known Chicago financier. Even an old Well House has been preserved (not in photo)—a small structure originally made from buckets of stone carried from the nearby Lake Michigan beach by house guests. The orchard has been replanted. Restored, 2004.

MR. DENGLER ORGANIZES HIS FARM
1934
Riverside Road
Saugatuck Township

Two drawings from an album from the C. H. Dengler Farm, Riverside Farm, Riverside (Wiley) Road, Saugatuck Township. "#2 Block" was an apple and pear orchard. The plat includes the farmhouse and kitchen garden. The letters indicate type of tree. An "x" indicates tree removed. The names given to the farm paths are fictitious. The property is now known as the Art Barn.

HOUSE'S ROADSIDE MARKET
ca. 1940
Blue Star Highway
Saugatuck Township

Harvey House established a fruit farm that eventually encompassed 140 acres in Saugatuck Township in 1867. The farm business eventually included a commercially marketed cherry drink and this roadside market. The Michigan Farmer magazine for August of 1922 reported that Mr. Edwin House sold over 200 crates of cherries from this stand in that year. Now artist studios.

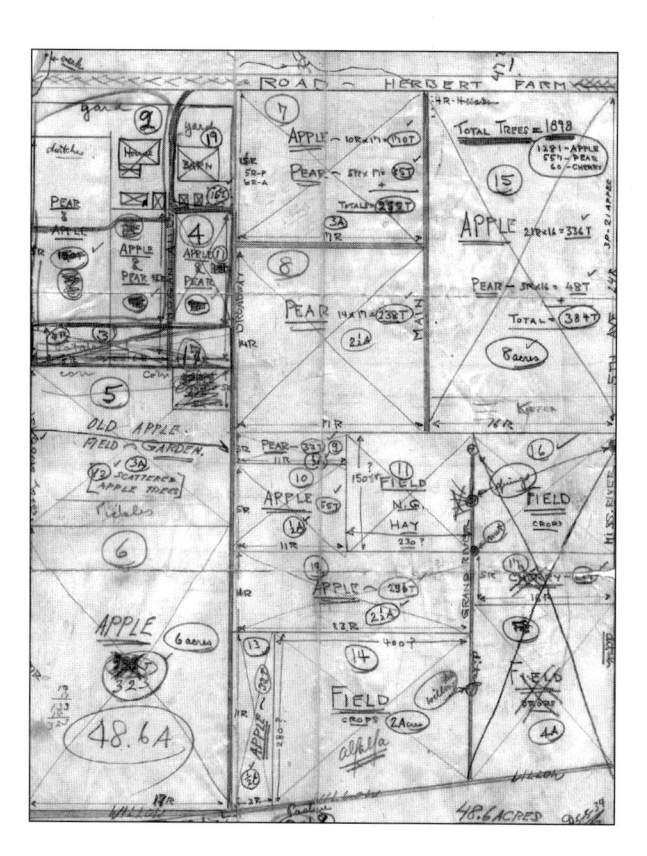

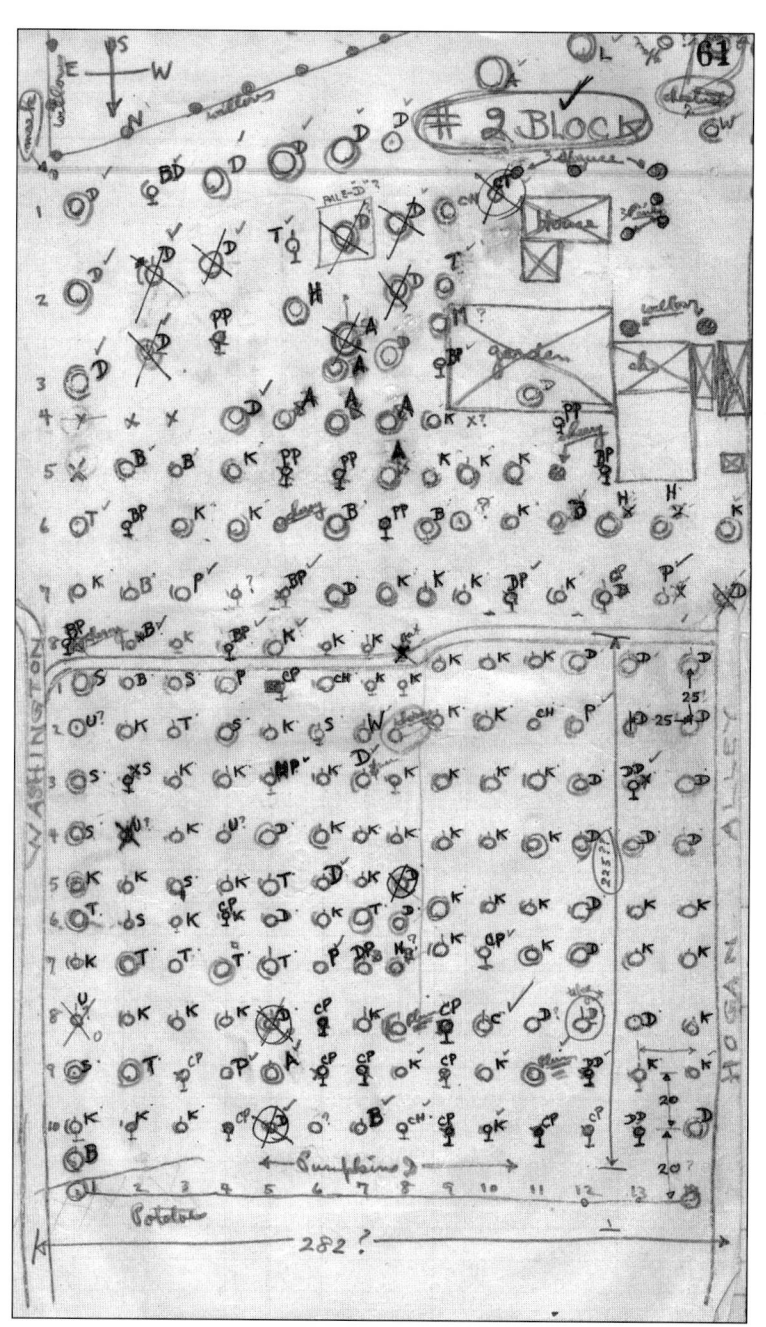

his two horses and two buggies and more recently they are used as artist studios, workshops, and garages. The recent careful restoration of Henry Till's barn on Spear Street is one of Saugatuck's most outstanding preservation efforts. *(Chp. 7)*

Few farm records exist to tell this story and most of the old barns have been destroyed, but Mr. C. H. Dengler's drawings of his orchard sites, carefully laid out according to field and fruit-tree type, building structure, and with clever names for farm paths, provide us with a view of an architectural universe constructed at the point where farmer meets nature itself.

A CHANGE IN FASHION BUT FEW TAKERS | By the 1890s the Italianate house was becoming old hat. A growth of wealth and urbanization in America, along with an increasing emphasis on "family life" and increasing availability of domestic appliances (including toilets and kitchen appliances), led to a demand for larger houses. The new fashion in houses was that of the "Queen Anne" style which had been sweeping the Midwest since about 1880 and which remained a popular house style for the twenty or so years after. Queen Ann reflected a less cautious and more consumption-directed society—and was, in effect, the swan song of "Victorian" house design. It combined a high-pitched roof

CAPTAIN PHELPS'S PORCH
1890
134 State Street
Saugatuck

An addition to house design—for taking the cooling breezes in an age that pre-dated air conditioning—the porch was also a symbol of respectability, welcoming passers-by, and informing all that the family could afford leisure and "style," this porch on the Captain W. G Phelps House is typical with its Victorian turned supports, railings, spindlework frieze, and roof pediment. (The porch has since been altered.) Pearl Phelps Brown is the third person from the left of the center porch support. It was Captain Phelps, a ship captain and school teacher, who in 1901 converted the local gristmill into the "Butler Hotel."

PLUMMER-JENNINGS/ GAMMONS HOUSE
1897
42 Spring Street
Douglas

Built by ship captain George Plummer. The lumber for the house was brought from Chicago by the steamer Aliber in October of 1897—soon after the first house on the lot was removed. Plummer was engaged in shipping, farming and was a partner in the McDonald grocery business on the northeast corner of Center and Spring Street.

RAISING THE ROOF

HOW TO IDENTIFY
A Queen Anne Building
ca. 1880 - ca. 1900 (locally)

1
steep-pitched roof; often of irregular form with cross gables

2
dominant front gable

3
elaborate overall detailing (shingles, spindlework, "gingerbread," columns, brackets)

4
porches, often of irregular shape, with pediment over entry

5
tower or "turret"

6
bay window (not shown)

7
large, broad windows—often surrounded by smaller (sometimes colored) window lights

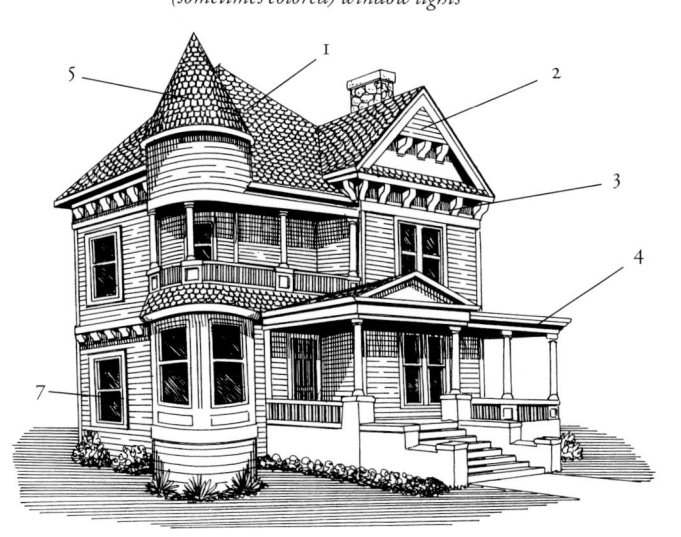

and irregularity of form with classical motifs in a highly decorative massing of towers, multiple porches, bay windows, eccentric extensions, and many layers of detailing. Regarded by later critics as the American style of "decadence" and ostentatiousness (Frank Lloyd Wright called Queen Anne "wood murder"[8]), in their day they represented to mainstream America the epitome of modernity and of the "luxury and comfort, softness and frivolity" that more and more people could afford. Inside, Queen Anne houses were even more complex—reflecting how specialized functions within the home had become: there were spaces for public use (the front hall and the parlor for greeting guests), spaces for domestic production (the kitchen, the sewing room, the pantry), and spaces for privacy (the bedrooms—separating boys from girls—and the bathroom, but also cozy private nooks and bays for contemplation or conversation). Separate rooms were designed for sewing, reading, storing food, for children and guests, and for servants who were usually relegated to a separate back stairway. Very large windows, bays, and multiple porches emphasized the link between outdoors and indoors—and provided good spaces for growing those big potted palms. The porch was a principal feature of the Queen Anne style—the bigger the better—as demonstrated in the house at 41 Mixer Street, Douglas (ca.1869-80), known as Captain Turnbull's house. As the Queen Anne house became the most common dwelling type in the United States in the final decades of the nineteenth century, it was mass produced as a pre-fabricated structure by many companies such as Sears, Roebuck and

KURZ HOUSE–SHERWOOD FOREST INN
ca. 1900
938 Center Street | Douglas

This was the house of the leading builder of the day, George Kurz. Since Kurz had no children, this large house was intended as a showpiece for his business. It has a small entrance hall opening into a large "front hall" with an open staircase to the second floor. Kurz built many of the cottages on the lakeshore.

TRADE ADVERTISEMENT

This small advertisement for G. E. Kurz, Douglas building contractor, appeared in The Commercial Record *in the early 1900s.*

G. E. Kurz
Contractor and Bulider

I am prepared to do all kinds of carpenter and cabinet work.
Estimates and plans furnished for all classes of buildings.

G. E. Kurz
Douglas - Mich

DOUCETTE HOUSE
ca. 1890 *(photo, 1930s)*
180 S. Union | Douglas

58

BIOGRAPHY OF A HOUSE

KIRBY HOUSE
294 West Center Street | Douglas | 1890

LIBRARY | The woodwork in this room—and probably throughout the house—was milled in Grand Rapids.

BACK STAIRWAY | The back stairway was for use of the maid, whose room was at the top of the stairs on the second floor.

FRONT STAIR | This grand staircase continued on to the third-floor ballroom (with its own cloak room) which occupied about half of the space on the third floor.

DINING ROOM & PARLOR | Mrs. Kirby undoubtedly used these rooms for entertaining on a smaller scale than the large parties she hosted in the third-floor ballroom.

BATHROOM | The house was well known for its advanced plumbing system. A second bathroom was located on the third floor; in addition, all four bedrooms on the second floor were equipped with their own sinks.

HALL | Though typical for fashionable Queen Anne houses of the day, this large entrance hall with wood paneling, open staircase, and fireplace was pretentious for Douglas at the time. Its owner was prominent in Douglas society and dance parties in the house were well known until the 1920s.

RESTORATION | The house was transformed into the community hospital in 1931 and existed as such until 1960 when a new hospital was built on Wiley Road. The house was then used for various purposes—falling into general disrepair and saw removal of many of its interior decoration. Restoration began in 1984 when it was a converted into a family home and B&B.

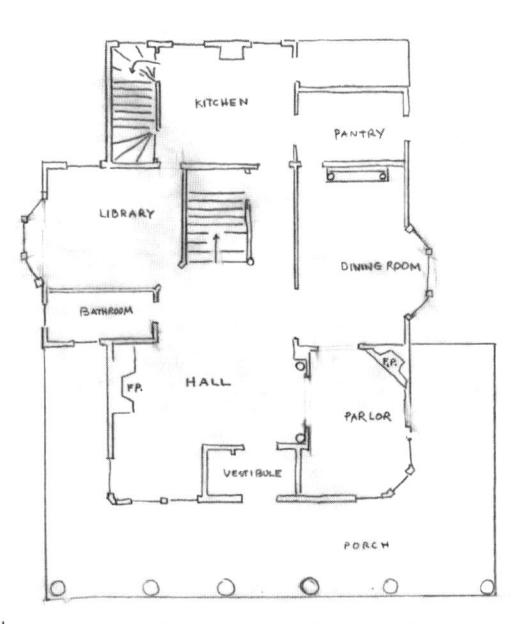

KIRBY HOUSE –
DOUGLAS HOSPITAL

KIRBY HOUSE
1890
294 Center Street
Douglas
J. H. Daverman and Son, *architect*

Sarah Gill Kirby, the wife of a Douglas businessman, built this house for her family when she was 35 years old. Her husband died a few years later and she continued to live here with her two children as one of the area's reighning social matriarchs. By the 1920s she was renting rooms to tourists and growing ginseng for commercial purposes. She moved to California in 1932 where she lived until her death in 1951. The house was used as the area's first hospital from 1931 to 1960. J. H. Daverman designed one of the grandest Queen Anne Houses in the American west. The builder was George Kurz. Now the Kirby House B&B.

KIRBY HOUSE
FLOOR PLAN

Company in Chicago and Aladdin Homes Company in Bay City, Michigan.

Although the Queen Anne style flourished in many Michigan towns, it is found less frequently in the Saugatuck and Douglas area—probably because the local economy was running out of steam by the 1890s. Nonetheless, there are a number of particularly interesting specimens including the Koning House on Butler Street, Saugatuck, the Wayne Coates house and store at 127 Hoffman which was given a Queen Anne addition to the front (later the home of Dr. Herman Kreager, Village President and now altered as the Uncommon Grounds coffee house); the house the carpenter George Kurz built for himself at on west Center Street (ca. 1900) (now "Sherwood Forest Inn,"), and the Doucette house on S.Union, Douglas. Sarah Kirby, the very modern daughter of a local farmer and carpenter, was the first woman in Douglas known to own her own car and to build her own grand house. The Queen Anne structure that architect J. H Daverman designed for her on Center Street was the village's most modern (and perhaps most costly) house of its time, complete with an impressive entrance hall with fireplace, a grand staircase, and running water. The house served as the community's hospital from 1932 until 1960 and was converted to "Kirby House Bed and Breakfast" in 1983.

THE STREET AS ARCHITECTURE AND ARTIFACT: BUTLER STRTEET GOES MODERN | The history of the commercial streets in our villages tells us that the decade just prior to World War One in 1914 was a golden age for the material well being of the villages—and a way to define what it meant to be modern in the early 20th century. Koning's Hardware Store (founded as Nies Hardware in 1868, now Wilkin's Hardware) is Saugatuck's oldest existing retail business. From its

| NIES-KONING'S HARDWARE STORE
1868
439 Butler Street
Saugatuck

It was described in 1880 as "large enough to hold the hardware stock for all of Allegan County." It acted as agent for the Hamburg-New York Steamship Lines and offered "all foreign money orders." [Saugatuck Business Directory, January 12, 1883.] Destroyed by a fire that originated in the implements building (to the left in the photograph) in 1903.

| KONING HARDWARE STORE
1904
439 Butler Street | Saugatuck
J. H. Daverman & Son, *architect*

John Koning's new store is of red brick, with white bands of galvanized iron. The upper floor was used by various renters, including the local Christian Science Society before they built their own structure nearby on the village square. The building now houses Wilkins' Hardware— with compatible additions—and remains just as "modern" as ever.

KONING HOUSE–VICTORIAN INN
1904
447 Butler Street
Saugatuck

A house for a prosperous merchant. Here is a representative of both the Queen Anne style of architecture and a very early Sears catalogue pre-fab house—and hence being very modern for its time. The house changed from family home to funeral home to gallery before becoming the Victorian Inn.

beginning the 1868 store had the latest and widest range of services and products, including everything from burial caskets and spokes for wagon wheels to building materials and hardware. But this rather simple wood-frame structure was completely destroyed by fire in the winter of 1903—partly because the fire department hoses froze—then replaced by the current brick structure, built in 1904. The new "John Koning Hardware" was the ultimate in modern for its day as well—complete with one of Michigan's earliest "counter-weight" elevators in a tall brick building crowned with a bold cornice and with the village's largest plate-glass windows. Today the store looks much as it did in 1904, with an agreeably designed addition to the rear.

At the same time, Koning demonstrated his modernity by buying a Sears and Roebuck mail-order house for himself, which he built next door. This up-to-date house, one of Sears's first, was packaged in pre-cut pieces and sent by steamer from Chicago. Like nearly 100,000 homeowners to follow, the Konings simply chose their house from the Sears catalogue, waited for the package to arrive by boat, and hired a local builder to put it up. Everything was included: lumber, lath, fireplace, kitchen cabinets, nails, flooring, and hardware, white paint for the exterior and red shingles for the roof!

Mr. Konings' modernizing kick was already in progress farther along Butler Street. An imposing brick Queen Anne building with a fashionable turret had already been put up at the corner of Mason and Butler Streets—first as a meat market and then with a new stone facade and impressive interior, it became the village's first bank building: the Fruit Growers State Bank. Adjacent to this new enterprise appeared another two story brick structure, a hotel on the upper floor and Jim Davis's restaurant at the street level—later to become the legendary "Soda Lounge" of the 1950s. Also making an appearance on this block was the largest retail establishment ever built in Saugatuck: Thornton Leland's Department Store, the first and only of its kind in Saugatuck. In its early years, the store was divided into various shops: groceries on one side and clothing and dry goods on the other side, a furniture department on the second floor, and, over the years, a multitude of consumer opportunities including a "Tea Room"— painted grey and lavender and which featured caged canaries which sang for the customers.

The same year that Thornton Leland put up his department store, the village's first large multiple-shop front building was erected by Doc Heath ("The Heath Building") and filled a large portion of the block bounded by Butler and Hoffman Streets. Another very modern structure for its time, Roger Reed's Livery and Transfer Line station (with a feed store) rose up on the corner of Culver and Griffith Streets. This two-story building was constructed of a new concrete block material—the latest in fireproofing—and in the process took the place of the village's most notorious saloon-boarding houses.

† THE YOUNG & THE OLD
ca. 1904
Culver & Griffith Streets | Saugatuck

Changing environments, changing generations. Children at play in front of Roger Reed's new feed and livery store, constructed of modern concrete block and with concrete sidewalks—being watched by an old man across the street in front of Roger's father's store, with its old fashioned wood front and wood sidewalk.

† DAVIS RESTAURANT, INTERIOR
ca. 1900
Butler Street | Saugatuck

The restaurant later became the well-known Crow Restaurant and still later the "Soda Lounge." The building was removed in 1968 and the site now is part of the Mize Rose Garden.

A History of the Buildings and Architecture in the Saugatuck and Douglas Area

COMMERCIAL AMBITIONS

Nothing is more symbolic of the new consumer culture of the turn of the century than the coming of the department store to small-town America. Accompanying Saugatuck's Leland Department Store into the world of modern design for the day were a number of specialty stores—and, ironically, a new structure for a very traditional business, a stage coach stop.

HEATH BLOCK BUILDING
1904 *(photos 1928 / 2006)*
306-312 Butler Street | Saugatuck

Built by businessman D. A. "Doc" Heath, the building has housed a variety of businesses, including a drug store, ice cream shop, "serve-self" grocery and bakery, local telephone operator (upper floor), and (recently) the "village news store." The sidewalk loggia was added in the 1980s.

LELAND'S DEPARTMENT STORE
1904
119 Butler Street | Saugatuck

Saugatuck's first and only "department store." Its developer was a ship captain, Thornton Leland. In addition to grocery and dry good departments, the original store had a shoe repair shop, a soda fountain, and a "ballroom" on the second floor (used by the local Masons). A jewelry shop and restaurant ("the John Ball') and Dr. Kreager, the dentist, occupied an addition built on the south end of the structure in 1910. Various businesses have occupied the building including restaurants, an antiques shop, a "smoke shop," and the "Duck Pin" bowling alley. The ballroom later became a factory for making pennants. Considerable interior modernization since the 1980s—including construction of "Leland's Alley."

REED'S LIVERY, TRANSFER LINE, & FEED STORE
1904
Culver Street | Saugatuck

Roger Reed was a feed and grain merchant, a liveryman and one of the last operators of the stage line to Allegan. Built on the site of the old Union House Hotel, this was an "exchange stable," which meant that one could rent a horse with buggy at this location and drop it off at another location. As the trade was overtaken by the automobile Reed began to phase out the business. By 1914 he had moved into auto repair. This later became a factory for making roller skates and then the beginning of American Twisting Company in Saugatuck. In recent memory, it was the Saugatuck village barn, fire department, and jail. Recently restored and now the Toulouse Restaurant.

L. W. McDONALD'S STORE
1890 *(photo 1998)*
Center Street | Douglas

Built by Daniel Gerber, this fine example of "commercial Italianate" architecture was one of the first (and few) brick structures in Douglas. It was originally L. W. McDonald's "People's Store" (on the left) and later Norton's Drug and Soda Shop (on the right), but then fell into disrepair and was later re-cycled as the St. Peter's School and then the Saugatuck Township Offices before being restored in the 1980s. Note the elaborate cornice detailing and brackets. Upper cornice decoration has been recently restored. See also, Chapter 7.

THE BEGINNING OF ITS GOLDEN AGE OF TOURISM

ca. 1910
Saugatuck

It was the Big Pavilion (far right), built in 1909, that made the Saugatuck area into Lake Michigan's best known summer destination. By the turn of the century the tremendous inflow of people of all classes was largely an urban migration—most of whom arrived by steam ship. Here we see the village soon after the opening of the new harbor channel: three big hotels (by Saugatuck standards)—the Tourist Home lower left and the Leindecker (now Coral Gables) and Butler hotels on opposite sides of the Big Pavilion dance hall; dozens of additional boarding houses, small hotels and cottages covered the villages and lakeshore. During summer months the Pavilion entertained a thousand people a day. The three interconnecting bridges linking Saugatuck and Douglas can be seen at the upper part of the photo: a long iron bridge on the left, a tree-lined causeway bridge and the swing bridge. The Douglas Basket Factory can be seen at the south end of the bridge. The large building on the waterfront in the foreground (left) is another (short-lived) dance pavilion, which was recycled for a variety of uses.

RICHARD NEWNHAM'S POST CARD SHOP
1909
Location unknown, Saugatuck

They were wild about postcards.

CHARLIE'S ICE CREAM SHOP
1880 (reconstructed, 2003)
Mason Street, Saugatuck

And wild about ice cream.

WRIGHT'S PAVILION
1923
Lake Street | Saugatuck

Until 1936 the only way to get to the Lake Michigan beach was by boat. This was the stationhouse, dock, and refreshment room (with a dance floor) for Captain George C. Wright's "Wright Line" of large boat taxis. (See Chpt. 7)

MINIATURE LOG CABIN
ca. 1920
Village Square | Saugatuck

Experiencing the past—and a photo opportunity—on Saugatuck's village square.

CHAPTER FOUR

Building for Leisure, Health, & Morality, 1880-1920

"Ellen," he said presently, "Chicago seems too big and lonely
for you and me. . . . Joe Conners was telling me the other day about a place on the east
shore of Lake Michigan where he has spent his last three summers,
twin summer resorts, called Saugatuck and Douglas.
I have been thinking, dear . . . that you might like this little lake trip."

—CHARLOTTE ELLIS MAC DONALD
A Message From the Hills, ca. 1910

A NEW WORLD OF LEISURE AND A NEW ECONOMY | In 1888 a popular American magazine declared that a new question was being heard in American homes: "Where shall we spend our summer?"[1] As the history of Saugatuck illustrates, Americans had discovered leisure in a big way—big enough to totally transform old fashioned port villages up and down the Lake Michigan coasts. Increased wealth (the average American income more than doubled between 1890 and 1917), shorter working days, and improved transportation all led to the invention of new kinds of leisure, many of which—such as ballroom dancing, golf, "resorting," and that new American institution, the "get-away-from-it-all" cottage—had become commercialized and called for new types of buildings. Summer vacations and weekend retreats became the norm for millions of urban families. As the expression "the Gay Nineties" suggests, more people, including the poorer classes, were having more fun, more often.

By 1900 Saugatuck, and to an extent Douglas and Pier Cove, were cashing in on this exodus from the city with great vigor. Tourism had great appeal because the villages were on shaky economic ground. Saugatuck and Douglas were getting poorer. A glance along the changing Saugatuck riverfront tells the sad story: the years between 1895 and 1920 saw the disappearance of a number of boatbuilding yards, a blacksmith and wagon shop, a lumber yard, fruit shipping warehouses, docks, and one of the local basket factories. The boat building and fruit growing eras were rapidly drawing to a close.

This is the point at which the histories of Saugatuck and Douglas begin to branch off in different directions. While Douglas dwindled to a one-industry town by 1900—and then to a no-industry town when the basket factory burned to the ground in 1927—Saugatuck successfully reinvented itself as one of the Midwest's great summer resort economies. From then on jobs and the tax base in Saugatuck would depend less and less upon boatbuilding and fruit growing and more and more on how many artists came to paint, cottagers to celebrate cottage life, and vacationers to vacation. Although Douglas annexed its Lake Michigan shoreline in an attempt to boost its economy, Douglas would need to wait nearly a century to bring its village center back to life.[2]

WHAT SORTS OF LEISURE? | Leisure, of course, was nothing new to the villages. However, unlike the old-fashioned "drink-and-brawl" sort of leisure which had been found in the rivertown taverns during the lumbering days, by 1900 those who flocked to Saugatuck were in search of leisure of a new order. They sought creative, artistic leisure—such as writing or painting—to regenerate the soul: leisure to build family life, sport and social leisure linked to the outdoors, or simply impressing the gang back home with the new-fangled thing called a "photo post card." It seemed like half the village was either opening a guest house or an ice-cream parlor.

Even more important, the rush of city folk to the woods and beaches went beyond "pleasure for pleasure's sake." Many Americans sought to escape the increasingly crowded, ugly, sometimes violent, and often unhealthy cities. Chicago was seen to be an abyss of moral and physical despair. Once famous for its parks, by 1880 the city had grown so congested that it had fallen to the bottom of the list for per capita park space.[3] To make things worse, high-pitched battles between workers and capitalists pushed cities like Chicago to the very center of the debate over what to do about life in America.

THE TOWER AT TERRACE PARK FARM
1920
Ferry (near Center) Street
Douglas
Demolished 1980s.

SIMONSON'S PHOTOGRAPHY STUDIO
ca. 1930
236 Culver Street
Saugatuck

Like most villages of its ilk, Saugatuck too had its resident photographer. Herman Simonson produced hundreds of photographs of the people and places of the Saugatuck area in his 45 years as Saugatuck's chief visual documentarian. In addition he operated several small shops in the area, peddling photo postcards to cottagers and tourists. This building, now a restaurant, uses his studio as a dining room.

TERRACE PARK LUNCH TAVERN
1920
Ferry & Center Streets
Douglas

Opposite West Shore Golf Club, it featured Chicken and Fish Dinners. Now a sign shop.

What followed was a rethinking of American life and values—and architecture. In Saugatuck, Douglas, and Pier Cove, the lake, river, and forest, which had always been viewed as dangers to be traversed or exploited, came to be viewed by city folks as objects of beauty and as moral and spiritual antidotes as well. Indeed, the spirit of life in Saugatuck, mused one admiring Chicago visitor, was "so very far . . . from the great, drab, hustling, ever-alien city of Chicago."[4] Therefore, following the lead of urban social activists such as Jane Addams, and reform-minded architects such as Frank Lloyd Wright and Thomas Eddy Tallmadge, urban ministers, professors, architects, and others looked to lake and countryside not as a form of escape, but as a place to rediscover and reinvent American life. Not surprisingly, the great Chicago city planner, Daniel Burnham, considered the West Michigan lakefront to be a key part of Chicago life.[5]

This rediscovery manifested itself in different forms at different places but all were linked together in a common spirit: first, the establishment of various cottage communities; second, experiments in the reconstruction of the natural landscape (this was first done in Pier Cove); third, the creation of spiritual retreat for Chicago's urban poor; and fourth, the establishment of an outdoor school of painting for artists. All of these took place between about 1890 and 1910 and all were rooted in the idea that the best way to confront the urban crisis was through a spiritual, moral, and aesthetic reawakening rooted in the ideals of nature and traditional village life—and they came at a time when Saugatuck area people were increasingly interested in providing more educational and cultural opportunities for children and adults.[6] All of these will be considered in this chapter. The countryside and village acted as teacher to the city—and in so doing, the countryside and village were re-made, giving a new idealized face to the landscape and townscape. A massive rearrangement of space was underway.

THE HAMMERS WERE HAMMERING | Local history has it that the first "tourist" arrived in 1871. At first they came in trickles, and bedrooms were the first new space requirement. At the same time a multitude of tourist-based services needed some sort of quarters, be it a summer camp, an art school, a dance hall, water-taxi station, a summer chapel, a golf clubhouse, a lunch restaurant, a photography studio, a crafts shop, or an elaborate water tower.

By 1900 Saugatuck and the surrounding area could boast 50 boarding houses (a number of which were called "resorts"), two hotels, 14 cottages, and 70 tents. The large number of tents suggests, perhaps, more a shortage of bedrooms than an urge to get closer to nature![7] Within a short time Saugatuck had them all: boarding houses, which were primarily private homes with bedrooms for rent, and resorts which were home-like and often family run retreat-like places which offered their guests food and access to various leisure activities. The names were reminiscent of a vaudeville act: Applecrest

Inn, Idler's Rest, Colonial Inn, New England Home, Utopia, and so on. The hotels were pretty much straightforward "pack-'em in" types of places, although they had some pretense to service and "resort-like" accommodation. In reality there was a thin line between a boarding house and a resort or even a hotel.

In 1885 the Park House in Saugatuck was one of the first family residences to be converted to a "resort." If it was not enough to advertise that it had a great view of Mt. Baldhead, by 1927 it was offering a pow-wow led by Chief Blue Sky of Mt. Baldhead (he was paid by the village to welcome visitors there), who, in turn initiated visitors into his "tribe," followed by playing the piano and harmonica, "imitating birds and animals, giving Indian dances, and telling the story of his life."[8]

The imposing Samuel Johnson House at 765 Allegan Street followed, was renamed the "Frolic Inn" by the Bartz family; Captain James Dole's former house became the "White House" inn; and the "Newnham Inn" and the "Twin Oaks" were fashioned out of older residences. The first resorts on the lakeshore were really of the farmhouse-cum-sleeping-rooms type invented by a number of highly energetic women who knew how to create new spaces out of old: Emma Trumbull's "Hedgerow Villa"(1899), Elizabeth McVea's "Homestead," Rachel McVea's "Beachmont," and Ellen Bryan's "Rosemont" (1886 and 1901). Most of these had little to offer in terms of "style" but they did offer old-fashioned charm and comfort, and that is what kept people coming back. Though Mrs. Bryan was known for hauling her organ out onto the Rosemont's front lawn on Sundays for evening vespers, all in all the lakeshore landladies did not have to provide much entertainment except to point the way to the walk to the beach, Mt. Baldhead, and (after 1909) the Big Pavilion.

PROMISES OF DANCING ON THE ROOFTOP | By 1900 Saugatuck was ready to go big time. During the next three decades the building-for-leisure trickle turned into a gushing torrent. Hotels and cottages sprung up all over the villages. Newcomers clamored to purchase vacation lots. The new three-story "Pokagon Inn" of 1899 was the signal to Saugatuckians that the future of the local economy was in cottages and big hotels. The Pokagon, perched on a dune near Mt. Baldhead in the Park Addition, faced the Chain Ferry at Park Street. The hotel's backer, E. S. Perryman, was a Texan who clearly beheld the future. His Pokagon Inn promised to accommodate 100 people in something on the order of forty "large and airy" rooms (many with private porches). In reality, soon after it opened, the Pokagon was packing in 125 persons. There were parlors, a smoking room, "bell service in every room," a 1,320-square-foot dining room, a riverside dance "pavilion," and promises of another dance pavilion on the rooftop.[9]

A number of hotels and resorts followed, some of them purpose-built, such as the Leindecker Hotel (1902-1906) which had a popular dance hall, and the

TWIN OAKS
1860s–1886
227 Griffith Street
Saugatuck

Home of John and Isabel Henry. Henry was a partner in Griffin & Henry Lumber Company and served as Village President and member of the Michigan House of Representatives. The house at one time probably served as a boarding house for his workers as well as a residence. In 1907 the front of the house was the west side, facing a large lawn all the way to Mason Street.

NEWNHAM INN
Remodeled with additions in 1900
(photo, ca. 1922)
131 Griffith Street
Saugatuck

The Allegan Journal reported in 1900 that this house had been "thoroughly rebuilt" for Samuel Reed and family. Reed owned the "SCR" livery and feed business next door and his son Roger owned a competing business on the opposite corner.. This photograph was taken in about the time the Harry Newnham family purchased the inn in 1922. Currently a B & B.

THE ELMS HOTEL
132 Butler Street
Saugatuck

Part of the old John Francis residence and store, "the Elms" became a popular boarding house in the 1920s. It was still operating in the 1950s— popular with the Saugatuck gay tourist crowd. It is said that at that time it was possible to rent one half of a bed—and should one not approve of one's bed partner, a 'bed board' was affixed to privatize the two halves. Now incorporated into a larger structure.

RAISING THE ROOF

68

IDLEASE HOTEL – VALENTINE LODGE
1906
653 Campbell Road
Douglas

Captain Campbell was a local ship's captain. His new hotel boasted 27 rooms, a dining room, and nearby cottage—all set among an orchard.

CLIPSON BREWERY & TWIN GABLES INN
1865 *(photo, 2005)*
Saugatuck
900 Lake Street

Once the site of a mill and a furniture factory, this is the old Clipson brewery. At the close of the Civil War Samuel Clipson proudly marketed his "Union Ale." The brewery was rebuilt to become a well known boarding house and inn in the 1920s, known for its orchestra and restaurant— and reputedly frequented by members of Al Capone's gang during prohibition era; restored in 1982. Listed on State Register of Historic Places.

LAKE KALAMAZOO HOUSE
ca. 1910
Park Street
Saugatuck

Destroyed by fire

BEACHMONT
ca. 1880 *(photo ca. 1935)*
294 Lakeshore Drive
Douglas

William and Rachel McVea began to take "resorters" into their farmhouse in the mid-1890s. Rachel McVea ran the business, which meant, among other things, providing for all the meals, including produce from the family gardens and orchards. By the mid-1930s the Beachmont had 14 guestrooms. The building was demolished in 1960.

POKAGON INN
1900
106 Perryman Street at Park Street
Saugatuck

Hotel and a dance hall, the Pokagon was Saugatuck's first large hotel. After it burned, it was replaced by the smaller (now) "Beachway" hotel. At the waterside was its pavilion Destroyed by fire in 1902.

LEINDECKER HOTEL
1901-06 *(photo, ca. 1910)*
220 Water Street
Saugatuck
Architect: W. K. Johnson

Built in two sections and replaced a hotel built in 1900. Founded by the Leindecker family of Chicago. In early years the hotel was known for its "German Orchestra." Hotel guests were transferred to the Lake Michigan beach by steam yachts. Later known under various owners as Kalamazoo Hotel, Columbia Hotel, Hotel Saugatuck, the Crow Hotel and now as "Coral Gables" restaurant and bar.

ROSEMONT RESORT
1901
83 Lakeshore Drive
Douglas

The Bryans were lake shore fruit farmers—and Mrs. Ellen Bryan took the family into the hotel business, catering to city folks from St. Louis and Chicago. The Rosemont was the first of original boarding houses to join the 1980s B&B craze. Enlarged and restored.

BEACHWAY HOTEL
ca. 1903 *(photo, 1944)*
Saugatuck
106 Perryman Street

Replaced the earlier Pokagon Inn after 1902. Known variously as Ferry Inn and Hillside Inn. Still occupies the site at the corner of Park Street and Perryman (Oval Beach road).

TOURIST HOME – MT. BALDHEAD HOTEL
1901 *(photo, ca. 1950)*
528 Water Street | Saugatuck

Originally the "Tourist Home Hotel" (later renamed the "Mt. Baldhead Hotel") had the advantages of being a few steps from the chain ferry (for a hike to Mt. Baldhead), a short walk to the Big Pavilion when it opened in 1909, and its own sizable dance floor. The hotel was destroyed by fire in 1959 and was replaced by the "Ship & Shore Motel Boatel."

TOURIST HOME – MT. BALDHEAD HOTEL
528 Water Street | Saugatuck | 1901

Recycling buildings was common in Saugatuck. The site (adjacent to the ferry station) had been used by commercial fishermen, blacksmiths, barrel makers, a horse livery. The hotel was created by bring together a number of buildings over a period of 40 years.

1. Old Nicholas Warehouse and Store (1834) moved from site across from the Old Lighthouse in 1860 *(left of center in photo)*.

2. Blacksmith Solomon Stanton moved his shop here from across the street and attached it to former Nicholas Warehouse and Store to make a new blacksmith shop. It later became a boat rental shop and then a fruit warehouse for use by Milwaukee-bound boats, and then a coal and wood warehouse.

3. In 1890 owner Robert P. Russell moved the large (120 by 30 feet) "ironclad" Basket Factory Warehouse (1888) to this site. The building was transported in two sections. *(not yet moved to this site when this photo was taken)*

4. A new porch was added to join all the sections together. The hotel opened on June 15, 1901.

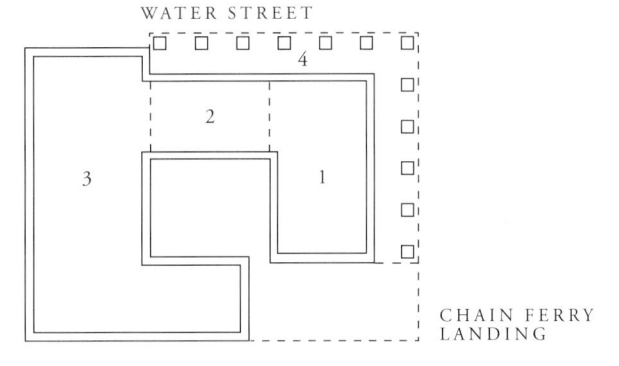

   In 1900 the buildings became the "Home Restaurant." *(far left in photo)*

THE RIVERFRONT IN THE 1890'S
Saugatuck

Looking eastward toward the Chain Ferry landing, with the structures that would become part of the Tourist Home hotel after 1901. (See photo, opposite page.)

RAISING THE ROOF

† BATAVIA RESORT–HALVERSON FARM
ca. 1911
Pine Trail Camp Road | Saugatuck Township

On the ridge above the harbor entrance. This was the old Nichols farmstead—established in 1855—later as the Halverson farm which became "Mrs. Halverson's Resort," with the rear addition added in 1902.

† RIVERSIDE REST
ca. 1875
3421 Riverside Drive | Saugatuck

The original James H. Bandle homestead, one of the earliest area fruit farms—converting the home into a summer resort in 1891—and by the 1930s boasted a private dock, tennis and shuffleboard courts. It was here that the Ox-Bow School of Art had its beginnings.

† HOWARD'S INN
ca. 1870 *(photo, ca. 1927)*
3409 Elizabeth at North Street | Saugatuck

Lillian Howard opened her inn in the late 1920s. It had a commanding view of the "Big Pool," which was built in 1927. The house was built in 1895 for Col. B. C. Chambers of Chicago who used the house as a summer home—although it is probable that a portion of the house was built earlier. The house still stands but the porches have been removed. The photo is a side view.

† CASABLANCA HOTEL
1923
Village Square | Saugatuck

This hotel, first known as the "Roamers' Inn," then as the "Grace Hotel," was built in 1923 and is shown here ca. 1945—and named after the World War Two battle site. Destroyed by fire in 1969

70

SPRUCEWOOD CABINS
ca. 1940
Water Street | Saugatuck

short-lived "Lake Kalamazoo House," which faced Saugatuck from across Lake Kalamazoo and the "Beachway" which replaced the Pokagon Inn. About this time ship captain John Campbell put up a large three-story hotel near the Douglas lakeshore and called it "Idlyease" (later Valentine Lodge). Still others were in recycled buildings. "Twin Gables" at 900 Lake Street, Saugatuck, was created by pulling together parts of a brewery, a tannery, a barrel factory, and a boatbuilding works. Three of Saugatuck's best known hotels, the "Maplewood" (1898), the "Tourist Home Hotel" (1901) (later known as "Mt. Baldhead Hotel") and the "Butler Hotel" (1901) were recycled buildings as well. The Maplewood started out as a general store in the mid-1860s, then a furniture store, a funeral home, and then beginning in 1898, a full fledged hotel with "big windows, commanding prominent views of Mt. Baldhead."[10] Its stately façade was added in 1923, making it one of Saugatuck's landmarks. Only two blocks away, the Tourist Home was cobbled together from a variety of existing buildings to become a hotel in 1901. It billed itself as having a big dance floor, a view of Mt. Baldhead and of being situated only a few steps from the Lake Michigan beach water taxis. In 1901 the Butler Hotel was carved out of a three-story 1892 flour mill by W. G. Phelps. Phelps kept the flat iron roof and added what was expected for the day: plenty of porches—including one on the second level with access from guestrooms. Rates in 1910 were $2.00 per day (or $2.50 with private bath). In the 1920s and 1930s Charles Redebaugh upgraded the Butler, and it remained one of Saugatuck's most popular hostelries until the top two stories were removed in 1973 and the hotel portion of the operation ceased.

The most eccentric of this building recycling began in about 1900, when two fellows by the names of Thomas Benton and Albertine Dates, swept up in the rush to take advantage of the new boom in tourism, took a chicken coop, an old one-room workshop stuck into the side of the hill and an old building moved from the village, and created a resort made of tiny cottages along Lake Street in Saugatuck. Their ingenuity resulted in what was initially called "Hillside Cottages"—eventually 17 of them each named after a different bird; hence, the collection became known as "Bird Center" cottage resort. Ingenious, indeed. Ironically but appropriately perhaps, in 1924 Cary and Elsie Bird purchased Bird Center.

Many other smaller resorts and hotels came into existence in the 1920s and 1930s such as the "Roamers' Inn" in 1923 (later the "Casablanca"); Howard's Inn on North Street, Saugatuck; and still later, "Sprucewood Modern Waterfront Cabins on Lake Street, Saugatuck. It is interesting how many of the larger hotels were built in the years just around 1900. The clientele of these establishments were generally middle-class and working

BIRD CENTER RESORT
584 Lake Street | Saugatuck | constructed 1900-1930s

A collection of cottages of various sizes (some recycled older buildings and some "pre-fabricated") brought together into what became known as Bird Center. Some of the original cottages still exist along Lake Street.

RIVERSIDE INN – OX-BOW SUMMER
SCHOOL OF PAINTING
1873-96
Park Street & Rupprecht Way
Saugatuck

The school was established in 1910 by a group of Chicago artists (John C. Johansen, John Norton, Frederick F. Fursman, Walter M. Clute, Thomas Eddy Tallmadge and Edgar & Isobel Rupprecht among them), some of whom had been summering in Saugatuck since the late 1890s and all of whom attained national prominence. They began holding classes in Saugatuck in 1910 and then at the Riverside Inn in 1913, by which time a re-routed river channel had shut the hotel off from commercial lake traffic. This isolation amidst the dunes, lagoon, and nearby woods provided the perfect spot for an "outdoor" school of painting. Several nearby fishing and ice storage shanties were relocated for use as artists' studios, and Tallmadge, Norton, Michael & Alice Mason (Alice taught lithography and was a one-time president of the Chicago Society of Artists) built cottages on the Ox-Bow grounds. The school now operates as the Art Institute of Chicago Ox-Bow Summer School of Painting and the Arts and has honed the talents of thousands of artists—including nationally known contemporary artists such as Wallace Kirkland, Ed Paschke, Bill Olendorf, LeRoy Neiman, Shel Silverstein and Claes Oldenburg. Changes and additions to the Inn occurred in 2005-6. It is the second oldest summer art school in the United States. Many of the families of Ox-Bow artists settled in the Saugatuck area.

class visitors who arrived by way of Lake Michigan steamer; some came by train into the Fennville Station; most sought to stay for a day or two. One of the more regrettable aspects of the village's history during these years was that some Saugatuck resort owners closed their doors to Jewish visitors. Lodging policy and practice was explicitly stated by the signs hung outside more than one local hostelry: "Gentiles Only" was posted at the entrance to the Grace Hotel, "Gentiles" before the Mt. Baldhead Hotel, and "Gentiles Only" on Mrs. F. H. Wicks's Maplewood Hotel advertisement. Even in a village whose cultural fabric was characterized by an interweaving of a diverse mix of social groups, this was a sad reflection of much of mainstream America and it lasted in Saugatuck up through the 1940s.[11]

All in all, much of the cultural and economic transformation from agriculture to tourism entailed the rearrangement of land use. The landscape and villagescape were being transformed from orchards and vacant forest land to parks, campgrounds, cottages, and hotels. This was promoted somewhat by the village fathers. For example, they set aside a huge acreage on the west bank of the Kalamazoo for what became Mt. Baldhead Park; they then platted and sold lots on an adjacent acreage, calling it the "Park Addition." Further, a number of Chicago businessmen worked out a land deal for Reverend George Gray that led, ultimately, to the enormously popular "Forward Movement Association Camp," now the "Presbyterian Camp," on the

A History of the Buildings and Architecture in the Saugatuck and Douglas Area

lakeshore. This resulted in a wave of westshore cottage building as well as the establishment of direct road access from the village to the present Lake Michigan "Oval" beach in 1936.

PAINTING THE TOWN | When the fishermen brothers Charles and Henry Shriver built their large family homes at the final bend of the Kalamazoo River before it flowed into Lake Michigan, they had no idea that their houses would become the nucleus of one of America's best-known summer art schools. "Uncle Charlie and Aunt Kit" as they were known, opened their plain, large Greek Revival house as a hotel they called "Riverside Inn." They catered to travelers arriving to and departing from the nearby docks. In 1893 they added onto the house—a large Italianate section to the south. Why the Shrivers and their builder chose an Italianate style, when it was already very much out of fashion by then is unclear, but all-in-all the addition of a porch across the entire front to tie the old and the new together was a success.

The Shriver enterprise was adversely affected when several hundred yards to the north of the inn the river channel was diverted to bypass the final "ox-bow" bend in the river, causing the old channel to become a landlocked lagoon. Without access to river traffic the Riverside Inn was deprived of its clientele. Within a few years the buildings were taken over by the "Summer School of Painting"—now known as "Ox-Bow." Today the "Ox-Bow Inn," as the former Riverside Inn is called, retains much of its original character.

The presence of the Summer School of Painting had an effect on the building and architecture of the broader area. On the Ox-Bow grounds several prominent American artists and architects constructed their own cottages, including Thomas Eddy Tallmadge and John Warner Norton. Across the Ox-Bow Lagoon Frederick F. Fursman, and later one of the school's backers, Arthur F.

CORA BLISS TAYLOR'S STUDIO & RESIDENCE
(photo, ca. 1931)
749 Holland Street
Saugatuck

The Taylor Art School was Saugatuck's best known in-town art education venue for a half a century. Cora Bliss was famous for her landscape and floral paintings—and for teaching hundreds of the village children and adults.

BIOGRAPHY OF A HOUSE

OX-BOW INN
Park Street & Rupprecht Way | Saugatuck | 1873-96

The Ox-Bow compound tells the story of how a beautiful harborside environment evolved from the home of fishermen to a tourist hotel and then to a school for the arts. The inn, first known as "Shriver's Inn," began as an expansion of the services the Charles Shriver family provided for passengers and goods arriving at their landing docks by way of Lake Michigan vessels. Over a period of years the Greek Revival L-shaped house (1873) was converted into the "Riverside Inn." The large addition to the south (1893) was built in the Italianate style, which would already have been at that time out-of-date—chosen possibly because the Shrivers wished to offer their guests the traditional "captain's watch" cupola from which to take the fine views of the lagoon and lake. The original gable of the 1873 house was leveled as a means of reconciling the old structure with the new, though the original windows remain; a new porch unified the several sections. Shriver and his brother Henry (whose quite similar Greek Revival house still stands just to the south) were fishermen, thus we may surmise that lodgers were not infrequently treated to tasty platters of Lake Michigan white fish. Guests were transported into the Village of Saugatuck by riverboat or were directed to the nearby footpath which led to the west-shore Chain Ferry landing near Mt. Baldhead.

Ox-Bow Inn, now used by the Ox-Bow School of Painting and the Arts, has 22 rooms, several sitting rooms, a dining hall, offices, kitchen, eating porch and service spaces.

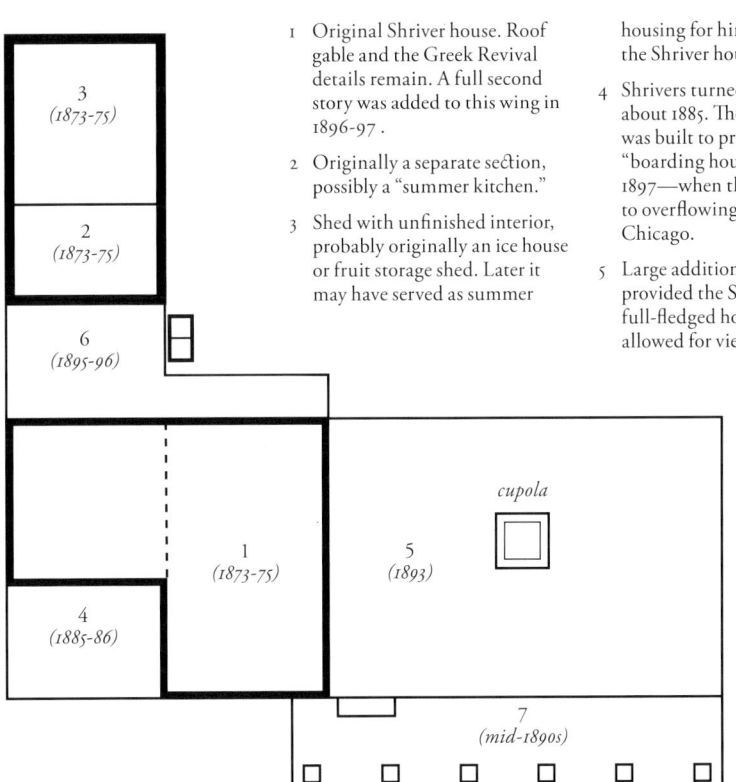

1 Original Shriver house. Roof gable and the Greek Revival details remain. A full second story was added to this wing in 1896-97.
2 Originally a separate section, possibly a "summer kitchen."
3 Shed with unfinished interior, probably originally an ice house or fruit storage shed. Later it may have served as summer housing for hired help. Predates the Shriver house.
4 Shrivers turned to tourism in about 1885. The 2-story addition was built to provide additional "boarding house" space about 1897—when the Hotel was filled to overflowing with guests from Chicago.
5 Large addition (30 ft. x 40 ft.) provided the Shrivers with a full-fledged hotel. The cupola allowed for viewing of the harbor, lake, and surrounding dunes. Hotel accommodated 90 guests in 1896. This part of the Inn now includes exhibit spaces and guestrooms.
6 New kitchen added for the Shrivers' growing summer tourist trade. Now the Ox-Bow School kitchen.
7 Porch added in the mid-1890s.

(Note: Considerable building addition and reconstruction in 2006)

[Research by Katherine N. Smalley, 1998]

73

BIG PAVILION
Constructed 1909
Water Street
Saugatuck

It was a sensation. Rising up on the site of an old coal yard and dock, nothing in the 20th century contributed more to Saugatuck's identity than that of the Big Pavilion—a brilliant statement in place-consciousness. Financed by a private company, it was built in less than 120 days. During its 51 year history its 100 by 60 foot dance floor was the scene of dance parties, contests, and later roller skating and professional wrestling. The Big Pavilion throbbed with the sounds of internationally famous dance bands—along with the hearts of the thousands who danced there. On May 6, 1960 the music stopped.

Deam, converted the old Saugatuck Lighthouse (1859) into a cottage. After the Lighthouse was destroyed by a tornado in 1956, Deam, himself a professor of architecture, salvaged some of the materials to build a modified adaptation of the old structure. In the villages artists set up studios and galleries, the best known being Cora Bliss Taylor whose two studio-residences became the place of art for hundreds of local children (and adults) from 1931 to 1980.

THE BRIGHTEST SPOT ON THE GRAT LAKES | Already in the 1890s ballroom dancing was "in" and city slickers seeking recreation in the Saugatuck-Douglas area were part of the craze. Indeed, Saugatuck hotel owners appear to have done well in giving the customers what they wanted. As we have seen, the Pokagon Inn advertised two dance floors (one on the roof-top), and beginning in 1901 the Tourist Home Hotel offered a large dance floor. A similar trend was taking shape in private houses as well. Sarah Kirby had a ballroom built on the third floor of her stylish new house on Center Street in Douglas, while O. C. Simonds had a dance floor installed in his cottage at Pier Cove. What better an idea than to build a big dance pavilion to serve the villages and cottages from Saugatuck to Pier Cove?—and well beyond, as it turns out!

The historical moment in this story is the 4th of July 1909, the day the "Big Pavilion" opened for business. Known as the "Brightest Spot on the Great Lakes," the Big Pavilion ballroom was opened to an audience dazzled by the thousands of sparkling electric lights which lined both the exterior and the interior of what was

BIG PAVILION
INTERIOR
(photo, ca. 1909)
Water Street
Saugatuck

The interior arches held 5,000 lights that changed color as the music changed. Looking west toward the bandstand. One of America's largest dance halls. The many lights lining the arches changed color with the music. In its heyday it entertained thousands of people a week—many coming by steamship or the Interurban train that ran from Grand Rapids-Holland-Saugatuck.

BIG PAVILION UNDER CONSTRUCTION
1909
Water Street, between Culver and Mason Streets
Saugatuck

The Saugatuck pavilion dance floor alone was 66,000 square feet. The nine wood arches were pulled into place and then tied together with wood planking.

TECHNOLOGY & BUILDING

How they built Saugatuck's Greatest Building
BIG PAVILION
Water Street | Saugatuck | 1909

SITE | *The east side of the Big Pavilion faced Water Street while the west side extended out onto a newly land filled river bank. Site provided for a striking view of the building from the water and the opposite shore. Large Lake Michigan passenger ships had docking access to the west side, and the east side faced the village. Soon it became a termination point for the Interurban railroad that brought visitors from Grand Rapids and Holland. Part of the site was formerly used for industrial purposes and part of it was landfill. The site today is a park area, parking lot and Singapore Yacht Club. All that is known of the architects is that they were from Kalamazoo.*

COST | *Originally to cost $25,000, construction costs mounted until the final price tag appears to have exceeded $50,000.*

ENTRANCE | *The main entrance was eventually re-oriented from the north façade to the east, facing Water Street.*

FOUNDATION AND SUBFLOOR | *The foundation was comprised of concrete piers on the landside and pilings driven into the Kalamazoo River on the waterside. The floor surface (105 by 200 feet) was of conventional wood construction, though the function of wedges on the completed sub floor is unknown. It was noted at the time that this was one of the first buildings in West Michigan for which the concrete was mixed by a gasoline driven concrete mixer. Henry Gleason & Sons of Saugatuck were contracted for the concrete work.*

STRUCTURE | *Nine laminated wood arches (86-foot radius) were constructed on the floor and raised by block-and-tackle to be attached to the concrete pilings under the floor and footings under the corner turrets. The arches were then braced diagonally with wood and then with roofing planks, and finally covered over with roofing material. The two poles shown in the photograph extend ropes for lifting roof lumber and workers. Steel cables were drawn across the breadth of the arches to strengthen the building. (These were used also to string radio station penants on during the years of the WLS radio broadcasts.) These cables were loosened or tightened to create more or less give to the building as needed. It was reported that during a high wind one could see the walls move.*

HEATING PLANT | *Originally built as a seasonal structure, a heating plant was added in 1929 to extend the building's use year-round. It proved less than profitable during the cold months and the Big Pavilion resumed its summertime-only schedule.*

WORKFORCE | *The Big Pavilion was erected in less than 12 weeks by 75 men, some of whom had worked on a similar structure in nearby South Haven. Overtime pay was necessary to get the work done by the 4th of July. One of the carpenters wrote a postcard home with the message:*

> Am now working on this building. I get 40¢ per hour and 60¢ overtime. It is 200+ something long and a little over 100 wide & about 89 ft. high. Went up on old baldy after work tonight. From its summit you can see the many miles down Lake Michigan. Will probably [. . .] here for a week or two. There are all of 50 carpenters working on it. Chas. Write and let me know how you are [. . . .] write soon. This is a beautiful place.

MATERIALS | *Nearly 350,000 board feet of lumber was transported by barge from the Hines Lumber Company of Chicago. Wood roof covered with tar.*

CORNER TOWERS | *The towers, or "turrets," are "battered" (flared toward the bases) except for the northwest corner. They had no function beyond dramatic effect.*

SIDING | *The building is basically a huge arched roof, the sides of which are filled in with batten board siding and 14 large windows with tilt-up shutters which provided the ballroom clientele with ventilation and views of the harbor.*

MOVIE THEATER WING | *At first open to the ballroom area (1919), then, with the advent of "talkies," it was made fully separate from the main building and given a separate entrance (1930 with theater seats and air conditioning).*

DOCK BAR | *A new lower level was added by a subsequent owner, George Barrett, in 1938. It featured polished wood paneling and a long "U-shaped" mirrored marble bar. Popular jazz venue in 1930s-1940s.*

COFFEE SHOP | *The coffee shop, which was added in 1953, provided for counter seating for 150 persons.*

LIGHTING | *Electricity had not yet come as far as Saugatuck in 1909, so a separate steam-powered generating station was constructed at the southeast corner of the Big Pavilion, which only multiplied peoples' fascination with the building. The electrical room, it was said, was like something out of The Wizard of Oz. Imagine dancing beneath 5,000 twinkling electric lights!*

FIRE | *Destroyed by fire on May 6, 1960. Origin unknown. Gigantic fire-fighting efforts. The Village was saved by shift in wind.*

RAISING THE ROOF

billed as the second largest dance hall in the America. Although it was preceded by a smaller East Shore Pavilion just south of the ferry landing, the Big Pavilion came to be regarded as Saugatuck's greatest advertisement. The original 105-by-200-foot wooden building was actually fairly simple. Painted red, with its vast height and soaring corner towers and its prominent position pushing out into the harbor, it became an immediate landmark. It was a sensation. Everything about it was big: On the harbor side it provided direct dock access for large passenger boats from Chicago; it included a vast movie theater; and a large "U-shaped" bar was added in 1938. Many still remember the Big Pavilion for its "big band" music (e.g. Erskine Tate's Colored Band, Dizzy Gillespie, Wayne King, Duke Ellington) and its radio broadcasts. In its heyday it catered to as many as 1,000 people a day.[12]

The Big Pavilion was a mirror of much of the history of popular culture in America over the half-century of its life. It helped usher in the dance craze of the turn of the century, the so-called 'jazz mad' 1920s, and the "big-band" decades that followed. It was where many learned how to roller skate and, following World War Two, its gigantic Dock Bar was the "in place" for a new generation that put alcohol at the top of its entertainment list—and its grand dock became the

BIG PAVILION INTERIOR
1909
Water Street
Saugatuck

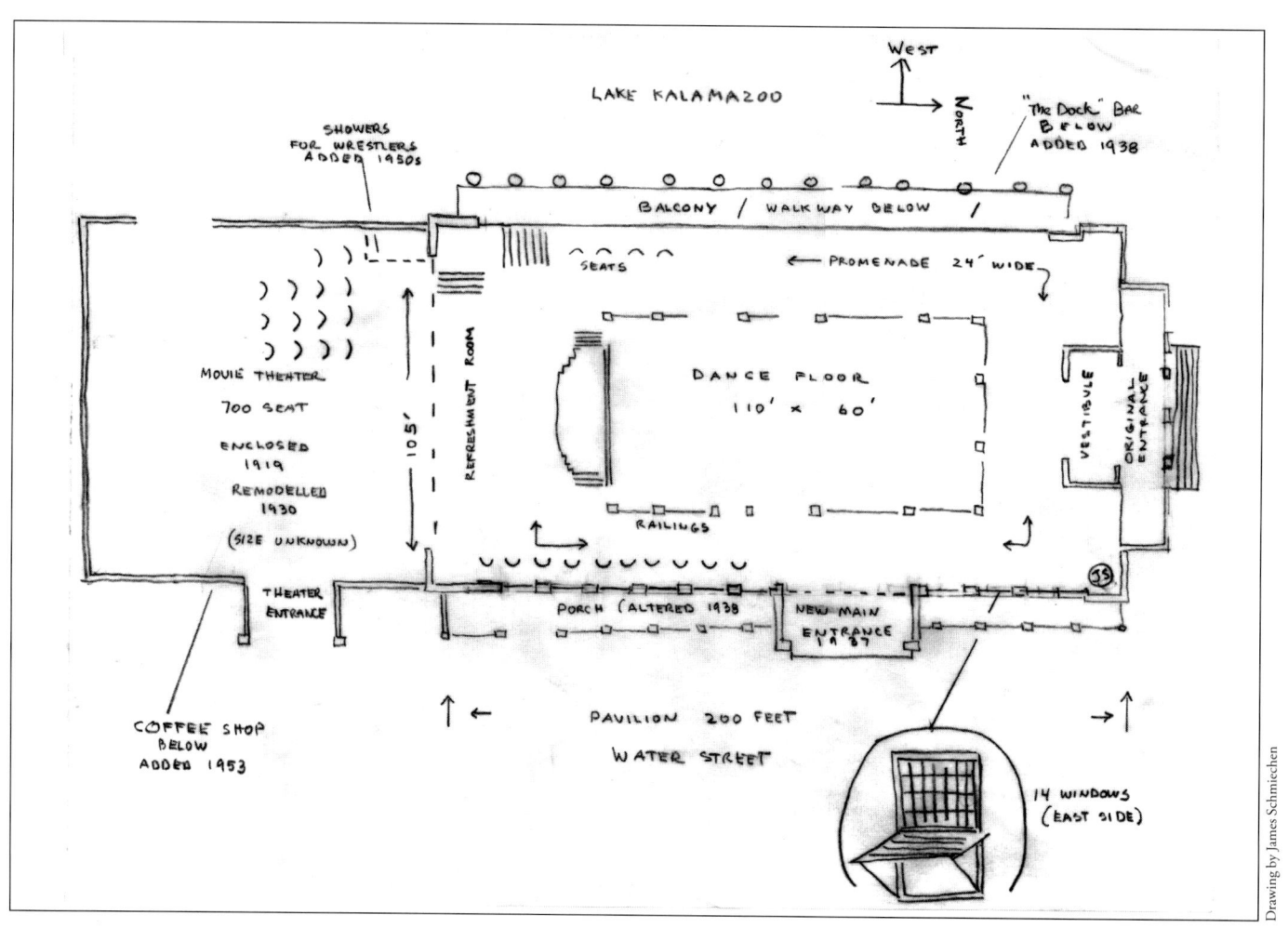

BIG PAVILION PLAN
1909
Water Street
Saugatuck

78

A History of the Buildings and Architecture in the Saugatuck and Douglas Area

BIG PAVILION INTERIOR
1909
Water Street
Saugatuck

From left, H. H. Engel, Fred Limouze, Andy Crawford, owners and managers.

viewing platform for a new sport, that of pleasure boating and water sport. Likewise, its decline in the 1950s mirrored the coming of television that did so much to privatize American life and culture. It was Saugatuck's most important building.

THE IDEA AND ROMANCE OF THE "SUMMER COTTAGE" | The people who rushed across the state and across the lake—and eventually across the nation and world—to this nature's paradise were both rich and not-so-rich. Some stayed a night and some stayed an entire summer. It was in the later 19th century that Americans began—in mass—to escape from the "daily grind" of ordinary life to find solace and enjoyment in a little house in the woods, among the fields, or by the water. The writings of Henry David Thoreau, Walt Whitman, and the transcendentalist Ralph Waldo Emerson encouraged a popular interest in the idea that a return to nature was the key to everything from building a moral society, writing music, building the perfect house and raising the perfect family. Emerson's portrait hung in the place of honor—above the fireplace—at the Forward Movement (now Presbyterian) Camp's main lodge.

Some cottages appeared as makeovers of a former house—such as the case with Ann Renaldi's charming cottage on Park Street—or an old shed, or even a fishing shack, but more often than not the cottage was built (and often rebuilt) from scratch to the fantasy of its owner. Nevertheless, it is often forgotten that one of the early forms of summer dwelling was the "tent-cottage." The first known artists to come to the area lived in tents as did George W. Maher, one of Chicago's leading architects, who with his family spent summers in a tent on the lakeshore south of Douglas before constructing their new cottage.[13] Heavy canvas tents were divided into rooms and almost always put up on elevated wood platforms; they were erected on both private and public land; the Saugatuck village square even had its share of tent people. In 1900 a community of 125 people housed in 30 tents, many of which had running water and rugs on the floors, stretched along the Kalamazoo riverbank north of Mt. Baldhead. Indeed, it appears that at that time there were twice as many people living in tents as in cottages in Saugatuck and Douglas. Each spring several local farmers hauled the wooden platforms down Park Street and placed the platforms and the carefully folded tents on the assigned spots to be assembled by their owners when they arrived from the city. The same process happened along the Douglas lakeshore where these platforms became the foundations for new cottages, as was the case with the Frank Woods family cottage.[14]

One Saugatuck summer resident, from a middle-class urban family, captured her memories of turn-of-the-century tent life in a fictional story based on her Saugatuck youth:

CAMP "UNEEDA REST"
Park Street (?)
Saugatuck

The tents in which they lived were a delight . . . for [they] were open at both ends to permit free passage of air . . . [and] were pitched where they received direct sunlight a part of each day, and the platforms were raised sufficiently off the ground to insure dryness underneath. Both the platforms and the flies [the doors] extended several feet in front of the tents to make a little sitting room where callers were usually received. Camp etiquette prescribed a discreet "halloo" when approaching a tent and the visitor stood at one side of the entrance until invited to enter. Meals were plain but ample, clothing plain and not too ample; floors were scoured by walking about on the particles of sand which seemed to be ever present.[15]

THE FIRST COTTAGES | The first cottages looked like farmhouses—because some of them actually were old farmhouses with a porch added here and there (e.g. Simonds's "Orchard House" of 1889) or because many of the early "purpose built" cottages were done in a traditional "folk-farmhouse" manner. The essential requirements here were cool interiors (often painted white), plenty of sleeping spaces, porches, and, of course, proximity to woods, dunes, and water. Porches ruled. No cottage better demonstrates the turn-of-the-century passion to bring the outdoors indoor than "The Porches" cottage built for John Butler Johnson and his family in 1897. Johnson, a St. Louis professor, and his carpenter (probably E. E. Schaeffer of Fennville) used a simple Folk-Victorian design but wrapped it with porches on all sides and on both floors—thereby providing the Johnsons and their guests with stunning views of Lake Michigan. Like many of these early two-story cottages, there was no interior

ORCHARD HOUSE COTTAGE
1855

2320 Lakeshore Drive | Pier Cove

O. C. Simonds purchased this "T-shaped" Greek Revival farmhouse in 1889 for his family's use as a summer cottage. Originally built by a Mr. Nichols, the house is set in an apple orchard and with its back to Lake Michigan. It is one of the earliest instances of the conversion of an existing house to a summer cottage. The 1855 house was built of white pine timber that was cut nearby at the local sawmill. It is of balloon frame construction with 1-inch sheathing planks covering the studs and finished with a layer of white pine clapboard. Simonds, a well-known Chicago landscape/garden designer (Morton Arboretum; Graceland Cemetery; parts of Lincoln Park, Chicago; Central Michigan and Michgian State University campuses; and Cranbrook Academy of Art in Bloomfield Hills, Michigan) created a 100-acre land preserve and arboretum at Pier Cove, partly as a way to repair damage done by clear-cut lumbering but also as a way to experiment with natural landscape design. He was one of the first to plant grasses to protect the dunes. He was friend to a number of prominent architects who were working in the Prairie Style at the time and was a partner in the Chicago architectural firm, Holabird, Roche, and Simonds. In keeping with the idea of cottage, he enlarged and refashioned the house interior in the Prairie Style, and made the principal living space face the lake.

THE PORCHES *(inset: Porches Second Floor Plan)*
1887

2297 Lakeshore Drive | Pier Cove

Looking directly out onto Lake Michigan, all four of the second-floor bedrooms in this very early purpose-built cottage open onto the 8-foot wide porches, which wrap completely around the 34-foot-by-40-foot house. A "back house" was added for additional room. The original cottage had its own water storage and gravity-flow system to supply the indoor plumbing. The walls were covered with random-size 3/4 inch planks, which were in turn covered with cheese cloth and wallpaper. The second-floor bedrooms had large "steamer trunk" closets to hold the luggage of the many schoolteacher family members who came to stay for the summer. The first owners, Professor and Mrs. Robert Butler Johnson, had five children.

A History of the Buildings and Architecture in the Saugatuck and Douglas Area

AVALON COTTAGE, INTERIOR
ca. 1900
Ox-Bow Hill
Saugatuck
Harbart family cottage. Destroyed.

JOHN NORTON'S COTTAGE LIVING ROOM
1923 *(photo, 2004)*
Saugatuck

This recent photo of the Norton living room shows several standard "cottage" features that draw upon the Arts & Crafts movement: the barn-sash casement windows, unfinished wood walls, the mandatory fireplace, Craftsman type furniture, plenty of nooks and shelves for books and mementoes, and support beams hand-carved by children on rainy days. As one of the proponents of the Arts & Crafts movement put it, "a generous amount of woodwork to give an effect of permanence, home likeness and a rich warm color in a room."

JOHN NORTON'S COTTAGE BEDROOM
1923 *(photo, 2004)*
Saugatuck

"Bless the bed I lie upon." John Norton's bed room door panels. Norton was one of Chicago's best known muralists. Here we see how he decorated his bedroom with the images of the gospel figures, Matthew, Mark, Luke, and John. The Arts & Crafts ideal held that when we return to nature, "the impulse to do beautiful and vital creative work is as natural as the impulse to breathe." (Gustav Stickley, Craftsman Homes. Architecture and Furnishings of the American Arts & Crafts Movement *(1908). p.199.)*

stairway from the first to the second floor, and as is the case with this cottage, each of the four second-floor bedrooms opens to the upper porch. Another porch extravaganza is the Allahee Lodge, Park Street, Saugatuck (ca. 1900), which has three levels of porches in a delightful sort of folk-stick style.

Most of these first cottages, including Professor D. O. Barto's cottage, 70 Lake Shore Drive, Douglas (1896), were plain and "very handsome" as the local newspaper called them,[23] but without a distinctive cottage style. Typically, Mrs. Bliss's cottage, Van Dalson Street (ca. 1896), just a stone's throw from the Chain Ferry in the new Mt. Baldhead Park neighborhood, the Park Addition, was built at the same time as Barto's in a similar folk-farmhouse manner, but with some "Victorian" trimmings. Her cottage was archetypal for its neighborhood: a multi-story clapboard house with high-pitched roof and generous porches, nestled against a steep dune. The price of the lot?—a whopping $25! It is probable that Mrs. Bliss's neighbor, Mrs. Van Dalson (after whom the cottage lane was named) was the proud owner of Saugatuck's first purpose-built cottage on Van Dalson at Park Street. By 1898 there were nine cottages in Mrs. Bliss's neighborhood.

83

SANDRIFT COTTAGE

1912
Shorewood
Saugatuck

Prairie style at its finest. False thatch rolled roof and half-timber upper story with a grand porch overlooking Lake Michigan. Large sleeping dormitory on upper floor. Lumber was shipped from Chicago by steamship to the dock at Douglas. Design close to that of Walter Burly Griffin of Chicago. Impeccably preserved.

MOORE–SMULSKI–NELSON COTTAGE
ca. 1908
3075 Lakeshore Drive
Douglas

Built for a member of a local lumber family (Moore), later owned by Chicago politician and banker who had a piano installed for a guest, the famous Polish pianist (and one-time President of Poland-in-exile), Ignace Jan Paderewski, in the 1920s. Paderewski played inside while lakeshore residents sat on the lawn. (Kit Lane, "Lakeshore Serenade" in The Popcorn Millionaire and Other Tales of Saugatuck. *(1991)*

TALLMADGE COTTAGE,
EXTERIOR
ca. 1922
Saugatuck
Watercolor by Judy Anthrop

TALLMADGE COTTAGE,
PAINTED INTERIOR DETAILS
ca. 1922 *(photo, 2004)*
Saugatuck

Hand-painted interpretations of Native American design were applied to the all-wood interior of this Arts & Crafts cottage by amateur and professional artists. The owner, Thomas Eddy Tallmadge, was an important Chicago architect known for his 'bohemian' lifestyle.

TREE TOPS COTTAGE
ca. 1920 *(reconstructed 2004)*
336 Park Street
Saugatuck
John Hurst, *reconstruction architect*

Part of an early community of cottages. A harbor-view cottage on a hill has shed its 1970s "modernization" and returned to a traditional cottage design, including an authentic stone fireplace.

WORTHINGTON COTTAGE
ca. 1903 with numerous additions
377 Lakeshore Drive

Like many cottages, this one evolved over time to meet the needs and design interests of various owners. Front porch became enclosed room with entry in 1938-39 and side porch added in about 1950. Knotty pine interior. The builder for the 1930s additions was Alex Campbell.

Bill Werme

Bill Werme

Bill Werme

Bill Werme

Bill Werme

Bill Werme

A COTTAGE GALLERY
(opposite page, from upper left to lower right)

SHAFROTH/ELAM
COTTAGE
1920s
Park Street | Saugatuck

RENALDI COTTAGE
1887
596 Park Street | Saugatuck

One of the oldest houses on the west shore, it was originally the home of the Joseph McGonagle family.

ALLAHEE LODGE –
HIGH CAMP
ca. 1900
Park Street | Saugatuck

The house of many porches. Built at a cost of $6,900 ca. 1896 by a U.S Senator from Michigan; it became a guest house in 1920s and 1930s. In 1965 it became "High Camp" cottage when purchased by a Chicago business man and former U.S Navy officer. For the next 20 years was locally known for its gay-straight parties.

VAN RAALTE COTTAGE
3081 Lakeshore Drive | Douglas

YELLOW COTTAGE
1901
Lakeshore Drive | Douglas

ROSE COTTAGE
1909
125 Elizabeth Street | Saugatuck

MC CORMICK COTTAGE
ca. 1940
88 Lakeshore Drive | Douglas

ALIBI COTTAGE
1920
127 Van Dalson Street | Saugatuck

GRAY/ZERATE
COTTAGE
1920s
541 Campbell Road | Saugatuck

ca. 1896

ca. 1900

ca. 1910

ca. 1925

ca. 1990

2006

BIOGRAPHY OF A HOUSE
No. 3

MRS. BLISS' COTTAGE
120 Van Dalson Street | Saugatuck | ca. 1896-1998

Mrs. Bliss built one of the earliest purpose-built cottages in the area (ca. 1896). The cottage was built in the Park Addition where lots were offered cheaply by the Village of Saugatuck in order to encourage people to build cottages on the west side of the river. It is of a folk-Victorian style.

The main living floor is the second floor, taking advantage of the Kalamazoo River views from the broad front porch. The back side of the cottage nestles into a sand dune. Antique photographs often give a grim appearance, but the flowers along the fence, painted clapboard siding, green roof framed by old oaks and the river nearby must have presented a perfect picture of the cottage by the water.

By the 1920s the porch was extended to the side and enclosed and an outdoor stairway had been added. The family car had begun to intrude into the picture thus necessitating a garage. The folk-Victorian look had begun to be superceded by a Colonial Revival image (which began Saugatuck in the 1920s). Later a screened porch was added below, beside the garage.

Today the house remains in use as a cottage. The garage has been removed and the lower porch has been filled in. The basic structure retains its good old bones and its skin has only been altered slightly to keep up with the times.

In the ca. 1900 photo *(upper right)* the cottage owner, Mrs. Bliss, is seated to the left, with her neighbor, Mrs. Van Dalson, who lived nearby in a nearly identical cottage, seated on the right. Now the Thieda-Masters Cottage.

RAISING THE ROOF

UPTON COTTAGE
1910, 1993
Lakeshore Drive
Douglas

90

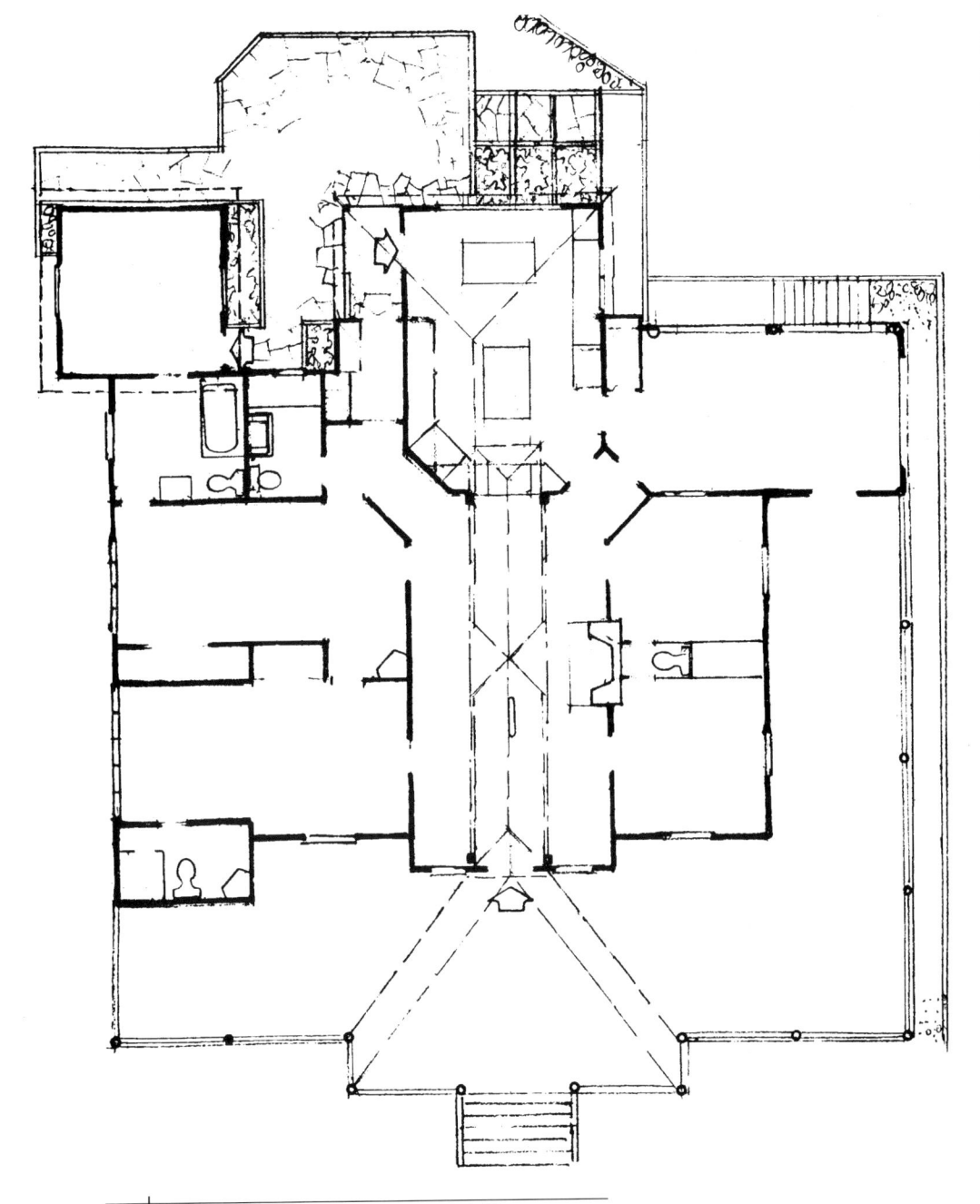

While Mrs. Bliss and Mrs. Van Dalson had to climb dunes to get to their houses, cottagers on the lower sand ridges of the Lake Michigan shore found it necessary to travel across ravines; thus, it is not surprising that their cottage plans included long and sometimes rather elaborate wooden bridges. In the Alvord and Delaney cottages the bridges became a part of cottage architecture. The "Leet Walk" bridge at Forward Movement [Presbyterian] Camp featured a charming log entrance pavilion.

ALVORD BRIDGE
332 Lakeshore Drive
Douglas
Design: John Alvord
A footbridge made of four stripped tree trunks, each 9 inches in diameter.

HELEN LEET WALK
ca. 1910
Forward Movement Park
(Presbyterian Camps)
Saugatuck

UPTON COTTAGE PLAN
1910, 1993
George Clark, *architect for 1993 remodelling*
The original layout consisted of a center core great room (far ahead of its time in current connotation) from which one entered four bedrooms and by diagonal passageways into a kitchen appendage and the porch. The house underwent remodeling in the 1910s and reconstruction in 1993—meeting the needs for modern plumbing and appliances, a new kitchen and dining porch—as well as addressing some structural problems

DUEX GOOSE COTTAGE
ca. 1930
649 Pleasant Street
Saugatuck

Built as the studio of artist Louise Crawford, daughter of captain Andrew Crawford.

Professor Barto on the lakeshore was the first of a large number of lakeshore cottagers from Oak Park, Illinois. His is the first known "purpose built" cottage on the Douglas lakeshore. The second was built next door by a Chicago businessman-journalist, and within a year the same area welcomed a pack of professors from the University of Kansas, ministers, architects, and businessmen, many others from Oak Park and Chicago, and then St. Louis, Cincinnati and so on. It is noteworthy that a number of early cottage builders and real estate investors were women, some of them single.

A NEW VIEW OF THE BUILT ENVIRONMENT | It has already been suggested that the building boom was very much tied to the belief that nature's paradise offered an antidote to urban—and, later, suburban—life. This made an allegiance to the preservation and, in some cases, even the restoration of the local landscape essential. In a reversal of the clear-cutting practices of the departed lumber barons, a new sort of relationship between man and the natural landscape was being devised, one in which man and nature coexisted and one in which man could learn from nature.

An early experiment in this sort of thinking and building was carried out at Pier Cove. In 1889 the landscape architect O. C. Simonds, an early partner in the Chicago firm of Holabird and Roche, purchased in Pier Cove a derelict farmhouse and orchard and a large tract of lakeshore land which had been decimated by clear-cutting (now known as "Pier Cove Ravine"). He designed the landscape as a series of "nature pictures," reintroducing native and some foreign species of plant and tree life. He was one of the first to protect the dunes by planting dune grass. He also established a

† O. C. SIMONDS ILLUSTRATION
ca. 1900

THE VENERATION OF TREES

THE TREATY TREE
Holland Street | Saugatuck

A local veneration of trees—sometimes assigning to them association with past events—was a part of the 'back-to-nature' experience, and remains a part of local lore. Such is the case with the story of William Butler's "Treaty Tree" on Holland Street (where it is said he signed treaties with the local Native Americans). Such cultural complexity is also found in how some public places were given a treescape—for example, the grand cavern of willow trees along the new bridge causeway, planted by Mr. Densmore soon after the Saugatuck-Douglas bridge was built in 1869, and the planting of trees along the east side of Mt. Baldhead to stop the dune as it pushed toward the river. Some of the many trees planted along Lakeshore Drive after the great fires of 1871 still stand. Walking trails were pushed through the woods for those who sought to combine hiking, conversation and nature. The Camp Gray (Presbyterian) camp trails were even given literary associations such as "Browning Path" and "Tolstoy Road."

nursery business to promote the use and protection of local trees and plants.

AN "ARTS & CRAFTS REVOLUTION IN BUILDING | O.C. Simonds was neither builder nor architect per se, but his passion for the natural landscape was shared by many who were. Indeed, what O. C. Simonds was undertaking at Pier Cove was also sweeping America—particularly the Midwest—by 1900. It was revolutionizing the way people designed and perceived buildings. It was called the "Arts & Crafts Movement," and it sent shock waves throughout the building industry. This was a new revitalizing approach to architecture, interior design, painting, furniture building, urban planning, and so forth. The movement which had its beginnings in England as early as the 1860s, had by the turn-of-the-century spread to America. It was founded on the principles of simplicity of form, honesty of materials, the virtue of hand craftsmanship, and an allegiance to locality—be it forest, sand dunes, farmland, or prairie. Rigorous simplicity became the middle-class ideal and fashion. At the same time, philosophy aside, the Arts & Crafts Movement had become a marketing strategy as well, especially in America. Specialized companies sold handmade products—such as hand-crafted tiles and "art pottery" of the Pewabic pottery in Detroit or "mission oak" furniture from the Stickley Brothers in Grand Rapids or from Charles Limbert's firm in nearby Holland, among a host of others in nearly every other region of the country.

A RESPITE IN THE WOODS
1909
Park Street | Saugatuck

What appears to be a scene of rural poverty to late-twentieth-century eyes is in fact a demonstration of a progressive social philosophy practiced by a particular stratum of affluent urban dwellers at the turn of the century. Typically this group turned to the countryside as a vehicle for simplifying and renewing their lives. This fashionably dressed woman and her son have just arrived to pursue the estival pleasures of the west Michigan shoreline.

More than anything the Arts & Crafts Movement was the dream that together the carpenter/craftsman, the architect, and the social reformer could re-link humankind to natural materials, the natural landscape, and (for some of its adherents) to The Divine Being himself. These were intellectuals who were forging an escape route from the perils and pitfalls of industrial urbanism. It is not surprising that in Chicago the great social worker Jane Addams joined with the great architect Frank Lloyd Wright at Hull House to establish the Chicago Arts and Crafts Society.[17]

But how did these "Arts & Crafts" principles translate into buildings and materials? To the Arts and Crafts mind, the ideal house was the minimal house. This idea found expression in the hugely popular "Craftsman" cottages and houses—the one- or one-and-a-half-story versions of which are still called "bungalows." The Craftsman designer totally erased the "Victorian" and farmhouse look. Instead, a low-pitched roof with wide overhang was preferred; as was natural wood for both interiors and exteriors, very often finished in dark stain; exposed rafter tails; brackets, beams; casement windows in cottages; open ceilings; few or no connecting hallways (the "open plan" was to bring people together) and exterior or interior trim in a rustic or "artistic" manner (derived from humble medieval detail), often with rustic hardware. Kitchens were small, windows were casements, fireplaces were of brick often with epigrammatic inscriptions with romantic associations above them, and porches were large (and screened) and always had square columns. No one popularized the Craftsman style more than did the Stickleys, two of whom, George and Albert, operated the Stickley Brothers furniture company of Grand Rapids which produced high quality "mission style" under the motto "Home of Quaint Furniture." Once again America had an all-American "home sweet home," but this time it was an architectural form which sought to complement rather than impose itself onto the landscape and townscape. Americans were becoming grownups.

ARTS & CRAFTS HOUSES AND COTTAGES | Two classic Craftsman "Bungalow" houses are found at 143 Elizabeth Street and 231 Water Street, Saugatuck. In each case the main roof extends over the porch. Both were possibly built from pre-cut packages of lumber (and detailing) which would have selected from one of numerous

A History of the Buildings and Architecture in the Saugatuck and Douglas Area

TAYLOR–WILCOX HOUSE
ca. 1910
231 Water Street
Saugatuck

This Arts & Crafts "Bungalow" was built by local banker, A. B. Taylor and came fully furnished with Mission furniture. It became the home of the Ross Phelps family.

95

HOW TO IDENTIFY
A Craftsman "Bungalow"
1900-1930 (locally)

The Bungalow originated in California but soon became one of the most popular house and cottage forms in American history. The style is found throughout the area, but particularly as cottages. Many pre-built ("catalogue") houses (Sears, Aladdin) offered variations on the style. It has the disadvantage of being difficult to add on to without destroying the original design.

1
low-pitched roof with wide overhang and exosed rafter tails

2
front porch, with columns, often square or flared ("battered")

3
"knee" braces at cornice or porch line, often triangular (see also Byrd House, next page)

4
windows in bands of three, often with multiple panes of glass in upper sash

5
fireplace of brick (not shown)

6
variety of "stick work" in gables and porch, use of shingles in gable ends (see "Landis Lodge, p. 78)

7
interiors emphasize an "open look" with fewer interior walls; built-in conveniences such as cabinets, fold-down tables, venetian blinds, built-in bathubs, and compact, efficient "home laboratory" kitchens (not shown)

THE BUNGALOW

"The word 'bungalow,' from the Hindi . . . [meaning] house in the Bengal style, originally referred to a type of colonial dwelling in East India. This was a single-story house whose well-ventilated rooms opened off a central airy hall, and which had a low-pitched roof and a verandah on all sides. For a time a form of the bungalow became fashionable in England. In the early twentieth century, the American Arts & Crafts Movement unofficially adopted it as the ideal Craftsman house." [26]

BYRD HOUSE
1918
143 Elizabeth Street
Saugatuck

A classic American Bungalow. The original owner of this house, Duncan Byrd, was a botanist and the foremost authority on azaleas in western Michigan. It is said that the azaleas at the front of the house may be the largest and oldest this far north in Michigan.

building magazines or retailers such as Sears in Chicago or Aladdin in Bay City, Michigan, and then have been purchased directly by the prospective owner or through a local builder. The Water Street bungalow (ca.1910) even came furnished—in Mission style, of course.

While "Craftsman" became a formula house in America from about 1905 to about 1920, a large number of idiosyncratic or vernacular Arts & Crafts houses and cottages can be found in the Saugatuck and Douglas area as well. In 1912 the William Allen family moved their farmhouse into Saugatuck and used it as the second story of very large new stuccoed Craftsman-style house, 423 Water Street, Saugatuck, which, in an altered form, still faces the village square.

Arts & Crafts variations were endless and were dictated largely by time, site, and personal taste. H. M. Bird created a trendy Arts & Crafts interior for his "Busy Bee" refreshment and souvenir shop on Butler Street. The Bavarian-born artist and architect Carl Hoerman created a distinctive Arts & Crafts house and studio for himself at 621 Pleasant Street, Saugatuck, with similar chalet-like details as he used when he used an old lumber yard site for the River Guild store and studio in Douglas in 1942. The River Guild building, which was a cooperative association of artists and artisans, reminds us that the Arts & Crafts tradition continued in the Saugatuck and Douglas area long after it went out of fashion in other parts of America.

CHALET STUDIO
ca. 1910
621 Pleasant Street
Saugatuck
Carl Hoerman, *architect*

On the Pleasant Street ridge overlooking the Kalamazoo. Arts & Crafts home of Bavarian-born architect and painter, Carl Hoerman, who designed the reconstruction of "Kemah" next door and the River Guild building in 1942, among other commissions in the Saugatuck Douglas area. This was his principal residence and studio. Earlier he had owned a farm on Old Allegan Road. The cast concrete railings are of Hoerman's design.

BUSY BEE CAFÉ
ca. 1904
233 Butler Street
Saugatuck

An interior shot of "The Busy Bee," decorated in Arts & Crafts Mission furniture which qualified it as possibly the most stylish café-shop on Butler Street. The proprietor, H. M. Bird, advertised "souvenirs, curios, pottery, and confectionery." The fountain menu tells us that a "Bread and Butter Sandwich" cost a nickel, while the "Home Boiled Ham Sandwich" cost a dime. Coca-cola was 5¢.

RIVER GUILD
1942
Blue Star Highway | Douglas
Carl Hoerman, *architect*

The River Guild building (later "Gray Gables" and more recently renovated as the "Joyce Petter Gallery") is a continuation of the local Arts & Crafts tradition in building. The interior "Gallery" featured a large "Oxbow Mural" painted by artists from the Oxbow Summer School of Painting.

MERRILL
COTTAGE
West Façade
1937 *(photo, 2005)*
Lakeshore Drive
Saugatuck Township
Carl Hoerman, *architect*

Overlooking Lake Michigan. Peterson D. Merrill was a South Bend industrialist who first came to Saugatuck in the 1920s to attend Camp Gray. This is one of the finest of a number of cottages designed by Saugatuck architect Carl Hoerman. It is in Hoerman's typical mix of Tudor Revival with American Arts & Crafts, with some Bavarian twists from Hoerman's German roots. Very fine mix of vertical and horizontal siding and with an exaggerated (16' x 12') version of one of Hoerman's familiar arched windows. Relocated on property, 2005.

MERRILL COTTAGE
ARCHITECT'S SKETCH OF EAST ENTRY
Lakeshore Drive
Saugatuck Township
Carl Hoerman, *architect*

The front (east) entrance of the cottage. The architect's drawing to celebrate the 25th anniversary of the owner's marriage.

MERRILL COTTAGE
INTERIOR
1937 *(photo, 2005)*
Lakeshore Drive
Saugatuck Township
Carl Hoerman, *architect*

KAMMAN COTTAGE
1936
2236 Lake Shore Drive
Saugatuck Township
Carl Hoerman, *architect*

Hoerman's distinctive translation of Arts & Crafts—with typical mixing of horizontal and vertical siding. Typically grand Hoerman fireplace dominates large living room.

RAISING THE ROOF

Here, as elsewhere in the country, the Arts & Crafts Movement inspired a romantic vision of American pioneer life, a log cabin building craze—pre-dating by many years Ralph Lauren's more recent reprise of this nostalgic era. A fine Douglas example can be seen in the W. H. Simpson family cottage, 11 Lakeshore Drive, Douglas (1903). It was designed by Charles F. Whittlesey, a Chicago architect best known for the design of one of the granddaddies of log cabin architecture, the "El Tovar Lodge" in Grand Canyon, Arizona, and was built by local builder George Kurz whose cottage-building business was flourishing during this period.

With its unfinished interior walls, bands of barn-sash windows and simple furniture, the Norton family's Saugatuck cottage still exists as a splendid example of the "home-made" cottage look. A number of Arts & Crafts cottages can still be found along the trails in the Mt. Baldhead area. Others were built in north of the village of Saugatuck in "Riverside Heights" (now Riverside Drive), a community of cottages platted in 1906 by Jesse M. House, but most have been destroyed. A more idiosyncratic Arts & Crafts cottage is the one that Chicago engineer John Alvord designed for his family at 332 Lakeshore Drive, Douglas (1903). It bears a number of stylistic affectations of the day: Gothic Revival and Stick Style with some pure fantasy details, such as colored glass window panes, gable finial and bracketing, and a "Juliet Balcony" gable facing Lake Michigan

Also in the Arts & Crafts mode, "Landis Lodge" 2593 Lakeshore Drive, designed by the renowned Chicago Prairie Style architect George W. Maher for his sister, Mary Hooker. The dwelling makes references to the English "Tudor cottage" but within a decided "Prairie" idiom. In so typical an Arts & Crafts manner, over the brick fireplace Maher's father-in-law, artist Alden Brooks, painted the

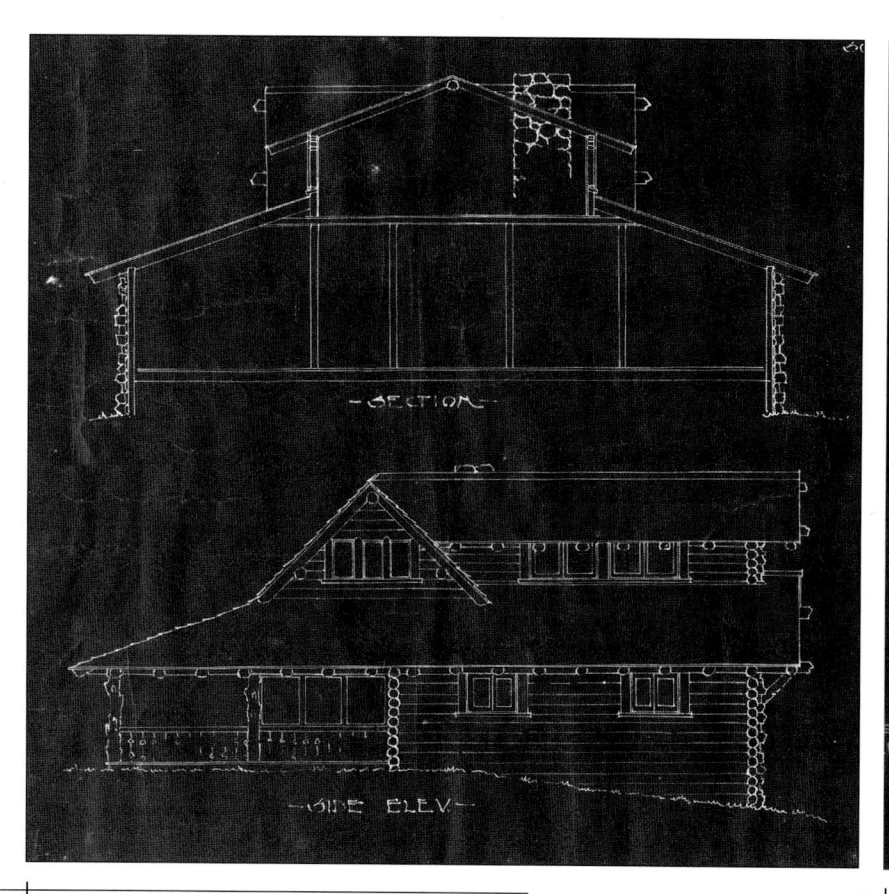

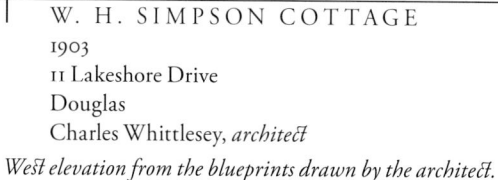

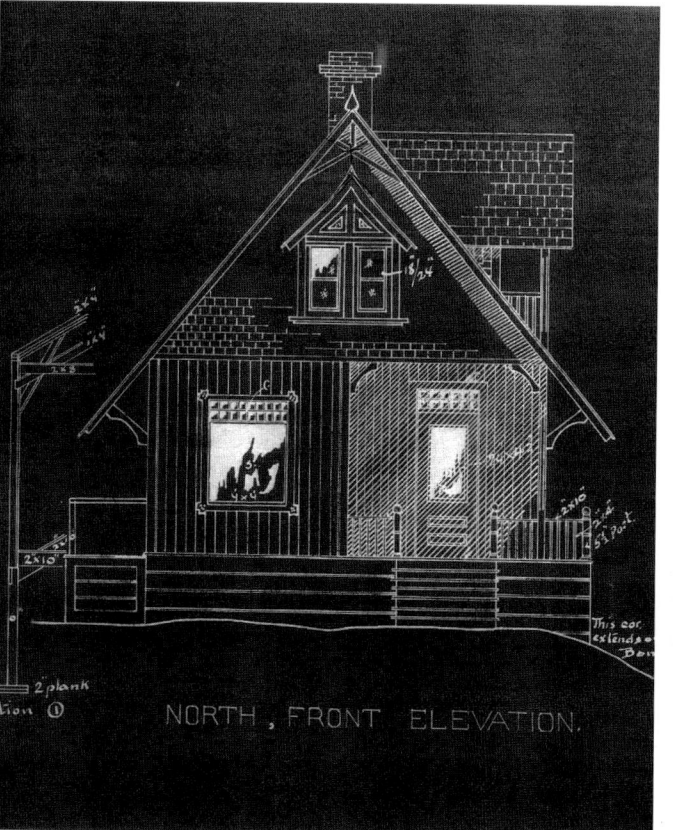

| W. H. SIMPSON COTTAGE
1903
11 Lakeshore Drive
Douglas
Charles Whittlesey, *architect*
West elevation from the blueprints drawn by the architect.

| ALVORD COTTAGE
NORTH ELEVATION
1901
332 Lakeshore Drive | Douglas
John Alvord, *architect*
This cottage, as well as the nearby Vossburg cottage, served as a Sunday school before the nearby Lakeshore Chapel was built. It is of vertical wood plank and shingle. The builder was local carpenter Arthur Weed. Alvord was a well known Chicago engineer—who collaborated on the design of Saugatuck's new water system and the Pump House of 1904 and that of the Chicago Columbian Exhbition of 1893

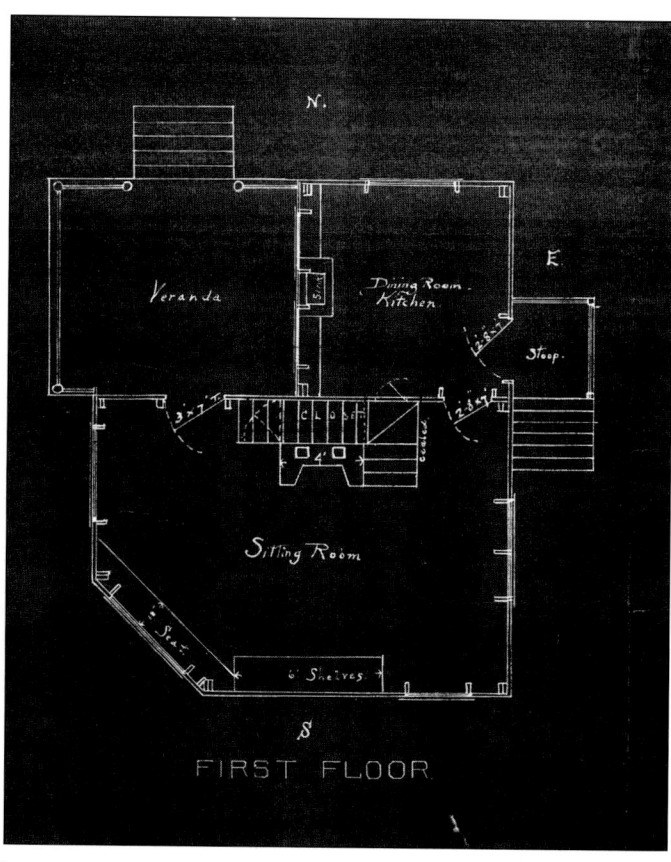

| ALVORD COTTAGE
PLAN, FIRST FLOOR
1901
332 Lakeshore Drive | Douglas
John Alvord, *architect*
No interior studding. Mr. Alvord's written instructions to the carpenter were that the cottage was to be built the old-fashioned way— with 4" x 8" braced corner posts and post at openings, rather with modern wall-studding system. On this framing was applied horizontal planks in order "to give the inside the appearance of paneled surface." The floors are 2 ½" pine. Two rooms and several sleeping rooms above. The "sitting room" is 20' x 14'–with a fireplace, built in bookshelves, and large corner window, with window bench, overlooking Lake Michigan.

A History of the Buildings and Architecture in the Saugatuck and Douglas Area

FRANK LLOYD WRIGHT ON CASEMENT WINDOWS

"Single-handed I waged a determined battle for casements swinging out, although it was necessary to have special hardware made for them as there was none to be had this side of England."[16]

ARTS & CRAFTS INSCRIPTIONS

During the Arts and Crafts Movement, it was common to find snippets of philosophy incorporated into furniture, needlework, or architectural detail, etc., such as:

East, West, Home's Best

was inscribed in tiles over the fireplace in one "hillside home."[23] *In Gustav Stickley's own log house at the Craftsman Farms the motto over the big stone fireplace read:*

The Lyf So Short, the Craft So Long to Lerne[17]

Stickley cites another overmantel example when speaking of the bungalow of an Indiana headmaster of a boy's school (the design for which was adapted by the owner from a published house plan, with assistance from architect George W. Maher): "Unconsciously one remembers the inscription above the chimneypiece downstairs:

To Teach Boys to Live

—and after all, to what finer purpose could any man dedicate his home?"[18]

| LANDIS LODGE
1910
2593 Lakeshore Drive
Fennville
George W. Maher, *architect*

Maher is best known as an architect of a large number of large and stylish Chicago area residences—particularly along the north shore. This was one of several Arts & Crafts cottages he designed for his family. He once said that low ceilings "convey the idea of privacy."

101

RAISING THE ROOF

motto: "A Summer Well Spent / Brings a Year of Content." Maher built a Prairie Style bungalow for himself across the road (now considerably altered). A less intellectualized but equally idyllic Arts & Crafts version of "cottage"—and more typical of our local pattern—are the Worthington and McCormick cottages (Lakeshore Drive).

The Arts & Crafts philosophy is perhaps best fulfilled when a cottage owner collaborated with a local carpenter to realize a combined vision. This is what happened when Mrs. Gage from Chicago teamed up with carpenter Mr. Allen from Douglas. The result was the delightful "Gage Cottage" (1931) which overlooks the Kalamazoo high on the northern-most hiking trail along Ox-Bow Hill. Designed by Jean Richardson Gage, Mr. Allen added hand-crafted, high-backed dinette benches, simple trims on doors and windows, wood boxes disguised as benches, bookcases, cabinets, shelves and a heavy front door in the vernacular rustic Arts & Crafts manner that Mrs. Gage desired. Some of the bedrooms are laid out with the efficiency of miniature Pullman sleeping cars. For a house that measures only 26 feet by 28 feet, it gives the illusion of space and privacy. Like many cottages of its era, it was given an Indian-sounding name, "Oh-Ja-Jo-Je."[19]

Nothing could be simpler or more straightforward vernacular cottage-beside-the-road than the "Alibi" Cottage, 127 Van Dalson Street. The original screens—not just the frames, but the original screen wire also—are

TONAWANDA– PORTER COTTAGE
1927
Riverside Drive | Saugatuck
Florence Ely Hunn, *architect*

Photo shows the rear (east) side. Built for the Jordan family of Chicago in 1927 and designed by Florence Ely Hunn, Tonawanda cottage is perched high on a bluff overlooking the Kalamazoo River and Saugatuck's Lake Michigan harbor entrance. It is of large brown salt-glazed brick from the Kalamazoo Brick Company, with over-sized divided-light windows in front and rear to provide a somewhat modern English Tudor effect. Hunn was one of Chicago's foremost interior designers, and practiced as an architect in her own right. She designed a number of other cottages in the area.

still painted biennially by the owners and nothing (not even the addition of a hot water heater) has been done to significantly alter the Alibi since Mr. Guild added a small "tip-out" on the east wall to accommodate the Alibi's refrigerator. Painted plank doors and shutters remain.

The best-known type of Arts & Crafts house (and cottage) is the more exaggerated and aesthete "Prairie Style" which was born in Chicago and is most commonly associated with the architect Frank Lloyd Wright. Wright, who said "democracy needed something better than the box,"[20] popularized houses with strong horizontal emphasis, but often with contrasting vertical lines (such as board and batten and Tudor-like wood framing). No architect in America has been as important in causing us to think about building houses that respect and conform to the natural landscape. One of the most important followers of Wright, the Prairie architect, Robert C. Spencer Jr. (also of Chicago), created a fashionable Saugatuck "Farm House." The house is typically Prairie in that he used wide roof overhang to give it a horizontal feel, divided-light windows and multiple porches to push the house out to embrace the natural landscape. It

| COMSTOCK FARMHOUSE
1905
Saugatuck
63rd Street
Robert Spencer, Jr., *architect*

Built for A. J. Comstock, it was purchased by Chicago executive John D. Williamson in 1912. Six weeks after Williamson's purchase, the house was destroyed by fire. Destroyed by fire 1912

| GAGE COTTAGE
1931
Saugatuck
Park Street / Ox-Bow Hill

High on a secluded path, a true "cottage" that still functions as a summer retreat.

KEMAH
1906
633 Allegan Street
Saugatuck
Thomas Eddy Tallmadge, *architect*

Overlooking Lake Kalamazoo, "Kemah" was originally built for Chicagoan Fred S. Thompson who had summered in Saugatuck since 1896. The porch wrapped around three sides. The women in the photograph are unidentified.

is an unusual house for the area because of its use of roughcast (stucco), although a more contemporary Prairie variation, the Schumann Cottage at 296 Lakeshore Drive, Douglas, uses concrete block. Another of the Chicago Prairie School masters, Thomas Eddy Tallmadge, designed an Arts & Crafts cottage called "Kemah," on Allegan Street, on the hill in Saugatuck in 1906 with porches on three sides. Carl Hoerman later enlarged and redesigned Kemah, adding Prairie windows and Arts & Crafts tiles—but with more of a sophisticated English look, making it one of the most unique summer houses in Michigan.

KEMAH – SPRINGER COTTAGE
1926 *(restoration, 2004-2006)*
633 Allegan Street
Saugatuck
Carl Hoerman, *architect*

Extensive remodeling and expansion of Kemah by William and Alys Springer of Chicago as a family "cottage" designed by Carl Hoerman, to become on of Michigan's best designed and highly crafted houses of the period. Hoerman drew upon Arts & Crafts, Prairie and Art Nouveau forms—with some references to the English Cotswolds and his own Bavarian roots. The house features a porte-cochere and colonnaded porch, a "false-thatched" roof, a grand fireplace, fine stained glass windows, hand-carved doors and includes a rathskeller and cavern. Finely restored, 2004-2006 with new stone entrances. Springer was a member of the Chicago Board of Trade. Hoerman, a local painter and architect who lived on the same street at No. 621 Pleasant.

KEMAH – SPRINGER COTTAGE
1926 *(restoration, 2004-2006)*
633 Allegan Street
Saugatuck
Carl Hoerman, *architect*

104

KEMAH – SPRINGER COTTAGE
1926 *(restoration, 2004-2006)*
633 Allegan Street
Saugatuck
Carl Hoerman, *architect*

LAKESHORE CHAPEL

1904
Lakeshore Drive & Campbell Road | Saugatuck & Douglas
Harry L. Walker, *architect*, with Frank Lloyd Wright

Mr. Walker (1877-1953) grew up in Oak Park, Illinois, attended the school of the Art Institute of Chicago and was employed by Frank Lloyd Wright. The building is reminiscent of earlier chapel designs by Mr. Wright and Mr. Walker for Wright's estate at Spring Green, Wisconsin. The Arts and Crafts/Craftsman conformation of the building reflects both his clients' desire for a simple chapel to complement the surrounding landscape as well as his own interests in English medieval and Chicago Prairie Style of architecture. Mr. Walker spent most of his architectural career in New York. The chapel straddles the dividing line between Saugatuck and Douglas.

The Chapel was the outgrowth of a Douglas lakeshore Sunday School begun by Mrs. Annie Vossburgh of Oak Park, who used her Douglas cottage as a Sunday School. The children of the School collected enough pennies for the Chapel to cover about half of its cost. A separate Children's Chapel was later built nearby. It continues today as an inter-denominational summer chapel.

Perhaps the very best example of the Arts & Crafts respect for locality is the "Lakeshore Chapel," Campbell Road and Lakeshore Drive, Douglas (1904), designed by a Wright student, Harry L. Walker. The chapel, with its dramatic flared roof, traditional clapboard siding, and simple barn-like windows, still speaks to us about how local cottagers sought a humble structure that would help them feel the presence of God in nature.

Many of the early Douglas and Shorewood cottagers were educated middle-class professionals, some were allied with the ideals of American "progressivism" of the day and many were involved with the Presbyterian and Congregational churches. In 1902 John Alvord (whose own cottage design was noted previously), was responsible for laying out Shorewood, a Douglas example of a planned cottage community, called a cottage "association," of a type not uncommon in resort areas such as this. By 1930 some 23 cottages, many in an Arts & Crafts/Prairie style, housed families from all over the Midwest, but especially from Chicago and Oak Park, Illinois—from which five of the original eight Shorewood incorporators hailed. Indeed, the story goes that the meeting that gave birth to Shorewood took place in the Walnut Room of Marshall Field's in Chicago.[21] With their attention to natural materials and simplicity of style, many of the Arts & Crafts cottages still mirror the turn-of-the-century desire to merge life with nature. So, we are fortunate now, at the opposite end of the century, that many of the early Douglas and Shorewood lakeshore cottages remain intact as fine examples of Midwestern cottage architecture.

At the same time that Arts & Crafts was in fashion there were also other sensibilities being expressed. As Shorewood was platted, the Douglas lakeshore was also becoming dotted with the new cottages of St. Louis cottagers who followed a Colonial Revival rather than an Arts & Crafts mode. An example of this is the patrician cottage of Mr. and Mrs. John O'Fallon Delaney, Lakeshore Drive (1902) which indulged itself in a higher visibility, and that of St. Louis architect George Helmuth, who built an equally large cottage for his family on Lakeshore Drive (1910). Many of these cottages were constructed by local carpenter George Kurz.

PLAN FOR SHOREWOOD
1902
Lakeshore Drive & Campbell Road
Saugatuck

A 27-acre property located on Lake Michigan, Shorewood is one of a large number of private "planned" resort communities in Michigan to have been established soon after 1900. While most villages and towns were laid out on the modern grid plan, Shorewood's planner John Alvord, a Chicago engineer and colleague of Daniel Burnham, was attracted to the more naturalist approach set forth by America's leading landscape architect, Frederick Law Olmstead, by having the roadways path-like and curved to suit the contours of the rolling and hilly dunes. The Shorewood Association built its own lighting system, and for many years had its own well and water works, sharing with neighboring cottages to the south. All but three of the original 26 cottages were built between 1902 and 1930. The layout of the road-path and lots and the scale and design of the cottages still remind us of the originators allegiance to the natural environment.

RAISING THE ROOF

BUILDING TO BRING PEOPLE CLOSER TO GOD | As suggested earlier, there is closeness in both distance and spirit in what was happening along the Saugatuck-Shorewood and Douglas lakeshore and what was happening after 1896 at nearby "Forward Movement Camp." The founders of the Forward Movement ("Camp Gray" / "Presbyterian Camps"), like those who built behind the Ox-Bow school, looked to lake, village, and countryside as locus for a moral, spiritual and aesthetic reawakening. To Reverend George W. Gray this was to be extended to the disadvantaged people of the city, particularly children, youth and women.

Exactly how Reverend Gray, the Chicago "city missionary" and founder of the Forward Movement, came to settle on Saugatuck's shore as the basis for his experiment we do not know, but we do know that a young Saugatuck man by the name of Edwin House, who was studying in Chicago and Oak Park, interested

SWIFT COTTAGE

"Swift Cottage, which will accommodate 100 if need be, will be opened to girls and young women who wish an outing and cannot pay more than $2.50 per week for board and room. This will not apply merely to Chicago people, but to any who wish to take advantage of the offer, as long as there is room. Each young lady must bring a recommendation from the pastor of the church which she usually attends, or principal of the school where she is acquainted. The propriety of the rule is manifest, and it is a guarantee to the mother that her daughter will be protected. Address Geo. W. Gray, Superintendent, Saugatuck, Michigan"[22]

SWIFT COTTAGE, FORWARD MOVEMENT ASSOCIATION
1900
Perryman Street & Lake Michigan
Saugatuck

Now known as Presbyterian Camps, the Forward Movement Association of Chicago was founded as a "Chautauqua for the Poor" by Reverend George W. Gray, with help from a number of wealthy businessmen. Boys and girls paid $2.50 a week for room and board. Within a few years Forward Movement had 87 buildings, one of which was this guest house called Swift Villa or Swift Cottage (named for its donor of Chicago meat packing fame). The camp included cottages, food and recreation halls and many outdoor spaces including trails, worship and recreation areas and beaches. Here nature was recast as the architecture of the soul and body. Destroyed by fire, 1954.

Reverend Gray in the Saugatuck area. Gray had the backing of a number of well-to-do Chicagoans, including W. S. Harbert, a wealthy land speculator, and David C. Cook, the famous publisher of religious materials. By 1900 Forward Movement had built a road west from Park Street and had constructed a large number of cottages and other buildings, including the large hotel-like "Swift Cottage," a gift from the prosperous Chicago meat-packing family0. Swift Cottage eventually accommodated over 100 persons at a time and had a dining room which would have made any urbanite feel at home. "The Camps," as the Presbyterian Camps are known today, are still dedicated to bringing urban people of all circumstances to experience God's woods and lake. Not only did Reverend Gray succeed in bringing the city's poor to Saugatuck, but he attracted the rich as well. Both Harbert and Cook built summer residences nearby. Cook's residence turned out to be the grand mansion of Saugatuck and Harbert's, a romantic vision called "Oak Openings," was constructed on a tall dune—but has since fallen victim to the wind, sand, and time. Another of the Gray patrons, William Gamble, built his "cottage" on Riverside Drive.

SWIFT COTTAGE, TUMBLE INN CAFÉ & RECREATION ROOM

SAUGATUCK VILLAGE HALL
Before & After
1880/1926
102 Butler Street | Saugatuck
Carl Hoerman, *architect (1926 reconstruction)*:

No local building better represents the 1920s effort to create a new village image than the remodeling of the finely proportioned exterior of the village hall in 1926. The Fire Department was organized in 1871 and this was built in 1880 as the village's second fire engine house, with meeting rooms above and a jail. In Hoerman's reconstruction of 1926, the bell tower was replaced with a gentle dormer with semi-circular window, corner pilasters (note pilasters between the upper windows as well) and an elegant recessed entrance portico with a small arched window to either side. The famed neon clock was installed in 1935, and the fire department continued to use the structure until 1954. It was here in 1931 that the Saugatuck Art Association staged its first regular exhibit (which included the work of Carl Hoerman). Addition of a basement in 1929 confirmed the site as former Native-American burial ground. Alteration to the structure was proposed in 1988 but was rejected in the face of strong community opposition.

CHAPTER FIVE

Inventing the Peaceful Village, 1920-1940

"Everyone who works amid the tumult of the big city will understand why Saugatuck, Michigan is my favorite town. Here is a restful, tree-shaded village which is off the railroad and off the main highway but which is not so remote that a person cannot go there frequently . . . the surrounding countryside is as attractive as the town, with the drowsy Kalamazoo River and Kalamazoo Lake close by and with Lake Michigan itself only a short distance away thru dunes and woods."

—FRED STEARNS
"My Favorite Town,"
Chicago Tribune, July 4, 1954

THE ROARING TWENTIES (WELL NOT QUITE SO ROARING) | After World War I, American cultural life took another "let's redefine America" turn. As we have seen, this was not the first—nor would it be the last—time that Americans attempted to trace a line around what it means to be American. Much of this was a reaction to the war (1914-1918), which was viewed by most as a huge mistake, needlessly costing millions of lives on the mud- and blood-soaked killing fields of France. Thus in a mood of disillusionment with all things European, Americans sought out what was good about American life—and architecture. Urban people of the 1920s saw escape to the countryside as a form of survival, as had the pre-war generation, but a new aspect of urban life called "suburban living" breathed new life into the "back to nature" movement. By 1925 Chicago, for example, had 57 suburbs, most of them full of standardized narrow houses and tiny suburban yards.[1]

In spite of "boom times" in Michigan's automobile industry, the 1920s were not the best of times for her small towns. This was partly because of declining demand for agricultural products and the 1930s, of course, were years of severe economic depression. By 1920 Saugatuck's population had fallen below that of 1870. Land values dropped, derelict buildings dotted the landscape and even the most visible local "gentleman farmer" (and Chicago executive), John D. Williamson, sold his "Belvedere" estate and moved back to Chicago. Overall the Saugatuck area had but a few things going for it—some fishing, a basket factory in Douglas (until 1927) and, of course, the tourist-resort trade. Because so much of this was seasonal labor, some hard-up residents had to sell off property and even take jobs as maids and laundresses with the local hotels. There were not many new houses during this period—with the major exception being the Felt mansion in nearby Laketown Township—but a few families could afford some remodeling, as was the case with the Prentice family at 34 South Spring Street, Douglas, who managed a new Kelvinator refrigerator and a newly remodeled kitchen.

On the idyllic side of this story, a slow and seasonal local economy meant that the villages retained the kind, old-fashioned

KRAEMER'S FEED MILL & STORE
ca. 1875 *(photo, 1940s)*
Corner of Wall & Washington Streets | Douglas

Remnants of former prosperity. In early years both Douglas and Saugatuck had several waterfront flour mills to meet consumer demands as well as meet needs of local farmers. The multi-story flour (grist) mill portion of the structure is hidden behind shop front. It is not known when the milling process ended, but John Kraemer offered the sale of flour, seed, and feed from this building in the 1910s.

MRS. PRENTICE'S KITCHEN
36 South Spring Street | Douglas

Modernism arrives. The door beyond Mrs. Prentice (in the kitchen) leads to a new laundry where the new "easy washer" was located. Photographed in 1936. The house was built ca. 1885 and became the home of the family of Joseph Prentice, manager of the Fruit Exchange in Saugatuck.

RAISING THE ROOF

FELT MANSION
1925-28
138th Avenue | Lake Michigan / Laketown Township
F. P. Allen and Sons, *architects*

The Roaring 20s brought millionaires as well as gangsters to West Michigan. A Chicago inventor, Dorr E. Felt began his fortune with the invention of the first adding machine-calculator and spent part of it here as a gentleman farmer. The thousand acre estate included an orchard farm, large forest and a half-mile of Lake Michigan beach—to which Felt built a road for public access. The family sold the property to the St. Augustine Seminary in 1948 which used it until the 1970s at which time it became a State of Michigan minimum security prison. Recent acquisition of the property by Laketown Township for public access. Under extensive restoration since 2004 by a volunteer organization.

A History of the Buildings and Architecture in the Saugatuck and Douglas Area

FELT MANSION
- *u* | In Its Heyday
- *ml* | Horseback Riding
- *mr* | Ballroom
- *ll* | Beach House on Lake Michigan
- *lr* | Carriage House

113

RAISING THE ROOF

sleepy character that the summer visitors, including artists, wanted. The Big Pavilion, with its dance and movie venue, and the growing Ox-Bow art colony meant that Saugatuck was poised to become an even bigger summer attraction during the "Roaring Twenties." But even as a resort economy, Saugatuck's future was not assured. For a variety of reasons, the days of tourists and cottagers being delivered portside by large passenger ships was over. With the rising popularity of other forms of transport, the golden hen of tourism had flown the coop. Improved passenger rail service (direct to neither Saugatuck nor Douglas), the proliferation of the automobile and a new Michigan "trunk road" called M-11 (later called U.S. 31, now a portion of which is the Blue Star Highway) made it easier for more and more people to reach other lakeshore destinations and, consequently, other lakeshore towns vied for the tourists' affections—and their dollars. Thus Saugatuck and Douglas were now largely dependent on automobile traffic and, although it was their good fortune that the M-11 went right down the main streets in both villages, the competition had stolen a piece of the tourist pie.

Also, by the end of World War I in 1918, Saugatuck and Douglas were looking a bit shabby and out-of-date. Some of the earliest hotels and boarding houses now seemed worn and old and prior to about 1918 only a few village streets were paved. To make matters worse, the village was beginning to attract a class of young people with "unspeakable" moral habits, as it was said at the time, whose moonshining and "profligate licentiousness" was turning away respectable resorters.[2]

What could be done? Obviously, "respectable" tourists traveling the new M-11 would stop and spend their money at any town they found inviting. Douglas tried in the 1920s to market itself as a resort "Town to Remember" and even built a "beach house" on the three lakeshore properties it acquired in 1907 for a public beach. In Saugatuck, Dr. W. B. House and architect George W. Maher proposed a facelift based on cleanliness, beautification and improvement of municipal services. In 1918 the Saugatuck Village Council initiated an extensive street paving project.[3] Then, in 1923, Maher pleaded before the Council that the village adopt planning and zoning ordinances. All of this, promised House, who was President of the Chamber of Commerce, was necessary to maintain Saugatuck's position as the "finest resort in the state."[4]

A COLONIAL REVIVAL FACELIFT | What happened was extraordinary. Saugatuck reinvented itself as a peaceful (but fun loving), picturesque, and respectable all-American village. It may not have actually been all of these things, of course, but this is what the tourists wanted and Saugatuck was willing to accommodate by providing the proper image. The most picturesque building in the village, the Carpenter Gothic All Saints Church, was given an equally picturesque addition by Carl Hoerman. Despite a touch of modernism

† THE TOWN TO REMEMBER
1924

Tourist Promotional Brochure. With fewer tourists coming by way of the big passenger boats and the advent of a new Michigan highway system, both Douglas and Saugatuck found it necessary to market their respective villages to a new breed of highway travelers who could choose from many Lake Michigan towns. Although it had become the center of a thriving cottage community along the lakeshore, tourists largely bypassed Douglas in favor of Saugatuck as a destination. This brochure promoted the fishing, golfing, and swimming opportunities in Douglas, as well as advertising local boarding houses and "resorts."

† THE COLOR WHITE
1920s

All Saints Church gets a "colonial" whitewash.

114

A History of the Buildings and Architecture in the Saugatuck and Douglas Area

ALL SAINTS EPISCOPAL CHURCH PARISH HALL
1946
Grand and Hoffman Streets
Saugatuck
Carl Hoerman, *architect*

Although "Gothic" architecture has European roots, this "Carpenter Gothic" period piece is very "American"—and very picturesque. It might be stated that Mr. Hoerman's design equals the extraordinary 1873 building to which this addition was appended.

RAISING THE ROOF

here and there—e.g., Jean Goldsmith's modernist cottage at 536 Butler Street (1938) and the Hotel Saugatuck's "Crow Bar"—the architectural formula for the two villages in the 1920s and 1930s was the "Colonial Revival" style. This was not difficult to achieve, since Colonial Revival was in harmony with the vernacular tradition of the two villages: simple wood structures with a stubborn attention to classical form, scale and style—and even color. It was easily adaptable to existing structures, if only a switch to the color white. Unlike many Michigan towns that by now had lost their traditional architecture to wealth and economic growth, Saugatuck and Douglas capitalized on their old-fashioned look.

WHY DID AMERICANS WANT COLONIAL REVIVAL? | Colonial Revival was the most common architectural and building style in America in the 1920s and 1930s—a trend that continued into the 1950s and beyond, sometimes under the term "neocolonial." It had been popping up here and there since the 1880s when certain trend-setting architects and interior designers began to look backwards for design inspiration to what they perceived as the simplicity, honesty and nobility of colonial America.[5] As its name suggests, Colonial Revival is fixed on a restoration of the building and architectural customs during America's nearly two hundred years of "colonial days," and has been freely interpreted by some to include just about any "classical" reference—even embracing the simple early colonial timber-frame salt-box building type. Although the occasional purist sought a replication of English colonial "Georgian" or "Adam" styles, or the classicism of the Dutch settlers of

FINKL-KNOLLENBERG/JONES COTTAGE
ca. 1942
609 Campbell Road
Douglas
Florence Hunn, *architect*

One of the most "modern" cottages of the area, designed by one of Chicago's pioneer modernists—for a well-known Chicago industrialist, Anton Finkl.

OLD CROW BAR
ca. 1939
220 Water Street
Saugatuck

On the outside the Saugatuck Hotel was painted gleaming white to accompany its "Dutch Colonial" roof and to fit into the village's 1920s classical image, but on the inside the new "Old Crow Bar" was tricked out in a modish "Art Deco" style, a popular American 1930s "streamlined" version of the Paris original. The "crow murals" surrounding the bar were by the artist "Doré." Remodeled.

COOK-BENNETT MANSION
1916
Old Dugout Road | Saugatuck Township

David C. Cook was a Chicago publisher of Sunday school literature and a financial benefactor of the programs of Reverend Gray's Forward Movement (now Presbyterian Camps) which provided excursions to the nearby lakeshore for poor children (and others) from Chicago. The Cooks purchased a sizable tract of lakefront property (which included the old Singapore site) and built a number of family cottages around the property before building the main house in 1916, which, with its grand ionic columns, faces southwest from a high dune toward Lake Michigan. The architect is unknown. Mrs. Cook donated to the Village of Saugatuck a considerable riverfront acreage, now known as Cook Park. The house was sold to David A. Bennett, a Chicago perfume manufacturer and friend to President Truman's chief advisors. Consequently, the guests at the house in the later 1940s included high-ranking Washington officials. When Bennett died in 1953 the property was put up for sale.

FURSMAN HOUSE
1855
246 Mary Street
Saugatuck
Thomas Eddy Tallmadge, *reconstruction architect*

One of Saugatuck's oldest structures, this was originally the Pine Grove School. In 1927 it became the residence of Frederick Fursman, artist and Director of the Ox-Bow Summer School of Painting. The Colonial Revival front was designed by Fursman's friend and colleague, Thomas Eddy Tallmadge. Detached studio at rear.

New York and elsewhere, a good builder, such as George Kurz in Douglas, was adept at running up a good looking Colonial Revival house or cottage.

This obsession with early American classicism took America by storm after World War I because it was viewed as both a way to supplant Europe and the mistakes of the War and as a way to conjure up a common "American Past" that could unify an increasingly diverse American population. Once again architecture was used to provide meaning for a society in search of an identity.[6] The key was a sort of spatial harmony that is totally out of character for us today. In Saugatuck this return to classicism found expression in a grand manner with the neo-classical summer mansion of D. C. Cook, a Chicago publisher—placed for all to see, high on a dune at Saugatuck's new harbor entrance.

Proponents of the Colonial Revival had something in common with the earlier "back-to-nature" generation who embraced arts and crafts architecture: a shared a creed of returning to the virtues of the simple and honest pre-industrial life and the use of historic, though not necessarily historically accurate, building types. At the same time they were strange bedfellows with the likes of avant garde Americans who favored the various forms of modernism (the "International Style," "Art Deco" and "Streamlining") in that they were each in their own way grappling with the runaway beast of industrialization.

SAUGATUCK'S NARROW BRUSH WITH MR. ROCKEFELLER | Could this Colonial Revival building craze have been simply an import of fashion? The architects who initiated the Colonial Revival momentum in the Saugatuck and Douglas area were people who lived here and were connected to and understood the traditional face of the villages. One of them, Thomas Eddy Tallmadge, a Chicago architect, was America's best known architectural historian and a Saugatuck summer resident from 1915 until his death in 1940. Tallmadge's keen understanding of American history and American architecture set high design standards for the village. This can be seen in his modest but graceful re-design of the Frederick Fursman house (the old Pine Grove School) on Mary Street, Saugatuck—a wonderful complement to Mr. Fursman who was, at the time, working on his "Saugatuck Anthology," a collection of portraits of ordinary Saugatuck people. The presence of Tallmadge in Saugatuck provided a direct link between the Colonial Revival burst in Saugatuck and its popularization throughout America: Tallmadge served as a design advisor to America's most important historic preservation project of the day: the "restoration" of Colonial Williamsburg at Williamsburg, Virginia, sponsored by John D. Rockefeller beginning in the late 1920s. Tallmadge was also the designer of the "Colonial Village" at Chicago's Century of Progress Exhibition in 1933, which, like Williamsburg, popularized Colonial Revival building. Who is to say that the colonial revival "remake" in Saugatuck and Douglas was imported? Indeed, as we have seen and certainly as Tallmadge himself saw, the dominant architectural theme in Saugatuck and Douglas was, from the beginning, plain and simple buildings, usually of wood, within classical form and scale and with classical elements of some sort—a vernacular interpretation of the "colonial" tradition. Home grown.

PRETTY AND PICTURESQUE BUILDINGS | Tallmadge's work not only carried on a local tradition of building with wood in a classical format, but it was picturesque. A walk down Butler Street, Saugatuck, in 1940, as today, tells part of this story. The Butler Hotel received new porch columns and an entrance (now removed) in the 1930s, and the Village Hall was refitted in a pleasing

| BUTLER HOTEL
1901 *(photo, ca. 1940)*
Butler Street
Saugatuck

The Butler, once the village flour mill, at its best: gleaming white with its colonnaded porches, manicured lawns, and graceful entrance. It was only a few steps away from the Big Pavilion ballroom and the Interurban train station. Miniature golf appears to be the sport of the moment, but someone has been bicycling. The structure has been radically altered.

HOW TO IDENTIFY
A Colonial Revival Building
1900-1940 (locally)

1
gable to front or side; many with gambrel ("Dutch Colonial") roof, with dormers

2
imposing entryway, usually centered and often with sidelights, pediment above, and with pilasters to the side.

3
occasional entryway porch ("portico") with columns; additional sun porch or screened porch to side.

4
windows double hung with six to twelve panes; restrained use of large " fan windows."

5
white painted clapboard siding (local); fixed shutters are common but not mandatory.

6
upscale versions have corner pilasters. (not shown)

7
locally, many applications of above are applied to older buildings with existing "classical" forms, such as Greek Revival and Italianate. (not shown)

RAISING THE ROOF

manner by Carl Hoerman in 1926; the Saugatuck Woman's Club Auditorium by Tallmadge was built in 1935, reminiscent of his own work in the design of Colonial Williamsburg. Facing the village square is the gleaming white and precisely proportioned Christian Science Church of 1924 by Howard Cheney and its equally classical neighbor, the new façade for Maplewood Hotel by George W. Maher for its owners Frank and Carrie Wicks. This scene of tranquility continues with the Ira Koning house at 507 Butler Street (1922) and a glance up to 246 Mary Street will reveal the already mentioned Colonial Revival restyling Tallmadge carried out on the little house of his fellow artist Frederick Fursman.

The story continues as one walks on. Fursman, like many artists who settled in the area, was attracted to the idea of the quaint village and the landscape which he captured in the American impressionist manner. Although he shied away from establishment exhibitions, Fursman frequently held exhibits in Saugatuck in the nearby Woman's Club facility and in a gallery on the second floor of the Village Hall. He was one of the Midwest's foremost Impressionist painters—the genius (with Tallmadge) of the Ox-Bow Summer School of Painting and teacher in Chicago and Milwaukee. Eventually his house on Mary Street was passed on to another artist, Elsa Ulbricht, and then to the artists Rachel and Emily Faucett.

| BELVEDERE FARMHOUSE
1912
3656 63rd Street | Saugatuck
Perkins, Fellows, & Hamilton | Chicago, *architects*

With its hipped roof, elaborate windows on the lower floor and raised terrace, the Belvedere is the only local example of an "Italian Renaissance Revival" house in the area. This house (west view) was built for John D. Williamson and family of Chicago. Williamson, the Vice-President of Peoples Gas and Electric Company, built the house on the site of the former A. J. Comstock house), and hoped to engage in a profitable farming enterprise. The house is of stucco over tile block with a roof of green slate. At the time of its construction one had a view of Lake Michigan from this verandah. Facing the agricultural depression of the post-war era, Williamson gave up his dream of profitable farming and sold the house in 1920. Throughout the 1920s and 1930s it was used as a summer home by a Chicago family and then, from the later 1950s it was a nursing home. It was subsequently restored in the 1980s and is now the "Belvedere Inn."

| KONING – WILEY HOUSE
ca. 1922
507 Butler Street
Saugatuck
J. and G. Daverman | Grand Rapids, *architects*

Ira Koning was a partner, with his brother James, in the hardware business nearby at 439 Butler. The arched dormer and arched porch pediment give this four-square 30-foot-by-30-foot house a sense of classical refinement, while the original large "picture window" gives it a modern twist. Comparing this house to that of his father of twenty years earlier (see chapter 2) illustrates how much house fashion had changed between 1900 and the 1920s.

A History of the Buildings and Architecture in the Saugatuck and Douglas Area

The house still stands to remind us of the influence that so many artists and architects had on the re-making of the villages in the 1920s and 1930s.

RE-CUTTING THE DRESS | Tallmadge's updating of Fursman's house was, of course, not unusual. A new house built here and there, one fine Colonial Revival example being the Frederick W. Job "summer house" at 212 Grand Street (now All Saints Church Retreat House), but, probably because of a lack of money for new buildings, an alteration craze of sorts took place in the 1920s and 1930s. A new porch here, new windows there, a garage stuck on here and a few new dormers there—all accomplished more often

SAUGATUCK WOMAN'S CLUB
1935
Hoffman & Butler Streets | Saugatuck
Thomas Eddy Tallmadge, *architect*

With Minnie Breuckman's house (attached) on the left. The "Woman's Club" is a principal "public" meeting and performing center—and the traditional power center for generations of Saugatuck area women. Mrs. Breuckman gave her house to the Club in 1934 and Tallmadge's auditorium was added in 1935. The Club was founded in 1904. The graceful entrance and the tall arched windows give the street side a dignified "colonial" air. The architect, Thomas Eddy Tallmadge, was a summer resident at the Ox-Bow Summer School of Painting and was one of the consultants to John D. Rockefeller's rebuilding of the colonial village of Williamsburg, Virginia, a project which undoubtedly influenced Tallmadge's design for this building.

Drawing by Margaret McDermott

CHRISTIAN SCIENCE SOCIETY
1925
12 Main Street
Saugatuck
Howard Cheney, *architect*

MAPLEWOOD HOTEL
1860 / 1923 façade
428 Butler Street
Saugatuck
George W. Maher, *architect (1923 façade)*

Having many lives and many owners, the building housed furniture and grocery stores and apartment dwellers before becoming a hotel in 1898. The architect of this new classical front was a Douglas lakeshore resident and one of the most sought after architects by Chicago's north shore rich and famous. He was part of a group of citizens in the 1920s and 1930s who sought to give Saugatuck a more fashionable look.

than not in a simple Colonial Revival manner—with the fortuitous outcome of leaving the village atmosphere intact and without disruption to the overall scale. One finds, for example, a new entry porch on the Pond-Winslow House at 446 Griffith Street, Saugatuck (1868), and a porch and enlarged dining room on Lillian and Scott Eddy's Beech-Hurst farmhouse, 121 Ferry Street, Douglas.

Beech-Hurst farmhouse has many fascinating chapters and the house itself tells us the story of the lives of several generations of people who have lived there. When Lillian retired from her career in government work in Washington D. C. and Grand Rapids and moved back to her Douglas farmhouse, she made a number of changes to the house to accommodate her needs while

BEECH-HURST FARMHOUSE
ca. 1872
121 Ferry Street | Saugatuck

An 1870s orchard farm in Douglas became the early 1900s home for a teacher and government administrator and her husband, a Civil War veteran, and succeeding generations of their family. A typical Greek Revival farmhouse of the 1870s, Beech-Hurst underwent changes in the 1920s when Colonial details were added, owing to the patriotic interest in Americana in the wake of World War I.

A History of the Buildings and Architecture in the Saugatuck and Douglas Area

BIOGRAPHY OF A HOUSE

BEECH–HURST
121 Ferry Street | Douglas | ca. 1872

DESCRIPTION | *An 1870s Douglas orchard farm, which in the early 1900s became the home of a writer and succeeding generations of her family*

STYLE | *Greek Revival Gable "L", ca. 1872 with Colonial Revival alterations in the 1920s*

FUNCTION | *Working farm; family home; summer cottage*

OWNERSHIP HISTORY | *Beech-Hurst has been home to four different families throughout its 127-year history:*

Family 1. Erwin and Abigail Hewett and daugher Netty of New York State. The Erwins purchased the 62-acre farm from Robert Helmer in the early 1870s and built the original house (ca. 1872)

Family 2. John & Elenora Finley and daughter Etta (1873-79)

Family 3. James & Caroline Williams and family (1879-1906)

Family 4. Lillian (Grimes) & Scott Eddy and sons Raymond and Benjamin (1906-present)

Fireplace of local stone.

6 *A built-in china cupboard was a part of the 1920s addition, though workmen smashed Mrs. Eddy's china during construction.*

Original clapboard siding of tulip wood

Shutters added as part of the 1920s addition.

1. *Original 2-Story House. Front door removed ca. 1880. No basement. Roof of wood shingles.*

2. *One-Story "L" Section added circa 1873, with basement.*

3. *A new (second) kitchen was added in the 1890s because the Williams sisters could not get along. It was enlarged after 1906 and the fireplace added. It is known as the "Civil War Room" to hold mementos of Scott Eddy and his brother who were Civil War veterans.*

4. *The library was originally the kitchen. Here Lillian composed poetry, wrote Betsy's Book, and translated Leaves from a Laurel Wreath from Latin to English.*

5. *When Lillian moved back to Michigan in 1922, she enlarged the dining room, kitchen, bathroom, and back porch.*

6. *A built-in china cupboard was a part of this addition. A new chandelier was also added at this time.*

7. *Porch enlarged with new columns, part of 1920s additions.*

8. *Breakfast Room added in the 1940s.*

9. *Water pump windmill.*

When Lillian Eddy was a girl she often accompanied her father to the Douglas area where they passed a farmhouse set amidst a grove of magnificent beech trees. Years later, in 1906, after holding several teaching positions and a principalship, and after marrying Ganges postmaster Scott Eddy, the family purchased the farmhouse on the Chase Road with its 300-year-old beech trees and named it "Beech-Hurst." Lillian became principal of Douglas Union School where she taught Latin and math. In 1918 she worked for the U. S. government in Washington D. C. and then beginning in 1922 held important Veterans Administration posts in Michigan. In 1933 she retired to Beech-Hurst, where she published Leaves from a Laurel Wreath, a translation from the Latin, and numerous poems which appeared in anthologies, newspapers and magazines. —*excerpted from a biography by Esther (Paton) Eddy.*

LILLIAN GRIMES EDDY
1853-1955

123

honoring the house's historic character—and added a room to honor the life and times of her father's Civil War experience. Also in Douglas a more ambitious Colonial Revival "re-do" was undertaken by a summer resident, Lillian Bendixon of Chicago, who carefully restored and embellished the large folk-Gothic Revival farmhouse at Union and Randolph Streets. A new classical face and graceful porch were added, which identify it today as the "Lion House." This house and its Coach House immediately to the west at 91 Mixer with its extraordinary classical detailing in wood, remain as two of the best examples of local Colonial Revival architecture of the 1920s.

Colonial Revival cottage variations were endless. In the case of some cottages the use of an American "colonial" prototype was just a short step away from the earlier Arts and Crafts tradition in cottage building and had the same sort of home-at-the-fireside appeal. On the lakeshore, the John O'Fallon Delaney's of St. Louis used local builder George Kurz to build them a pleasing barn-like version of a

LION HOUSE
ca. 1867
90 Union Street | Douglas

The original house was a folk Gothic farmhouse built around 1867 and at one point it had a large porch across the front. Its tall pitched roof with tall gables is typically folk Gothic, while its arched window hoods, porch with pediment and arches, and the corner pilasters are Colonial Revival additions, including the open porch (right), made in the 1920s by its new owner, Lillian Bendixon of Chicago, who used the house as a summer house until 1935. The Colonial Revival entrance with its sidelights under a broad frieze-band was recently added. The board-and-batten garage-studio, also a recent addition, is in a manner that respects the scale and size of the original house. Bendixen also remodeled the Coach House to the rear of the property at 91 Mixer Street to an equally fine Colonial Revival standard.

ANTHROP HOUSE
1860s – 1920s
91 Mixer Street | Douglas

This structure was built as the coach house for the Lion House next door at 90 Union Street—with a ballroom on the second floor. Perhaps the quintessential Colonial Revival structure in the area, it was given its present form early in the 1920s by Lillian Bendixen at the same time she remodeled the Lion House. The garage-studio is a recent addition that shows great respect for the scale and design of the original. It was, in the 1950s, the Artist Guild shop of the Walter A. and Miriam Dienhart—advertising that "good taste is not expensive."

DELANEY-THIELE COTTAGE

1902
254 Lakeshore Drive
Douglas
George D. Barnett, *architect*
George Kurz, *builder*

While the cottage design is in a reserved Colonial Revival manner, its original owner, Mrs. Delaney, was known on the lakeshore for her ostentatious display of wealth, including her annual arrival from St. Louis with an entourage of servants. Barnett, of St. Louis, was one of the best-known Midwest architects at the time, having designed the new Cathedral of St. Louis and the Illinois Athletic Club, Michigan Avenue, Chicago. The bridge is a brilliant way to allow the visitor to view the Lake while approaching the house from the rear.

RAISING THE ROOF

HELLMUTH COTTAGE
1914
204 Lakeshore Drive
Douglas
Harry and George Hellmuth, *architects*

Overlooking Lake Michigan along the Douglas shore, the cottage was the home for a family of famous architects—founders of the international architectural firm, HOK.

A History of the Buildings and Architecture in the Saugatuck and Douglas Area

"BIG POOL" &
BATH HOUSE
1927
North & Elizabeth Streets
Saugatuck

Swimming and beach going became increasingly popular in the 1920s and 1930s. Advertised as the largest swimming pool in Michigan, the elliptical "Big Pool" was the brainchild of a Saugatuck/Chicago resident by the name of Robert Marriott. Its location near the M-11 highway made it a favorite tourist attraction. The Spanish Mission style bathhouse was typical of its day. Recreational bathers needed changing rooms, partly because many of them used rented swim wear. When the Village of Saugatuck carried out a long awaited proposal for a road to what is now Oval Beach in 1936, the Big Pool's days were numbered. (Now filled in.)

BALUSTERS & URNS AT
MASON STREET LANDING
1927 *(photo, 1950s)*
Mason Street at Water Street | Saugatuck
Carl Hoerman, *architect*

Inventing a classical stairway. The reconstruction of this little lagoon boat landing, where Indians once beached their canoes, was undertaken by the Village at the behest of the Saugatuck Chamber of Commerce for the "beautification" of the Village and to provide better facilities for skiffs and other small pleasure boats. [The Commercial Record, March 28, 1924.] *Hoerman designed the cast concrete balusters and vases. The Hotel Saugatuck (formerly Leindecker's and now Coral Gables) is in the background.*

Colonial Revival cottage at 254 Lakeshore Drive, Douglas (1902), and Harry and George Hellmuth, internationally well-known architects, followed with a similar large and imposing cottage for themselves at 204 Lakeshore Drive, Douglas (1914).

Such activity extended throughout the 1920s and 1930s and included public amenities as well. Streets were paved, tennis and shuffle board courts were built, as was a soldiers' memorial and public demand for swimming facilities led to a gigantic swimming pool, the "Big Pool" in 1927 and the creation of "Oval Beach" in 1936. In 1924 a new public boat landing at the end of Mason Street was designed by Carl Hoerman, complete with a classical balustrade with hand-cast concrete balusters, and a new Chain Ferry landing was built about the same time with similar detailing. The Hotel Saugatuck itself erased its increasingly dated Arts and Crafts look and was re-sided and painted white. The Van Syckel store, 32 East Center Street, Douglas (1941), and the "Dutch Colonial" house at 620 Butler Street

VAN SYCKEL'S STORE
1941
Center Street | Douglas

This classy Colonial Revival with six bay windows and a tall pedimented hood over the door was the village grocery store. Note the gas pump. The VanSyckel family operated this store for many years, at first as a combination grocery and hardware business, then exclusively as a grocery. It later became the IGA store operated by Ed and Marge Burns. Now retail space and apartments, slightly altered condition. Destroyed by fire, 2006.

and the Heath-Edgcomb House, 336 Hoffman Street (ca. 1930), illustrate the popularity as well as the variations of the Colonial Revival style. The Heath-Edgcomb house was a popular Sears catalogue house, called the "Verona," which came complete with everything from "Colonial shutters" to "Kitchen DeLuxe Outfit," all for $4,347. To top off two decades of "colonialization," Frank and Carrie Wicks created "Wickwood" in 1940 at the corner of Butler and Mary streets. Saugatuckians would henceforth look at their village as "Saugatuck, The Beautiful," and see themselves living in a "charming little village."[7]

THE GOLDEN AGE OF LOCAL ARCHITECGTURE AND BUILDING? | As we have seen, Saugatuck and Douglas were economically poor in the 1920s and 1930s but they were not culturally depressed. In fact, it might be said that the Saugatuck-Douglas image of today— what can be called its "traditional face" of picturesque villages was an invention of the 1920s and 1930s and a great deal of its impetus came from nationally known artists and architects who called these quaint hamlets "home." The fact that much of the building of the era was "re-building" meant a continuity in materials and style, and thus the humane "village scale" was allowed to remain intact. Cora Bliss Taylor's little studio-home was, like the artist herself, part theater *(Chapter 4)*. Indeed, the two villages, particularly Saugatuck, had become, in a sense, theater. But it was good theater all round. By 1940 the Milwaukee Journal could report to its readers that even the grocery clerks in Saugatuck wore smocks and berets,[8] "just to help along the atmosphere of art," and by the 1950s a visitor from New York City would send a message home announcing "having such a nice week in this sleepy little old town with a wonderful beach . . . ."[9]

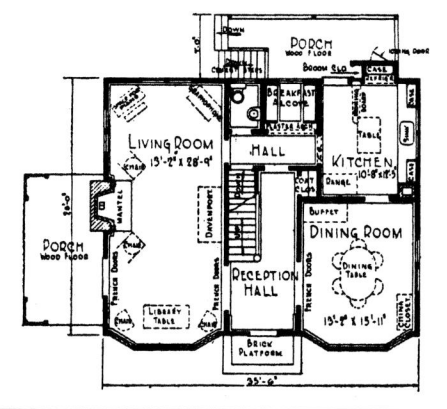

HEATH-EDGCOMB HOUSE & PLAN
1929
336 Hoffman Street
Saugatuck
Sears, Roebuck, and Company | Chicago, *design*

This Sears catalogue house, the "Verona," was among the top of the line in the 1926 catalogue. This version of the model varied slightly. It was sent to Saugatuck by railroad by way of New Richmond. Its cost was $4,347, about 15 times the price of a 1926 Ford Model T automobile. Most of the 80 houses in the 1926 catalogue were of some variation of the Colonial Revival style. The first owners of the house were Doc A. and May Francis Heath. Mr. Heath was fond of saying "Real Estate is sure," and Mrs. Heath is Saugatuck's best known historian.

WICKWOOD INN
1920s / 1940
510 Butler Street
Saugatuck

Built on what was once the site of the second residence of the founder of Saugatuck, William Butler, the "Wickwood" home and apartment house of Frank and Carrie Wicks, was one of the more fashionable new structures of the village when it was constructed in the 1940s. The Wicks' (right) were volunteers in nearly every community activity, and their house, along with the nearby Koning houses across the street at 447 and 507 Butler, suggest that as the smoke and noise of the old riverfront industries disappeared, it was popular once again to live on what was becoming a charming Butler Street.

POND–WINSLOW HOUSE
1868
446 Griffith Street
Saugatuck

Typical of many area houses, this Italianate house had numerous additions and alterations over the years but it retains its basic footprint and scale. The first owner was J. M. Pond, a Civil War veteran and a carpenter. At one time the house had a view of the river. Porch added in ca. 1935.

THE ARCHITECTS

The Saugatuck and Douglas area has been favored with the presence of a sizable number of architects, some of them among America's best known; many of them were summer residents but some settled here year-round. Here are a few of the most prominent known architects of the 1920s and 1930s and later who lived here and designed buildings in the Saugatuck and Douglas area.

"FISH TOWN, SAUGATUCK"
Drawing by Carl Hoerman

THOMAS EDDY TALLMADGE | 1876-1940
We have already met Thomas Eddy Tallmadge as the Saugatuck summer resident who popularized the Colonial Revival style of architecture not just in the Saugatuck area, but in America at large. As a young architect and an amateur painter he came to Saugatuck in 1915, staying at the Riverside Inn (later Ox-Bow Inn). From this time on he made Saugatuck his summer home, becoming one of the three principal organizers (and benefactors) of the Ox-Bow Summer School of Painting. At the time of his death in 1940 in a railway accident, he was considered one of America's greatest teachers and historians of architecture. He wrote a number of books on architectural history, including the popular *The Story of Architecture in America* (1927) and *The History of Chicago Architecture* (published posthumously, 1942)

Tallmadge received much of his training from the famous Chicago architect Daniel Burnham and is known for his successful designs in various "styles," as well as being an expert on early steel skyscraper construction. His Chicago architectural firm of Tallmadge and Watson is best known for its Prairie Style work, a fine local example being the Marigold Lodge (Lake Macatawa in Holland) that was built as a summer home for a Chicago industrialist. Tallmadge himself became a master architect of gothic revival churches. His masterpiece is the First Methodist Church of Evanston, Illinois. He was a teacher at the Armor Institute (now Illinois Institute of Technology) and lecturer at the Art Institute of Chicago. He designed the "Colonial Village" for "A Century of Progress Exhibition" in Chicago in 1933, and was one of the architectural advisors for the restoration of Colonial Williamsburg, Virginia. In Saugatuck he remodeled the façade of the old Pine Grove schoolhouse in 1927 and designed the original "Kemah" cottage on Allegan Street, as well as the Auditorium for the Saugatuck Woman's Club and a pleasant Prairie Style cottage for himself on the Ox-Bow grounds.

CARL HOERMAN | 1885-1955 | The most active local architect and painter of his time, Carl Hoerman came to the United States from Bavaria, Germany in 1904 to study architecture in Chicago and first came to Saugatuck with his wife Christiana, also a painter, in 1910. They stayed at Bandle's Farm. He practiced architecture in Chicago until 1919 when he moved to Saugatuck, where to all appearances he made enough of a living on architecture to support his painting. Indeed, he is best known as a landscape painter, particularly of the Saugatuck area and the American West. The Hoermans occupied a farmhouse on Old Allegan Road as well as a house and studio, in a rather eccentric Arts&Crafts design, called the "Chalet Studio" at 621 Pleasant Street, Saugatuck (ca 1926), from which for more than 30 years Hoerman and Christiana operated a shop. The living space was on the street level and the studio and gallery occupied the lower level overlooking the harbor. Hoerman was also an accomplished photographer and some of his glass negatives were used as windowpanes in the house.[8] He worked from a second studio in a log cabin, which is still standing off Holland Street along the east bank of the Kalamazoo River. There, it is told, he displayed two notices: "Visitors Unwelcome," and "Work is One's Best Companion."

Along with a number of large lakeshore cottages designed in an idiosyncratic Arts&Crafts style, his architectural projects included "remodelings,"—creating new spaces and façades that fit into the local historical context while meeting modern needs. In this sense, Hoerman was Saugatuck's master "vernacular" architect. His buildings spoke softly, treating Saugatuck's villagescape, history, and people with respect. extraordinary is the Parish Hall addition in a Carpenter Gothic manner for All Saint's Church, Hoffman and Grand Streets, Saugatuck (1946) which replicates the scale and materials in a flawless vernacular manner. Hoerman also designed the new front and addition to Saugatuck Congregational Church and the reconstruction of "Kemah," which is acclaimed as one of Michigan's finest houses.[9] He designed the makeover of the Saugatuck Village Hall and created the River Guild shop and gallery—and his interest in the vernacular led to his drawing of a series of historic illustrations for May Francis Heath's book, *Memories of Saugatuck*. His decorative cast concrete vases and railings still exist in various places. One of his later works was the Children's Chapel of Lakeshore Chapel, Campbell Road, Douglas (1948).

GEORGE W. MAHER | 1864-1926 | George W. Maher is recognized as one of America's premier Prairie Style architects and furniture designers, working largely for well-heeled Chicagoans who moved into northshore suburbs such as Kenilworth and Evanston in the first decades of the twentieth century.

Maher began his summer excursions to Saugatuck with his family—his wife, Elizabeth, was the daughter of the Chicago painter, Alden Brooks—in the 1890s. Here in this "back-to-nature" climate that was influencing so many of his contemporaries, Maher built several local versions of Prairie

Style cottages, including one for himself and one for his sister (p. 74) and established a fruit farm called "Hilaire." Living in Michigan underscored his life-long philosophy that buildings should be designed to fit the habits of the client and the nature of the site. He once wrote:

> Large, old fashioned fireplaces, ease of stairs, nooks with settees; heavy oak beams leave the impression of solidity; low ceilings convey the idea of privacy; all contribute to make life a matter of ease. This style of building suits the taste of the better class of American people . . . .[10]

After World War I, when the Prairie Style was on the wane, like many of his contemporaries, he turned to revivalist architecture. During this period he designed the new (present) façade for the Maplewood Hotel in Saugatuck for the Wicks family. Locally this was a significant project in that it was the earliest major Colonial Revival influence in the center of the village. As an architect, Maher was interested in the welfare of Saugatuck and other small towns and he was one of the first to urge Saugatuck to adopt planning and zoning policies.

GEORGE HELLMUTH | 1852-1931 | George and Harriet Hellmuth began their summer treks from St. Louis, Missouri to the Douglas lakeshore in about 1909. The brothers George and Harry Hellmuth were architects for a large number of St. Louis houses, many in some sort of classical or Colonial Revival manner, for wealthy St. Louis families who wanted houses in various exclusive districts of the city. They followed their well-heeled clients, Mr. and Mrs. John O'Fallon Delaney, to Douglas where the Delaney's had already built a cottage. George and his business partner and brother Henry designed a large ten-bedroom cottage for themselves at 204 Lakeshore Drive, Douglas, and another at 408 Lakeshore Drive (the Lodge-Stutzman cottage). The builder for both of these cottages was George Kurz, who provided a beautiful end product but reputedly refused to read the plans. George Hellmuth recalls that his father had a passion for fishing and found a fisherman's paradise at the so-called "hobo" camp at the east end of Center Street in Douglas, presided over by a somewhat derelict fellow named "Blackie" who guided architect Hellmuth and his son, George Jr., through the backwaters of the Kalamazoo River and Lake Michigan. It was, for the younger George, who became one of America's best known architects in his own right as a partner in the prominent St. Louis/New York architecture firm of Hellmuth, Obata and Kassabaum, a lesson in snapping turtles, Lake Michigan Whitefish, and how to row a boat.

The Hellmuth, Marie Garesché (217 Lakeshore Drive) and Delaney cottages were the first of the uncommonly large cottages. When asked about the family cottage, George Hellmuth, at age 92, called it a "big barn, and if I were to do it over it would be smaller." But the historical context was different then. The arrival of the St. Louisians must have come as something of a shock to the Chicago-Oak Park "back-to-nature" crowd who were comfortably settled into their cozy Arts & Crafts cottages. Here came their new neighbors with their big cars, big cottages, domestic servants—and a different religion, for the Hellmuths and many of the St. Louis cottagers were Catholic.

FLORENCE ("DANNIE") ELY HUNN | 1887-1983 | Florence Hunn first came to Pier Cove in 1913. She had spent some of her school years in Germany, France, and Greece. She was a graduate of University of Chicago and attended the School of the Art Institute of Chicago. She desired to become an architect but at this time women were not admitted to architecture schools, so instead went into interior design, eventually owning one of Chicago's most prestigious interior design firms, specializing in design for wealthy north-shore Chicago apartment dwellers and other clients all over the United States. Her design forte was in the American Colonial and English 18th century styles, but she was one of the first designers in Chicago to favor modernism—even opening her own modern design shop in New York City. She was one of the founders of the American Institute of Interior Designers. She lived, with her companion Mabel ("Jims") Warren at her Pier Cove cottage during summers until she made it her permanent home in 1956. She designed a number of cottages locally, including the Kamman cottage on Lakeshore Drive, one for the Chicago industrialist A. Finkl (now the Knollenberg-Jones Cottage) on Campbell Road and one for the South Bend industrialist, Peterson Merrill (the Voegler Cottage, recently relocated) in 1937 on Lakeshore Drive. She undertook the important restoration (with additions) of the Martel House on Grand Street for a Chicago industrialist, and carried on a variety of local interior design works, including murals for the Tara Restaurant in Douglas. In 1960 she designed highly customized modern house for Edward and Mary Curtis at 2278 Lakeshore Drive. Her own cottage, now partially destroyed and partially relocated, in a rambling English Arts & Crafts cottage manner, near Pier Cove, is built around a small 1858 house made of tulip wood clapboard secured with wooden pegs (or hand-made nails). Her additions replicate the old, even to the point of copying the hand-made nails. She built a separate studio nearby. She wrote for the *Chicago Sunday Tribune*:

> That charming, lived-in quality which some homes possess and some do not, comes not from the size of the house, nor from the money spent upon the furnishing of it, but rather from the gracious living of those who dwell within it.[13] The experienced and intelligent decorator can create for these a fitting background whether the amount to spend on furnishings is much or little.[11]

In 1927 she was the architect for one of the area's most unusual cottages, a very tall multi-story cottage high on the ridge overlooking the Kalamazoo River and Lake Michigan. Named "Tonawanda," it was constructed in a rather modernist interpretation of an Arts and Crafts cottage of over-sized glazed brick and casement windows.

FLORENCE HUNN'S ADVERTISING BROCHURE

Hunn was one of Chicago's foremost interior designers and also had a retail design shop in New York City—but most of her architectural work was done in the Pier Cove/Saugatuck area where she lived.

SAUGATUCK OVAL BEACH ENTRANCE
1958
Lake Michigan at Oval Beach Road
Saugatuck

The coming of the automobile culture in the 1950s led to a rearrangement of village life and work. Here we see how a new "beach culture" accompanied a new automobile culture. Although the village of Saugatuck acquired some beachfront property as early as 1902, it wasn't until 1936 that the road (now Perryman Street) to the Presbyterian Camps was extended to Lake Michigan and the Village of Saugatuck created "The Oval" as it was referred to. Parking was 25 cents.

CHAPTER SIX

Buildings for the Automobile and Television Age, 1940-1970

"Why on earth do you need to study what's changing this country?
I can tell you what's happening in just four letters: A-U-T-O"
—a Muncie, Indiana Resident
1920s1

"WE'D RATHER DO WITHOUT CLOTHES THAN GIVE UP THE CAR."[2] | There has been endless debate in America about the effect of the automobile on American society. Sociologists, historians, urban planners and architects, government officials, clergymen and so on, many with an ax to grind, have looked at the good and the bad from seemingly every possible viewpoint. The only certain conclusion, however, is that the automobile has democratized American culture, providing more people with more choices—from fast food to suburbs to vacations—and totally changed how Americans use physical space.

Between 1920 and 1929 automobile ownership in the United States increased from 8.5 million to 23 million. The price of a car in 1908 was $1,000; by 1929 it had dropped to $295. America became a nation of tourists. By 1929 almost a third of the American population took vacations by automobile.[3]

THE ARCHITECTURE OF THE ROADSIDE | The automobile created several new and numerous roadside building types. Not all were intrusions of the natural landscape; the pleasant WPA-type "roadside table" picnic pavilion set amidst the pines along the Blue Star Highway is a local case in point. But overall in the tug of war between landscape and automobile, if the automobile has not already won, it was certainly in the lead.

No new building type of the automobile age is as ubiquitous as the "filling station." The new M-11 (later U. S. 31 and, still later, a portion was designated the "Blue Star Memorial Highway") was the major access to West Michigan's growing kingdom of resorts, drawing urbanites farther and farther northward along Michigan's lake coast. Many gas stations started out as offshoots of hardware stores and grocery stores, such as that connected to the McVea family grocery on Lakeshore Drive, Douglas, and the VanSyckel Grocery at Center and Washington Streets, Douglas (chapter 5) and then mutated to simple free standing structures, as the one seen for years at Center and Blue Star Highway, Douglas, known as Lundberg's "Dew-Drop Inn." By the early 1930s this simple station type had added a repair garage, and soon thereafter restrooms. Before long they were selling soft drinks, food and cigarettes. The most modern versions, the 1938 Millar brothers' Standard Oil station at the foot of the new Blue Star Bridge and the Rassmussen station at the other end of the highway, were built to a standardized company design, Some, like Freeman and Newnham's Garage at 302 Culver Street, Saugatuck, became an automobile dealership as well. Even though the gas station, like the automobile, grew up as a male preserve, the "Saugatuck Service Station" on Holland Street had a stylish drive-through pergola that announced its family and tourist friendliness. By the 1940s function had determined the gas station form, as witnessed in Gus Reiser's service station on the Blue Star Highway. Reiser's station design included eight white cement finial ornaments on pedestals, but was not unusual in an era when many gas stations were built in a variety of fantasy styles to appeal to travelers looking for something new.[4] Today the repair function of the garage has all but disappeared, replaced perhaps because of better made cars, stand-alone mechanics' shops and specialty muffler outlets. Thus, the fueling station has come full circle—once again a combination

ROADSIDE TABLE
ca. 1936
Blue Star Highway
Saugatuck
Origins unknown

FILL`ER UP?
A STORY OF GAS STATIONS

By the 1940s the gas station as a building type had become a standard feature of the highway and village landscape—first growing out of the Mom and Pop "general store" then evolving into highly specialized "service stations" presided over by uniformed clerks ready to fill the tank, check the tires, wash the windows and even to provide skilled repair and refreshment service—most of which could take place while one remained in the car. "Filling Up" had become a ceremony of sorts presided over by a staff-in-waiting. In so doing, the architecture of the gas station became increasingly standardized—and eventually the oil corporations incorporated all the station functions into a standardized design and offered it as a franchise. Today we have come full circle. The gas-station has become a brightly lit self-serve grocery store-coffee shop with a huge automobile landing field that provides self-service purchase of gasoline.

MCVEA'S STORE & GAS STATION
Photo ca. 1950
279 Lakeshore Drive
Douglas

Early filling stations were often appended to grocery stores, and in this case a grocery store and post office. Bill and Gertrude McVea established the store in the 1920s and it played a meaningful role in the summer life of many lakeshore cottagers from then until the 1960s. It has now been incorporated into a residence. One local cottage resident, Dorothy Garesché Holland, wrote:

In the 1920s, Bill McVea opened a grocery store. And it was a marvelous store, [having] any staple anyone wanted or asked for, fresh vegetables and fruit from the nearby farms or even closer. One day my mother wanted some fresh corn and Bill turned to one of his helpers and said, 'Go out and pick a dozen ears for Mrs. Garesché.' For many years there was a wonderful butcher at the McVea store, old Charlie, a Czech who had been a Chicago butcher until he retired and bought a little place down on the shore. In one corner of the store were newspapers, Chicago, Detroit and St. Louis, these could be reserved, marked with the person's name and put in a large pile. There was also a branch post office, and the morning mail distributed about nine-thirty was the focal point of the day. Everyone gathered there, everyone knew who had recently arrived, bridge dates were made, teenage gatherings arranged and it was almost as good as a club.[11]

MILLAR BROTHERS STANDARD STATION
1938
U. S. 31 at the Blue Star Bridge

A coke machine, restrooms, night-time lighting—and Mr. Orville Millar in his uniform. It was of ultra-clean, cream colored glazed brick and featured a large display window. Lubrication took place on an outdoor hoist and one of the as pumps was of the new "computing" type. Design by the Standard Oil Company. The station closed in 1942 when the Douglas brothers, Orville and Stephen, went off to serve in World War II. Building stands in altered form.

REISER'S SERVICE STATION
1939-40
U.S. 31 (Blue Star Highway)
Saugatuck
Mr. Scharf, Hamilton, *contractor*

The concrete finials and red tile roof trim were local inventions, but are typical of many 1930s gas stations of the time which sought roadside appeal. Gus and Pauline Reisser had come to Saugatuck to work at the Big Pavilion and later founded the nearby West Winds Camp Grounds. Photograph ca. 1946.

A History of the Buildings and Architecture in the Saugatuck and Douglas Area

(from upper left to lower right)

FREEMAN & NEWNHAM STATION & GARAGE
Later 1920s
302 Culver Street | Saugatuck

The pump on the left is a "visual gravity" Tokin pump. The building now houses a restaurant.

ED FORCE'S SNUG HARBOR STATION
ca. 1928

Constructed on site of old Interurban station. Ed Force lived across the street and it appears that he was in the tourist souvenir business as well.

AUBURN STATION & GARAGE
ca. 1930
Main & Wall Streets | Douglas

Became Lundberg's Douglas Garage. Formerly the Douglas Livery Barn for village carriages and horses. The view is from Main Street looking east. Subjects in the photographs are unknown.

SAUGATUCK SERVICE STATION
1927
Holland & Francis Streets | Saugatuck

Mr. McGraff's Saugatuck Service Station stood on the northwest corner of Holland and Francis Streets—then U.S. 31. The rocks bordering the drive remain as in photo.

WRIGHT'S GAS STATION
ca. 1945
Lake Street | Saugatuck

LUNDBERG'S STATION
ca. 1936
Center Street at U.S. 31 (Blue Star Highway)
Douglas

Carl Lundberg's new station, the "Dew Drop Inn."

RAY RASMUSSEN'S LIGHTHOUSE SERVICE STATION
ca. 1940
Washington Street at U. S. 31 (Blue Star Highway)
Saugatuck Township

Art Moderne comes to Saugatuck. Neon signs (and clock), a sandwich shop, and "clean restrooms." Living quarters for the Rasmussen family on upper floor. The sandwich shop was converted into Elwin Johnson's truck repair shop in 1945.

gasoline station and "mini-mart" or "quick stop" grocery store, just as it began in the 1920s but of much greater size—and occasionally with inviting landscaping.

THE ROARING 50S | The combination of the automobile with a post-World War II youth culture had a big impact on nighttime Saugatuck. A "liberated" generation became more and more spatially separated from their parents generation; a new mix of dancing, drinking and the automobile (and a new openness in sexual expression) meant, locally, a retreat away from the formal dance floor of the Big Pavilion to the night spots such as the Tara, the Crow Bar in the Coral Gables Hotel and the Dock Bar in the lower level of the Big Pavilion. A youth invasion meant not only fast cars—and in the case of one hotel, bus loads of party-makers from Chicago—but concerns that the streets were being taken over by the 'roughest class of people ever to resort at Saugatuck.' Sleeping in the car or piling into boarding houses, drag racing, beach parties and drinking on the streets—all changed the summer-time character of Saugatuck.[5]

THE DECLINE OF THE RESORT ERA? | By 1960 the era of the old and venerable Saugatuck resort businesses had mostly come to a close, although some of the buildings continued to house other ventures. The Maplewood Hotel closed its doors to tourists in 1954 when it became an apartment building and about the same time the Butler Hotel saw a decline in demand for rooms. Hotel Saugatuck faced a dwindling demand for hotel rooms and, when it became the "Coral Gables" bar and restaurant in 1959, it gradually ceased operation as a hotel. Most of the 36 "resorts" listed by the local Chamber of Commerce in 1952 were actually rooms and small cabins for rent.[6] The relatively short-lived Harding Hotel[7] at 338 Park Street, Saugatuck (1945) went by way of fire in 1954 as did the aged Mount Baldhead Hotel (formerly the Tourist Home) in 1959; the Casablanca succumbed in 1969. Some hotels and boarding houses, such as the Elms Hotel on Butler Street, hung on for a few years longer, but when the Butler Hotel's top floors were removed in 1973 and the business shifted its focus to

THE OLD CROW BAR
ca. 1945
Coral Gables, Water Street
Saugatuck

Part of the Hotel Saugatuck (Leindecker Hotel and now Coral Gables), the Crow Bar was, along with the Dock Bar in the nearby Big Pavilion and the Tara supper club in Douglas, one of the popular "night clubs" of 1940s and 1950s.

Artwork by Emily Parks.

food and drink only, it seemed as though Saugatuck's days as a major hotel venue had become history.

TOO MANY CHOICES | Although fire was the immediate reason for the disappearance of many of these buildings (including the Big Pavilion on May 6, 1960), in reality the death of the resort business—like the declining interest in ballroom dancing—had its beginnings with new American social and cultural habits following World War II. Night clubs had replaced ballrooms and looking out at the world from inside the Big Pavilion in its last days one could see that part of this cultural revolution was that millions of Americans were now sitting in their private boats. Indeed, yacht clubs and marinas had added a new "boating" face to the harbor. Another part of the story is that some people simply stayed at home because of the seductiveness of television as a private and inexpensive

THE DOCK BAR
ca. 1950
Big Pavilion, Culver & Water Streets
Saugatuck

Under the dance floor. Saugatuck's best known drinking place—and known for its live music.

BIG PAVILION IN FLAMES
May 6, 1960
Kalamazoo Riverfront
Saugatuck

The End of an Era: By the 1950s the ballroom was only occasionally used for dancing and the only profits were from the Dock Bar and restaurant. Maintenance of the structure had been neglected, but the owners had contracted to have the entire structure painted as soon as weather permitted that year. The fire began shortly before noon and within minutes the entire structure was in flames. The heat became so intense that windows in a nearby restaurant exploded and the paint peeled on a local fire truck. At one point 24 streams of water were poured on the building from the Saugatuck and 10 nearby fire departments. The roof collapsed in less than an hour. Many feared that the entire village would catch fire, but luckily the wind shifted from its usual westerly to a southeasterly direction. Various theories exist as to how the fire originated.

entertainment. But television also broadened Americans' travel expectations as did bigger, better, and cheaper cars along with better highways and increased real wages in the era of postwar prosperity. Americans could drive to farther and more exotic places. There was another "back-to-nature" movement in the making, but this time it was millions of Americans navigating popular highways, such as Route 66 westward and later the Interstate highway system, to see a grander America than old-fashioned Lake Michigan harbor towns. The "vacation" had changed from an extended stay at a particular destination to a "trip" whereby a family would travel from place to place, staying in a different town each night.

A PART OF THE VILLAGE'S SOUL DISAPPEARS | At the same time one of Saugatuck's most picturesque settings, an array of commercial fishing settlements that peppered the waterfront, disappeared without much registered lament. These markings of a century of comings and goings of fishing tugs and fishermen had been scrutinized by several generations of tourists and residents—not the least being a host of painters and photographers looking to document the heroes of the lake and their places of abode and work. After about 1960, the old docks, fish shanties and net-drying yards gave way to pleasure boat and sport fishing docks and harbor-side inns and condominiums. The architecture of a way of life was gone.

SLEEPING NEXT TO THE CAR | These changes in the spatial and architectural appearance of the village did not mean that tourists completely abandoned West Michigan, but when families now came to stay overnight they wanted to be modern: they wanted "motels." The motel was a phenomenon of automobile culture, invented for easy access by motorists— thus, the name motel. Motels were able to offer some things Americans wanted in the 1950s and 1960s: privacy, en-suite facilities and, in place of "nature" luxuries such as swimming pools, "Free TV" and "Phone in Room" and eventually "air-conditioning."

Nevertheless, the motel crept in quietly, first as an ordinary economy "cabin" for a few travelers in the 1920s—as we have seen at Bird Center (chapter 4)—or as a source of small change for the farmer living adjacent to the roadway. Any resort town had them all, documented by the countless picture post-cards with the automobiles lined up out front which make dating these structures easy. Some were primitive little boxes, other larger "over-night cabins" and then those with "modern kitchenette apartments"—all arranged so that the automobile was just a step away. Each unit at the now forlorn "Pine Crest Tourist Inn" had an attached garage. As different as these early motels were, each unit had its pair of outdoor chairs facing road and public activity—a testimony to the still public centeredness of life in mid-century America.

THE LAST OF THE COMMERCIAL FISHING SHANTIES & DOCKS
Photograph 2005
720 Water Street
Saugatuck

The Lou Gotham and George Sewers' docks, now owned by Demi Demerest, the last of the commercial fishermen. This architecture of commercial fishing—made up of docks, net-drying yards, fish shanties and ice houses—began to disappear in the later 1950s as the local commercial fishing trade declined. In its place came pleasure boat marinas and sport fishing docks, as well as new shops, condominiums and waterside hostelries.

A History of the Buildings and Architecture in the Saugatuck and Douglas Area

† DUNES VIEW CABINS

ca. 1940
U.S. 31 (Blue Star Highway)
East Saugatuck

"Located 1 1/2 miles north of Saugatuck. Scenic setting. Fully modern overnight and housekeeping cabins. Private showers. Shuffleboard, outdoor fireplace and picnic table. Mr. And Mrs. Jousma, Props."

† SAUGATAUCK LODGES – TIN CRICKET

ca. 1940
3291 Blue Star Highway
Saugatuck

Small in scale, with neither concrete parking lot nor mile-high advertising sign, the early "cabin-in the-woods" motel type was less intrusive on the natural landscape than motels of today. Removed from site, 2002

† PLAZA TOURIST COURT – PINES MOTEL

(above) photo ca. 1950 | *(below)* reconstruction 2004
56 Blue Star Highway
Douglas
Charles Kenneth Carlson, *architect*

One of the earliest area "motels," it was first known as the Plaza Tourist Court. Guest registration complex recently remodeled to reflect local Arts & Crafts tradition.

139

RAISING THE ROOF

† ARROWHEAD RESORT MOTEL
ca. 1940 *(photo, ca. 1948)*
840 Lake Street | Saugatuck

Owner, Robert J. Rogers. Post–World War II structure of modern design and materials. Rates in 1949 were $40 per week for a unit for two, which included kitchenette. Recently altered.

† AMITY MOTEL – DUNES RESORT
1965
U.S. 31 (Blue Star Highway) | Douglas

The Amity was one of the area's first double-decker motels of the 1960s, offering free TV and air conditioning. It was refashioned and expanded in 1982 to become the "Douglas Dunes Resort," which became one of the Midwest's most popular gay and lesbian vacation destinations. Exists with extensive additions. See chapter 7.

† PINE CREST TOURIST INN
1938
U.S. 31 (Blue Star Highway) | Saugatuck

This motel was considered up-market for its time when it opened in the fall of 1938 and was proclaimed "a new innovation" in overnight cabins. Each unit has a separate garage. Board and batten siding contributes to an appealing 1930s Colonial Revival style. The original owners were Miss Mildred Dvorak of Spring Lake and her mother. In need of restoration.

† MIRO MOTEL POOLSIDE – CABANA
ca. 1962
U.S. 31 (Blue Star Highway) | Douglas

"Joseph P. Megis, owner. Air-conditioned rooms, equipped with radio and wall-to-wall carpeting; tile shower tub combination bathroom. Air-conditioned restaurant. Recreation and conference room"

140

Another reason for the decline of the resort industry was that, with the decline of the Big Pavilion and finally its destruction, there was no longer any grand spectacle to pull in the tourists, many of whom were more difficult to impress as television replaced their naïveté with notions of worldliness. Consequently, when motels came in the 1950s there were but a few large ones to replace the disappearing traditional resorts. One of the largest motels was the Amity Motel: 22 units and a swimming pool at 333 Blue Star Highway in Douglas (1965). It is interesting that the largest motel of the age, the Ship 'n Shore, 528 Water Street, Saugatuck, reflected the rise of boat ownership as much as that of the automobile: it dubbed itself a "boatel" when it first opened in 1960 and had "Lanai units" for those who slept on their boats (appealing to returning veterans who had spent time in Hawaii during the war). Boaters, it was clear, were good for business. From an architectural standpoint the Ship 'n Shore is a textbook example from the 1960s: with its long, low gable roof, popular at the time as a "California ranch" type, its use of concrete block and with a central lobby open to the waterside, it is the luxury motel version of the modern ranch house being constructed at the time all over America.

Equally interesting, the riverside Holiday Hill–Marina resort, Park Street, Saugatuck (1964) served a boat-and-automobile clientele, in this case with a structure of modular construction inspired by the International Style which included "sky villas" reached by "our quaint little cable car." Like the Ship 'n Shore just across the river, the Holiday Hill complex was reaching for a new generation of tourists who sought high-class accommodation, with boat and automobile facilities to boot.

The life of the Amity Motel tells another part of the story. Even speedier transportation and better highways by the 1970s turned Saugatuck into an ideal getaway from the big cities of Detroit and Chicago. In 1982 the Amity Motel became the "Douglas Dunes Resort," one of the Midwest's most popular weekend resorts oriented to gay and lesbian clientele. Its club portion became the area's busiest dance spot since the close of the Big Pavilion. The "Dunes Resort" illustrates an important part of the area history, that of a growing gay and lesbian population of tourists, second-home owners, and full time residents. How far back this culture existed in Saugatuck's history is unclear (some undocumented accounts date a gay presence as far back as the turn of the 20th century). Certainly by

SHIP 'N SHORE MOTEL–BOATEL
ca. 1960
528 Water Street
Saugatuck

Built by Walter and Betty Coburn following the destruction, by fire, of the Tourist Home Hotel (chapter 4), which had been on the site since 1901. Of its forty rooms, thirty-eight had views of the Kalamazoo River and were decorated with blond furniture with tones of aqua and carpets the color of the sea. The street side had large nautical paintings featuring mermaids and sea plants by local artist Fred Stearns. Its first swimming pool was added in 1982. The building included a number of separate "lanai" (porches) for guests.

TIMBERLINE MOTEL
1953
U.S. 31 (Blue Star Highway)
Saugatuck

Concrete block construction, with additions in 1978, 1982 and 1986; it now has 29 units on spacious wooded grounds.

**BLUE TEMPO BAR &
MOTEL**
1960-76
Culver Street | Saugatuck

Advertising itself as "Tops in Music," the Blue Tempo was a popular gay and straight venue in the 1960s-being, perhaps, the first "gay bar" in West Michigan. Having its beginnings as an old ice house, a number of cabins overlooking Kalamazoo Lake were added to the rear; this "hotel" was first known as the "Ed-Mar" (after its owners Ed and Marie Demeter) and then became the "Blue Tempo" when a new owner, Donald "Toad" Davis, took over in 1960. It is remembered as cramped, noisy and crowded—and at times even wet, when the lake overflowed into the bar room and dance floor. At the time this photo was taken, the front portion of the building housed the "Cozy Kitchen." Destroyed by fire July 1976

TASTEE FREEZE – M&M'S
1957
Blue Star Highway | Douglas
Tastee Freeze Corporation, Chicago, *design*

Probably the area's first fast-food franchise. Drive-up roadside food shops of the 1950s forever changed the eating habits of millions of Americans. This was one of the first "Tastee-Freeze" franchises in Michigan, established locally by the Smith family. The Chicago-based company offered "minimum capital" franchises in 1956 for $3,500 (about the cost of a new car). It was subsequently operated as "Tastee-Treet" and is currently called "M&M's." Addition of indoor café in 2000.

the pre-Stonewall 1960s a gay subculture was well established, and a number of local hotels and bars were known to cater to gay clientele, including a Butler Street bar called the Log Cabin, and the most famous and notorious, the "Blue Tempo" on Culver Street, Saugatuck (destroyed by fire). The Blue Tempo was by all accounts West Michigan's first "gay bar." As one of its many former Grand Rapids patrons reported, "Driving to Saugatuck was like driving to freedom, but we could never tell anyone where we were going."

THE RISE AND FALL OF THE "MAC BURGER'S" | The new building most associated with the automobile age is the ubiquitous fast food franchise restaurant. As a building type, it started out small scale—to serve the day-tripper and weekend folks. The village became filled with little restaurants with wild and exciting menus to hook the tourists, such as "Chicken-As-You-Like-it" shop on Saugatuck's Mason Street. The Blue Star Highway in Douglas saw one of Michigan's first "Tastee-Freeze" frozen custard stores in 1955. It was an "eat on the lawn"—or in the car—restaurant; the scale was much like the old Root Beer Barrel drive-in on Center Street. These arrived at a time in local history when most people welcomed such businesses. The former Tastee Freeze from the 1950s, now "M&M's"—like the "Round the Corner" (now "Charlie's") ice cream shop at 132 Mason Street and "Uncommon Grounds" coffee shop at 127 Hoffman Street (both in recycled buildings)—still provides the sort of "mom-and-pop" product, service, and nostalgic atmosphere that have great appeal to those who seek to bypass today's supercharged world of the synthetic in favor of a more authentic experience.

By the 1970s America had changed: small-scale drive-ups became large-scale "MacBurger" type restaurants with considerable requirements for parking spaces. At first limited to suburban and highway spaces, they began to invade traditional small town centers. When the McDonald Corporation submitted a proposal to open in the very center of Saugatuck in 1985 (in fact, just a few yards away from where William Butler had established his log house and store in 1830), they encountered considerable public opposition. They were eventually denied zoning approval and abandoned their plans. As the villages and surrounding areas continue to grow, this sometimes contentious dance between traditional landscape and modern roadside commercial interests (and between long-term and short-term economic gains) will continue.

SPREADING OUT | Entering and leaving most of America's small towns, one experiences an abundance of strip-mall, fast-food, and gas-station architecture. The outskirts of neither Saugatuck nor Douglas have fallen victim to these homogenizing forces; neither of the villages during the 1950s and 1960s was growing fast enough to experience this sort of commercial blight. For Saugatuck a traditional sidewalk-centered village district was fundamental to its tourist economy.

Nevertheless, while the strip malls did not move in, many non-tourist businesses serving the local community disappeared. Just before World War II Saugatuck's Butler Street buildings housed one dairy store, two hardware stores, four grocery stores, a department store, and two beauty shops. By the late 1960s, with the exception of one hardware store, these businesses had closed. The Wilson Ice Cream shop in the distinctive brown tile-brick building on Butler Street had closed when its owners went off to World War Two. Over time the abandoned buildings found new tourist-oriented occupants. "Chicken-As-You-Like-It" became Ted Kimbels's Port-O-Call Antique Shop—and with a wink of the eye to Saugatuck's retail spirit, Ted's pug dog Elizabeth was on hand to welcome visitors. Some new owners worked to preserve the character of the old village. Others didn't.

The same sort of exodus occurred on Center Street in Douglas but already by the 1950s Douglas was just a shell of the vibrant village center that existed half a century earlier. The two principal commercial buildings on Douglas's Center Street became non-commercial: the original "Peoples Store" grocery and drygoods building on the NE corner of Center and Spring Streets became St. Peter's School in the 1950s and the Kerr building across the street at 33 Center, switched from a hardware store to an apartment building about 1975. The Burn's IGA grocery building at Center and Washington (chapter 5) was converted to apartments in 1967. With the school having moved to another location (see below) and the old Methodist Church building underused, Douglas's Center Street appeared derelict. Taft's supermarket (now SuperValu) was opened in 1966 at Center and Blue Star Highway. Attempts at a drugstore and various other businesses in the complex failed. The nearby bowling alley was built in 1947. It was only natural that in Douglas two of the most popular building types of the age, the community bowling alley and the

| PORT-O-CALL
ca. 1940
Mason Street
Saugatuck

Ted Kimball's Port-O-Call Antique Shop—and with a wink of the eye to Saugatuck's retail spirit, Ted's pug dog Elizabeth was on hand to welcome customers. Tile brick construction. Formerly Chicken-As-You-Like-It restaurant.

| LAKEVIEW LANES
1947
229 Center Street
Douglas

Ordinary 50s architecture, now a classic.

RAISING THE ROOF

DOUGLAS ELEMENTARY SCHOOL
1957
Randolph Street
Douglas
H. E. Beyster and Associates, *architects*

With four classrooms (left in photo) and a multipurpose room (right in photo), this school was built to replace the Old School of 1866 on Center Street. The cost was $90,000. At the time, the attention to proper lighting, temperature control and ventilation, lavatory facilities, interior colors and even chalkboards was considered advanced for a "country school." For this it won an Association of School Administrators award for excellence in design. Additional classrooms were added in 1963 when the Douglas and Saugatuck school district was combined and then again in 1994. The original "new school" is now incorporated inside of these additions. Extant (with extensive additions)

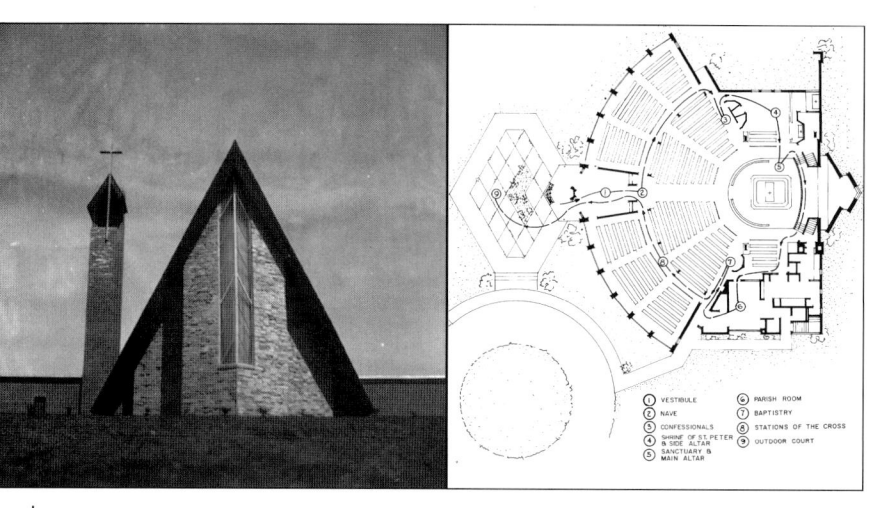

ST. PETER'S CHURCH & FLOORPLAN
1958
St. Peter's Drive
Douglas
Richard Drury and Carter Strong, *architects*
Howard Field Associates, Martin VanDyke & Sons, *contractors*

St. Peter's was founded in 1984 and continued as a mission church until becoming a parish in 1938, having as its place of worship the structure at Washington and Wall Streets, Douglas. By 1952 the parish had grown so large that a metal Quonset annex was erected next to the original church to provide for the summer crowds until such time as a new church could be built. Reverend William J. Hoogterp was pastor of the parish at the time of the building. Stained glass windows from the original church were moved to this site.

supermarket, found their homes close by the highway.

Douglas also saw its school and two of its churches gravitate toward the highway, bowing to the automobile and escaping their cramped quarters. In 1957 the Douglas school district moved its elementary school from its old four-room schoolhouse at 130 Center Street to a modern school of four classrooms plus a "multipurpose room" on a large field alongside what is now Randolph Street (the street was extended to meet the school). St. Peter's Catholic parish moved from its 1900 building on Washington Street, Douglas to a modern stone and brick A-Frame on the Blue Star Highway in 1958, and the Douglas Community Church, which had acquired the old St. Peter's building in 1965 and added to it in 1969, moved into a new suburban-appearing church complex along Wiley road in 1992. Subsequently, the old church was pulled down in 1998 after years of searching for adaptive use occupants.

BUILDING FOR LEISURE | One of the advantages of the automobile was that it gave more people access to a growing variety of activities. While the 1950s saw a shift in loyalties from the traditional "main street" to the more impersonal supermarket and mall shopping, one traditional public space that not only held its own but boomed in popularity

OVAL BEACH HOUSE
ca. 1950
Lake Michigan & Perryman Street
Saugatuck

"Sandwiches, Drinks, Ice Cream, Popcorn, Suits for Sale or Rent." The beach was established in 1936 and this beach house was constructed in the mid-1940s by the Pluim family. It has the natural look of a "beach house," but unfortunately, the large gable roof section was later removed (following tornado damage in April of 1956) and the concrete block walls were extended up to create a two story building, with a flat roof. It stood until it was replaced by a new octagonal structure in the 1980s.

A History of the Buildings and Architecture in the Saugatuck and Douglas Area

was Saugatuck's beach. It was cheap, it served food, and the automobile made the beach easy to get to—and they came in crowds. The Saugatuck beach's new entrance arch and collection booth was an architectural message announcing that one was entering not just a leisure zone but a commercial zone. Indeed, with its screened porches overlooking Lake Michigan, the Saugatuck "Beach House" at Oval Beach offered food, dressing rooms and even swimming suits for sale or rent.

Local summer stock theater had its beginnings in the high school in 1948. It then moved to a barn on Lawn Street in Douglas (now the Petter Sculpture Gallery) in 1951, and then moved to the livestock barn (built 1921) on the Belvedere estate in 1954. The "Red Barn Theatre," was a summer stock theater, which in 1958 advertised 12 weeks of summer stock, all Broadway Hits, played by an all-star professional New York cast. It closed its doors in 2002, but a new professional theater company, the Mason Street Warehouse, took the stage in the new Saugatuck Center for the Arts (SCA) in 2003. The SCA provides the area with a cultural center, proving once again the merits of adaptive re-cycling of buildings—in this case the old Lloyd J. Harris Pie factory on Culver Street—and confirming Saugatuck's status as one of Michigan's "Cool Cities."

RED BARN THEATRE
1954
3667 63rd Street
Saugatuck Township

A Saugatuck institution for a half century, the Summer Players moved to this site from Douglas and converted the old livestock barn of the Belvedere farm into a new "Red Barn Theatre" in 1954. It was expanded to provide more seating a few years later and again in 1962 to seat an audience of 500.

One of the most observable changes in riverside building in the 1960s and after was the replacement of the Big Pavilion with what was, eventually, one of the longest harbor-side boardwalks in Michigan. Complete with boat slips, the walk was eventually extended along the Kalamazoo Lake, down river from Butler Street to the Chain Ferry. As an important tourist promenade, it encompassed the new marina of the Singapore Yacht Club (1960). Indeed, a switch from the public boat taxi to the private boating became a public exhibition. The Saugatuck Yacht Club stands on the west shore of Lake Kalamazoo, and several large marinas were built along Kalamazoo Lake and River. In 1964 R. E. Peterson constructed a new, but authentic, grist mill on the old lumber millpond near Holland Street, thus providing an appropriately picturesque scene for the part of the village which had formerly been home to the village's largest lumber mill. Another new "structure" of the 1960s was a new Chain Ferry (1965) to replace the old ferry of 1857 that had relied on a succession of various wooden scow-type chassis over the years. The new ferry, the creation of R. J. Peterson, is a steel frame scow with white Victorian riverboat scroll-work. Once again the Chain Ferry became one of the riverside's principal visual features and a mirror of the village's history.[8]

HOUSES OF THE 1950S AND 1960S | The population of the villages of Saugatuck and Douglas grew modestly in the 1950s and 1960s; from 1,217 in 1950 to 1,868 in 1970.[9] Some new housing came in the form of a number of "ranch" style houses, many of them with vaguely Colonial Revival references. It is not known how many of the area's post-World War Two houses were prefabricated, but one of the popular "National Houses" by an Indiana builder may be seen at 160 North Street, Saugatuck. The often bland ranch house has been widely criticized for the homogenizing effect it had on American culture. However, this may be a somewhat unfair criticism since it was no more or less standardizing than the "formula" or "pattern-book" houses of past eras—such as the Italianate box or the craftsman bungalow. In fact, much of the objection, it appears, arises less out of the ranch style design than from the context in which it is often found: the bland and anonymous suburban sprawl that surrounds America's cities. This criticism cannot be levied in the Saugatuck-Douglas area, for in fact, the well designed ranch interweaves quite naturally into the scale and sentiment of the village streetscape. Two local examples of this American classic are the Galligan House on Butler Street, Saugatuck, and the Millar-Cummings House at Randolph and Washington Streets, Douglas. The Millar House is of an uncharacteristic, but charming material: glazed brick.

Looking at what happened to the house in the 1950s and after tells us something important about how village life—and the rest of America—was becoming more and more private, increasingly attached to the television set and the home computer, and more reliant on the automobile. During this period, something calamitous happened to the "modern" house: the garage. The garage had a humble beginning as an outgrowth of the stable or carriage house, relegated to the rear or side of the house and hidden from view. First regarded as a "service" building, it was not allowed to interfere with the design of the front façade. The garage grew from single-car to double- and triple-car size, and eventually it was appended to the house after which it moved to the side and then to the front of the house. The front porch gave way to the garage as the primary visual feature of the street façade and outdoor living and recreational activities, which traditionally took place on the grassy front lawn, were moved to the more private and protected back yard. A disproportionate amount of green space was converted to concrete or asphalt as driveways were widened to

† SAUGATUCK MARINA
ca. 1950
Saugatuck
Docks and boat slips, with a series of large boat storage sheds and boat services.

† SAUGATUCK YACHT CLUB
1937
Park Street | Saugatuck
Overlooking Kalamazoo Lake, Saugatuck area's first private yacht club was organized to give individuals access to docking facilities, a social venue and sailing lessons.

correspond to the size and importance of the garage. The age of the traditional street was history.

Although in the 1950s the "picture window" with its ubiquitous table and lamp in full view proudly announced to the outside world that family life existed inside the structure, by the 1960s domestic activities were increasingly conducted at the rear of the house in "family rooms" which opened to the back yard—in closer proximity to that wonderful 1950s invention, the patio and its requisite "barbecue." All of this, of course, is part and parcel of another re-invention of American life, the new and improved "Family," with Mom in the kitchen, Dad at the office and the kids safely playing games in the back yard, sheltered from the uncertainties of the streets. Whatever the case, the automobile and then the invasion of TV and air-conditioning contributed greatly to this privatization—and led to the view that "home sweet home" was a means for society to save itself. This meant bigger and bigger houses. The need, use and respect for public space, whether it be the Pavilion or the common public sidewalk, declined. Despite some efforts in Saugatuck to bring back the dance hall in the 1970s, Americans were entrenched in their love affair with home, automobile, and television.

Did the automobile muddy the visual difference between traditional village and modern city as some have claimed? Did it result in dramatic changes in the built environment of the two villages of Saugatuck and Douglas?[10] The answer to both questions is a qualified "yes." While it is true that the automobile brought many more people to Saugatuck and Douglas to discover an increasingly varied culture of leisure and, as in earlier eras, many buildings were recycled, in the main Saugatuck and Douglas saw considerable change. They were at the same time largely isolated from the sort of building ventures that were common in other towns: malls, strip malls, highway businesses and suburbs. The relative paucity of resources in both Saugatuck and Douglas partially explains this phenomenon, as does the positioning of the new main thoroughfare by 1940, the Blue Star Highway, away from the Village centers, which spared the villages from the sort of post-World War II highway commerce which was happening to Main Streets elsewhere. Also acting to preserve the traditional environment was an understanding of the economic value of the village character and scale. There were fewer shops for everyday goods than ever before, but a few of the old buildings still functioned in the same manner as a decade earlier, only the products had changed. The villages were nevertheless still villages.

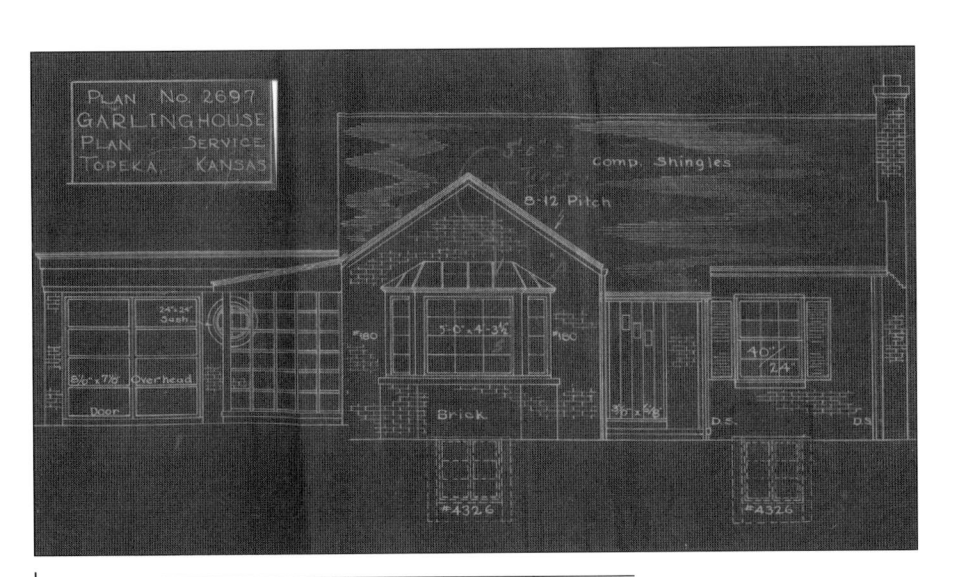

OOSTING'S HOME FURNISHINGS STORE
1957
Butler Street
Saugatuck

Showroom interiors photographed by Bill Simmons in 1957.

MILLAR–CUMMINGS HOUSE
1946
29 Randolph
Douglas
Garlinghouse Plan Service, Topeka, Kansas, *design*

Although the 'ranch house' was the post-World War II innovation in house design and American living, it was not a part of the common scene in Douglas or Saugatuck—largely because of the weakness of the economy and slow population growth. Built of Kalamazoo glazed tile-brick, with a few deviations from this original plan, this is one of the first of the American ranch house designs--an important "classic." Orville Millar was a World War II veteran (see page 134).

GALLIGAN HOUSE
1959
526 Butler
Saugatuck

Fifties Modern with the signature picture window, adding to the lineup of architectural styles found on this street.

DESTRUCTION OF THE
BRITTAIN HOUSE
1967
Griffith & Mason Streets
Saugatuck

The Brittain House, Saugatuck's best-known house, was dismantled to make way for a parking lot. The cupola, seen in the photo being removed, was salvaged and can now be seen at the Kalamazoo River's edge about one-half mile north of the Chain Ferry. The house, built ca. 1868 for O. R. Johnson, one of the area's prominent lumber mill owners, later became the home of Captain Ralph C. Brittain (d. 1905), Saugatuck's preeminent ship captain and boat builder.

CHAPTER SEVEN

Suburban vs. Traditional: Looking Forward and
Thinking Backward, 1980 to the Present

*"The crisis of the American home is not one of interior organization
or technological innovation—these problems have largely
been solved—but of how it relates or fails to relate to a town."*
—JAMES HOWARD KUNSTLER, *The Geography of Nowhere*

THE BATTLE: THE TRADITIONAL BUILDING VS. URBAN SPRAWL | The late 1970s were the beginning of an astonishing improvement of fortune for the Saugatuck and Douglas area. First at the doorstep was a new generation of Midwestern tourists who had considerable money to spend and were interested in regional travel. By the 1990s smart shops, galleries, restaurants and cafes were omnipresent, and Saugatuck was soon to be named by the Governor as one of Michigan's "Cool Cities." Visitors wanted to look at real villages and real landscapes—and, of course, new shops. Second was a renewed presence of cottage lovers, some of whom who were in search of a new type of cottage, more appropriately now called a "second home," which would eventually become the place for retirement. All of these newcomers were part of a growing American search that went beyond a desire for country and waterside living but included a pursuit for "real" and "genuine" experiences within "natural" or "historic" environments. It is clear that, as in the past, many Americans were frustrated with urban and suburban life, but unlike cottagers of earlier times, many of these cottagers wanted amenities that range from heated driveways to high-speed internet hookup and air conditioning. In the meantime, a third bag of gold was thrown at the doorstep, that of the housing developers who sought to cash in on the everyday housing demands of a growing West Michigan population, often without much respect for sense of place in terms of design or materials. Development, of course, threatened to bring with it all the features, both good and bad, of what is called urban sprawl: wide streets, big lots with big houses, strip malls, fast food outlets, and truck stops-convenience stations, increased traffic—and anonymity. Suburbanization appeared to be inevitable, and thus a battle for control of the landscape and townscape was underway. Not since the days of the lumber barons were the villages so capital rich or so endangered. Improved sewer and water access along with skyrocketing land prices and relatively weak tri-community attention to land preservation caused a shocking speedup of sprawl development beginning about 2004. Will Saugatuck and its surrounding villages become, as Gertrude Stein once said of urbanization, a place where "there is no there, there?"

TRADITIONAL VS. MODERN: AND THE WINNER WILL BE . . . ? | While such growth pressures were universal for most Lake Michigan coastal towns and for much of the "countryside" throughout Michigan, the Saugatuck and Douglas area was an especially attractive destination because time and modernity had largely passed it by during the 1950s and into the 1970s when the suburbanization and highway culture had run amuck in those areas that had the wealth to afford it. In the Saugatuck and Douglas area, although not in the best of condition, the "traditional" physical substructure—houses, cottages, shops, former hotel buildings, the chain ferry landing, and the like—was still in place. It was also the villages' good fortune that what we termed earlier as "intellectual capital," was still present in the form of the Ox-Bow school, the Presbyterian Camps, cottagers resolute in preserving the summer cottage and its culture, a lively and revitalized art-gallery industry, and a tradition of landscape preservation begun by O. C. Simonds.

| WELCOME TO SAUGATUCK
1937
The ultimate in identity construction. Porcelain on metal. Artist's pallet sign—probably part of a WPA project. Restored, 1994.

Newly added to this cultural mix, was the presence of a growing number of individuals and groups interested in the preservation and documentation of the area's history and buildings, including an increasing number of bed-and-breakfast entrepreneurs (a movement that had begun in the early 1980s), an historical society and museum, and a remarkable preservation-reconstruction "renaissance" in Douglas. Unlike the 1920s and 1930s when local architects such as Thomas Eddy Tallmadge, Carl Hoerman, and George W. Maher led the way in preserving and re-making the area's historic image, architects were conspicuously absent among the first ranks of the latter-day preservation-restoration movement. Nevertheless, efforts were promising: the late 1990s found 14 local buildings placed on either the State or National Register of Historic Places and Saugatuck had designated an "historic district," and business owners and real estate agents were coming to the realization that "authentic" sells. Both Saugatuck and Douglas were awarded national "Preserve America" status, partly because of their fine "traditional" townscapes.

THE BUFFALO HOUSE
527 Butler Street
Saugatuck

An ordinary house, once the Post Office, with an interesting tale. One day when the circus came to town and staged a parade down Butler Street, a buffalo broke loose from the parade and charged into the Post Office causing great fright and the fleeing of citizens. Onetime home of Butler Street watchmaker, Miller Robinson, then his descendants.

STUDIOS AT OX-BOW
(photo ca. 1955)
On the Ox-Bow Lagoon
Saugatuck

These former fish shanties/ice houses at the water's edge were converted to studios for students at the Ox-Bow Summer School of Painting and the Arts, and for nearly half a century they were part of Ox-Bow life. They were called "the Waldorf and the Astoria." They were pulled down in 1969.

BUILDINGS LOST: GOODBYE TO THE HISTORIC—AND THE ORDINARY | Those whose connection to the Saugatuck and Douglas area began only recently have little idea of how many physical links to the past have been lost to fire, irretrievable decay, "modernization," or destruction. Some of these "lost" structures, such as the Brittain House, the Terrace Park Tower, the Dutcher House, Leland Lodge were notable traditional structures, while others, such as Florence Hunn's charming Pier Cove workers' cottage were more offbeat but had value as local color. Many picturesque old barns have gone by the wayside and other lost structures such as the old Tara Restaurant had stood as narratives of ordinary experiences of days gone-by. The house on Butler Street that was invaded by a stray buffalo is long gone, as are Gerber barn (chapter 3) in Douglas and the Saugatuck Fruit Exchange where locally grown fruit was sorted and packaged for people all over the Midwest. Few buildings at the Ox-Bow school conjured up the scenes of picturesque rusticity more than did the fishing shanty artist's studios (affectionately called the "Waldorf," the "Astoria," and the "Drake") which stood at the edge of the lagoon for over a half century. The destruction of the charming Van Syckle store building on the Douglas Center Street in March of 2006 left the village bereft of one of its prime examples of Colonial Revival architecture.

HURRAH FOR QUIRKY | The wild stallion commercial statute on the Douglas stretch of the Blue Star Highway is gone (to the satisfaction of some), but there

A History of the Buildings and Architecture in the Saugatuck and Douglas Area

are other existing landscape oddities: the Root Beer Barrel refreshment stand (under restoration) along Center Street, Douglas; the barrel bird houses on brick plinths at 135 Union Street, Douglas, the giant signs calling for repentance on Center Street and the old Blue Star motel sign (recycled) on the Blue Star Highway. Their sentimental value is considerable and these peculiarities give the villages uniqueness and character, interweaving with the "important" structures to give the landscape texture and meaning—and to make this place "home." Everyone has their favorite. In 1994 one determined resident persuaded the City of Saugatuck to rehabilitate and relocate one of its most famous landmarks: the neon-lit 1937 artist's pallet sign that identifies Saugatuck; it now stands proudly at the city's south entrance.[1]

THE ROOT BEER BARREL
1946 *(photo ca. 1952)*
Center Street | Douglas

The Barrel was operated in early years by George and Joann Gallas, well-known vaudevillian dancers. Nearby was a miniature golf course and outdoor movie theater (a screen suspended between two telephone poles). The Barrel closed for business in the mid-1970s. Under restoration in 2006.

FAREWELL TO AN OLD HOUSE IN DOUGLAS
December 2005
Tannery Hill, South Water Street | Douglas

An 1860s vernacular Greek Revival house bows to the wrecking ball to make way for new construction—and an opportunity for adaptive use or relocation is lost. Built by Daniel Gerber, probably for workers at the nearby Douglas-Gerber Tanning Mill.

VAN SYCKEL BUILDING UP IN FLAMES
March 29, 2006
Center Street | Douglas

In a town made of wood fire is a constant threat. The Van Syckel building succumbed to this peril following an explosion from a broken gas main. Firemen were able to contain the blaze and save the adjacent strucure, the old Walz barber shop.

151

RAISING THE ROOF

PLAIN, OLD-FASHIONED PRESERVATION | Common sense has left a number of buildings marvelously functional but also as lessons on the history of American architecture. All Saints Episcopal Church remains as good an example of Carpenter Gothic architecture today as when it was created in the early 1870s, just as the hillside cabin on Pleasant Street sits as a splendid reminder of the 1920s "log cabin" craze. The Maplewood Hotel, the Thew House (Bay Building), the Landmark Building (Kilwins), and the Dole House (Good Goods) in Saugatuck's business district, along with the Old School House, the Lion House, Windover Farmhouse, the Flint and Doucette houses on Union Street, Douglas, make up part of a long list of buildings that deserve local historic structure designation and protection.

A number of structures have been spared the bulldozer by being rehabilitated to their original state or "reconstructed" as a friendly nod to the original in terms of style and scale. Noteworthy restorations include the Douglas Village Hall-Dutcher Lodge, the Martel House on Grand Street in Saugatuck which has gone through a series of restorations, the Felt Mansion, and the Kemah House. The range of restoration and preservation is wide and includes the everyday familiar in the Engleman-Fox House at 443 Grand Street, Saugatuck (ca. 1870); the restored 1920s cottage at 337 Ferry Street, Douglas; and the commercial fishing dock and shanties at 720 Water Street, Saugatuck. The Streamland and Henry Till barn restorations testify that Saugatuck area residents want to live in environments that have connections to the past.

SUMMER COTTAGE
1920s
337 Ferry Street
Douglas

Restored in 1997, basement added in 2006.

RESTORATION OF HENRY TILL'S BARN
2005-2006
Upper Spear Street | Saugatuck
Lesa Werme, *owner/designer*
David Ciolek & Dave Scholten, *restoration contractors*

SIGNIFICANCE OF THE STRUCTURE | The Saugatuck and Douglas area was one of Michigan's first major fruit growing area. It dominated the production of peaches, apples, and other fruits for export to Chicago for re-export throughout the Midwest and as far as Europe. Many local orchards have disappeared and most barns have been destroyed. Thus, this barn stands as an historic artifact—preserving the memory of the landscape, including the many people who tended to the orchards, picked the fruit, and transported the fruit to urban markets.

THE TILL FAMILY | Henry Till (b. 1864, d.1940) was a local shipbuilder who worked for the shipbuilders Martel, Heath and Williams. Like many others in his trade, he invested and worked in the profitable fruit industry of the time *(see chapter 3)*. In about 1895 he purchased the 23-acre Nies farm at the east end of Spear Street, Saugatuck—described at the time as well adapted to the culture of small fruit. Much of the Saugatuck "hill" area, eastward to what is now the Blue Star Highway, consisted of fruit farms. Till was also an officer in the Village fire department. He married Olga H. Shumann (b. 1873, d. 1942) in 1890, and they had a son and daughter. Part of the farm property was held by his daughter Augusta ("Gussie") until her death in 1994 at age 100.

Tucked away at the very end of upper Spear Street, Till built his barn in 1895 when he purchased the farm. At some point he acquired an additional 5 village lots (numbers 28-32). The farm is adjacent to that of his father-in-law, Andrew Shumann. The barn was used for storage of farm produce, packing crates, tools, and the necessary horse and wagons used for the transport of produce to nearby docks—or to the railroad at Fennville. The barn's upper floor appears to have been used for raising pigeons with a space for corn feed storage.

CONSTRUCTION | The barn's unusually steep roof pitch suggests the gothic-like barn style popularized by Andrew Jackson Downing in the mid-nineteenth century, and its balloon frame construction is unusually modern for an age when most Michigan barns were post and beam construction. The barn was probably built from a mail-order catalogue kit that was shipped in by steamship or railroad. The nearby Till farmhouse is a Sears Roebuck catalogue-packaged house.

REHABILITATION | This was a tricky project. Believing that the barn held a treasury of memories of how people have related to the natural and man-made environments, the owner wished to retain the age-old feel and patina of the structure. Hence, the goal was to restore and repair the badly deteriorated structure and avoid adding any but absolutely necessary new construction or materials— including paint. A portion of the barn interior was designed for use as the owner's workshop-studio.

RAISING THE ROOF

HENRY TILL'S BARN LOFT
2006 *(before restoration)*

A History of the Buildings and Architecture in the Saugatuck and Douglas Area

HENRY TILL'S BARN LOFT
2006 (restoration in progress)

THE ARRIVAL OF SUBURBANIZATION AND "DEVELOPMENT": A WALL OF GARAGES? | Suburbanization patterns produce pictures of townscapes that are all too familiar: wide streets set in even wider clearings of woodland for speedy entrance and egress, large lots with over-sized houses, huge setbacks, large expanses of perfectly manicured lawns with few trees, no sidewalks, abundant use of synthetic materials, enormous garages that dominate the facades of houses (giving rise to the term of mockery "snout houses"), and so on. Much of the countryside in the greater Grand Rapids area (and elsewhere) has fallen to the bulldozer or is certainly doomed to its arrival. Although it is the antithesis in scale, size, and even "style" to the traditional village and waterside houses and cottages of Saugatuck and Douglas, without a serious refocusing of civic thinking—including that of environmental issues—dwellers of the 21st century Saugatuck area will undoubtedly be left with little choice but to live amid considerable suburbanization. And once it is in place, there is no going back.

Although suburban-type developments are generally incompatible with woods and dunes, some recent developments, such as that of "Pier Cove Forest," "Cottage Home," and "Saugatuck Woods," have integrated roads and houses amongst rather than in spite of the woods. Similarly, the "Summer Grove" development in Douglas emphasizes traditional village organization and has constructed an homogenous neighborhood of dwellings in the folk-Victorian style. It achieves a small-town attitude by placing houses in close proximity with each other, with emphasis on the traditional front porch, front yard, and by downplaying the garage. The complex is unified by sidewalks and picket fences and a "commons."

THE GARAGE | Perhaps the aspect of the suburban house most incongruous with the traditional village is the modern garage. Earlier village folk placed the garage to the rear or side of the house, sometimes with a degree of charm and interest. The suburban way of garage design is to place an oversized garage to cover much of the front of the house— with a massive concrete driveway. Not only does this obliterate the traditional house façade with its front porch and front yard, it interrupts the streetscape and sends an unwelcoming "house-as-garrison" message. By 1990 this invasion of garages was underway in the Saugatuck and Douglas area, sounding the alarm for the decline of aesthetic (and in the long run, economic) value of certain neighborhoods.

The good news is that some homeowners and some developers have seen the light. This new view of the garage, attached and unattached (and some serving as studios as well), stands as proof that the garage can become an asset to the property— and the community's identity.

AVOIDING THE DEATH SENTENCE: THE MAGIC OF RECYCLING | History shows us that few buildings remain functional for long and most buildings fall out of favor in terms of style at some point in their lives. As we have seen, much of the history of building in Saugatuck and Douglas has been a history of recycling and remodeling of buildings, often, but not always, with a generally pleasing result in terms of compatibility of scale, size and style. The Peachbelt School, now used as an artist's studio and gallery, is an example of how adaptative re-use has saved some local buildings from destruction; as are the conversion of a local gas station in Douglas into a retail space and a century-old boat taxi station in Saugatuck into a residence. All of theses are models of how historic presence can complement and add value to a structure and how recycling buildings can join the environmentally responsible "green" parade in America. Unfortunately too often the act of recycling old buildings for new uses while holding to traditional material, scale, and style, is easily dismissed as impractical and uneconomic. This death sentence is commonly rendered with the dictum "the numbers just don't work" or "structurally unsound" or "no historic value." Equally frustrating, some preservation minded property owners find themselves up against zoning or building regulations that don't allow them to protect (or add onto) structures that pre-date existing regulations. Throwing away and starting all over is often easier—but not always the best value.

2004	2004	2000
521 Butler Street Saugatuck	751 Simonson Drive Saugatuck	42 Union Street Douglas
2006	2006	2004
201 Washington Douglas	633 Allegan Street Saugatuck	6594 Old Allegan Road Saugatuck
2003	1999	2005
562 Weirich Drive Saugatuck	254 Water Street Douglas	860 Simonson Drive Saugatuck

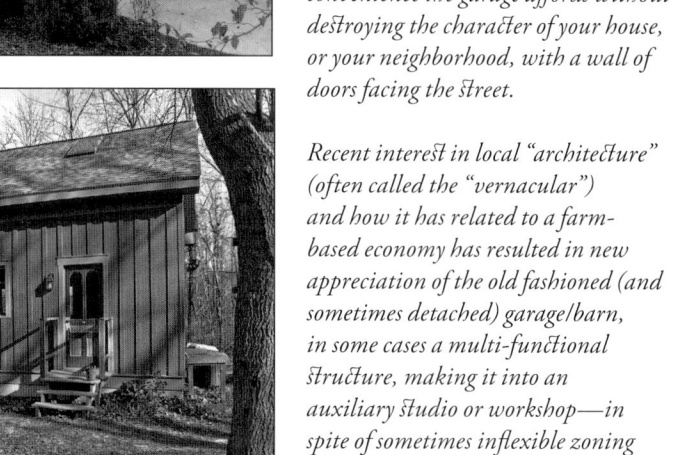

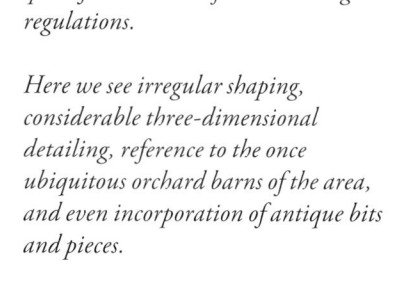

A History of the Buildings and Architecture in the Saugatuck and Douglas Area

all photos: Bill Werme

A NEW GARAGE—AND BARN—CONSCIOUSNESS

Without question the garage is a fact of modern life in America, but the problem is how to have the convenience the garage affords without destroying the character of your house, or your neighborhood, with a wall of doors facing the street.

Recent interest in local "architecture" (often called the "vernacular") and how it has related to a farm-based economy has resulted in new appreciation of the old fashioned (and sometimes detached) garage/barn, in some cases a multi-functional structure, making it into an auxiliary studio or workshop—in spite of sometimes inflexible zoning regulations.

Here we see irregular shaping, considerable three-dimensional detailing, reference to the once ubiquitous orchard barns of the area, and even incorporation of antique bits and pieces.

Once again the garage becomes an interesting contribution to the villagescape.

KEEPING NATURE AT THE CORE: NEW AND RESTORED "COTTAGES" | Much of Saugatuck's identity as a spirited, "laid back," and friendly place is connected to its large community of summer and week-end cottages. The "cottage" is, after all, one of the modern world's survival strategies and, although it is a dying breed, a good number survive in their original or near original state. The local cottage building recipe continues to follow the traditionally modest scale and use of natural materials. Plenty of variation in façade and roof line variations provides an excellent way to obtain square footage while retaining small scale appearance (see "1 Grand Street Cottage"). The Arts & Crafts Mellander cottage at on Helmer Street, Douglas was moved in 1992 from its former site on Park Street and then enlarged with a new but inconspicuous upper story. The reconstruction of several Park Street area cottages, among them Belle Rive, the large turn-of-the-century river-view cottage and the nearby Tree Tops cottage, were transformations from deteriorating seasonal to year-round "cottages," and on the lakeshore the remarkable collection of summer cottages, called Timber Bluff, has been brought back to life by a pair of dedicated cottage lovers—and smart businessmen. Admittedly, in many ways these sorts of "sympathetic reconstructions" are more difficult and often more costly than starting from scratch. But the results can insure that the fabric of a neighborhood is kept intact, maintaining also the integrity of surrounding structures and the sense of community and a higher property value.

Many "cottages" are in reality small but charming full-time residences or second homes. A good collection of these are found in the Ferry/Park Street-Mt. Baldhead area, along Campbell Road and Lakeshore Drive, in the Shorewood

NEW MEETS OLD
2004
440 Spear Street
Saugatuck

This carefully crafted rear addition to the 19th century Italianate Masterson/Spooner House is the perfect way to preserve the traditional and meet the demands of modern living.

BURNHAM HOUSE
2005
415 Lake Street
Saugatuck
Carl Miskotten, *developer*

Formerly Wright's Pavilion. A historic boat taxi station and refreshment pavilion has been converted into a contemporary residence—an example of preservation collaboration between developer and local Historic District. (The original structure is shown in Chapter 4.)

PEACH BELT SCHOOL
1867
124th Avenue (M-89) at 63rd Street
Ganges Township

Oldest one-room school house still existing in Allegan County. Brick veneer added in 1898; Restoration, 1970s, 2004-5. Now an artist's studio.

Painting by Dawn Stafford.

COTTAGES
Reconstruction & New Construction

MELLANDER/DEEM COTTAGE
1920s (1991)
392 Helmer Street
Douglas

PIKE COTTAGE
2005
164 Lakeshore Drive
Douglas

BARTO-IBSEN-BENOIST
1890s
70 Lakeshore Drive
Douglas

HUFF COTTAGE
2005
378 Lakeshore Drive
Douglas

GRAND STREET COTTAGE
1920s (1990s)
1 Grand Street
Saugatuck

MACK COTTAGE
1920s (2005)
303 Lucy Street
Saugatuck

BELLE RIVE COTTAGE
ca. 1897 (1991)
128 Van Dalson Street
Saugatuck

TIMBER BLUFF COTTAGES
1920s (2003-2006)
Lakeshore Drive
Saugatuck Township

RAISING THE ROOF

district, and in the Saugatuck Historic District area of Lucy and Spear Streets. One of these Lucy Street cottages, the Mack Cottage, is a former two story cottage that became a one-story cottage in the 1920s and brought back to its former self as a two-story home in 2005. Comfortable old structures on the opposite (north) side of the same street are destined to meet the bulldozer, partly because the Historic District includes only the south half of the street. Except for those buildings in the Saugatuck Historic District, there is no preservation protection for any structures in these old cottage neighborhoods. Indeed, the days of the quaint summer cottage along the Douglas Lakeshore may be numbered—and so its oldest and first cottage, the Barto Cottage (1896) at 70 Lakeshore Drive was the first cottage to be built on the Douglas lakeshore; still used as a seasonal residence, it is not only a model for this building type but a truly an endangered species.

A DOUGLAS RENAISSANCE | The restoration and rebuilding boom that has transformed Douglas since the mid-1980s demonstrates that the age-old tradition of re-cycling/restoring buildings remains vital and, in fact, still makes both aesthetic and economic sense. It is difficult to say why the Douglas transformation began. The economic and population decline of the village since the 1930s, and then the exodus of two schools, two churches, and a number of businesses since the 1950s left the village center largely abandoned of village life. Many of its buildings had fallen into decay. There

L. W. MCDONALD BUILDING
Before and After Restoration
1890 (restored 1992)
36 Center Street | Douglas

The structure was built by Daniel Gerber, one of the founders of the baby food industry. The west (left) front was the well-known "People's Store" from 1896 until the 1920s, under the ownership of L. W. McDonald (who lived in the house behind the store at 41 Spring Street). The east front was Ed Norton's Drug Store and Soda Fountain (Norton eventually moved to 48 Center Street, recently rebuilt). The upper floor had various uses, including as the meeting place for the Maccabees Lodge. The structure later housed St. Peter's school and then Saugatuck Township Office. Carefully rehabilitated in 1992 as a series of shops/galleries. (See also p. 31.)

POINT PLEASANT GARDEN HOUSE
1989
201 S. Washington Street
Douglas
Bud Baty & Doug Wierenga, *designers*
Lake Home Builders, *builders*

On the site of Douglas's first lumber mill and later the Douglas (Weed's) Basket Factory, this little classical summer garden house is a perfect complement to the earlier vernacular translations of Greek Revival and Colonial revival architecture of Douglas. It is part of a residence-marina complex.

was little interest in capturing the local tourist dollar and local consumer needs were met elsewhere. Back in the 1950s, for example, the Douglas village fathers did not believe a supermarket would be an asset to the Village.[2] By the mid-1980s collaboration between established residents and newcomers, many of whom were urban people and some a part of an increasing gay population in the area, occasioned a boom in residential and commercial construction, reconstruction and restoration. The results of this renaissance have been impressive.

In 1984 a university professor and his family and friends began the restoration of the Kirby House on Douglas's Center Street and converted it to a bed & breakfast. About the same time two Grand Rapids businessmen converted a 1950s house into a combination home and private marina, called Point Pleasant, in a manner complementary to the traditional "classical revival" townscape. In 1992 the Octagon House (1857) nearby on Mixer Street underwent a complicated rehabilitation project that was to last for over a decade and in the same year, Edwards Limited partnership initiated the revitalization of Center Street with the rehabilitation of the 1890 Gerber building at 34 Center Street and its return, once again, to shops. This was followed by reconstruction of a line of older buildings, with some new infill, on the remainder of the block and a return of the Kerr Building to its former glory. The old Norton drugstore building on at the corner of Spring and Center Streets was reconstructed with the addition of the Respite Coffee House as was Center Street's earliest retail structure, Marsh's General Store of 1862. An addition to the old Douglas Dinette café on the south side of Center Street gave Douglas an expanded home for an award winning restaurant, Everyday People Café. The EPC building provides an open window into Douglas history. It began in 1861 as George and Chris Walz's Meat Market, became the Douglas Soda Bar and Grill (in the 1950s and until 1958), and then Douglas Dinette in 1961, and since 2001 Everyday People Café, with additions in 2002 and 2006.

CHESTNUT HOUSE
ca. 1920s *(reconstruction 1997, addition 2004)*
60 Chestnut Street | Douglas
Duane Brown, *reconstruction designer*

This was probably originally built as a worker cottage for local mill and basket factory workers. It had been added to at several points in time. Extensive interior and exterior reconstruction, converting it into a contemporary house but of a scale, style, and materials that are fitting for the neighborhood.

OCTAGON HOUSE
1859
90 Mixer Street | Douglas
After and before restoration (see also page 34-35).

RIVER GUILD – JOYCE PETTER GALLERY
1942 *(renovation 1993)*
161 Blue Star Highway | Douglas
Carl Hoerman, *architect*

This well-known Arts & Crafts building was constructed for the River Guild (see Chapter 4) in a vernacular Arts and Crafts manner in 1941. It was later altered in form as its function changed and was restored with some modifications in 1993 to become the Joyce Petter Gallery. The gallery has retained the original River Guild logo.

By the mid-1990s Douglas's Center Street had become a West Michigan destination for strolling, shopping and eating—with a new waterfront park thrown in the mix. Much of this was encouraged by local government that worked alongside the Downtown Development Authority and the Douglas Heritage Preservation Committee. Some new developments were underwritten by making city owned property available at bargain prices to developers. Although no protection exists for Douglas's traditional streetscape or waterfront views, beginning in 2006 a DDA district will begin to use a portion of Douglas property tax revenue for specific DDA district projects.

A number of houses in Douglas's village center have been returned to their former state or reconstructed in a manner compatible with the village's past, replacing or correcting out-of-character additions or materials applied to the structures in the 1950s and 1960s. Included on this list are a number of modest but appealing houses in the neighborhood immediately south of Center: 36 Union, 62 Wall, 43 Wall, 26 Wall, 10 Wall, 15 Wall, 118 Spring, 41 Spring, 31 Spring, 60 Chestnut Street, 13 and 39 Washington, 37 Main, and the Bayou House at Center and Water. A reconstruction of the home of the village's most famous Civil War veteran, George Dutcher home (Dutcher-Mark House) at 148 Union (chapter 2), and the Bayou House on Water Street are exceptional. The Doud–Sax House at 34 Wall is a model for how to recycle an older structure by using traditional materials and keeping within the scale and style of

BIOGRAPHY OF A HOUSE

DOUD–SAX HOUSE
pre-1863 | 34 Wall Street | Douglas

Restoration & Reconstruction by Rick Haver

A HOUSE OF MANY LIVES | The Doud–Sax House is a pre-Civil War one-up-one-down mill worker "box house," built by nearby mill owner Johnathan Wade and perhaps used by a family member and by mill workers. The second owner was Judson Doud (in 1863) a house and carriage painter. It was later owned by Daniel Gerber. Reconstruction in 1996 allowed the builder to trace over a century of construction changes. The house retains the exterior form of its last incarnation—but with extensive exterior and interior repair and upgrading of materials and rearrangement of interior space.

CONSTRUCTION HISTORY | This 16-x-24-foot "box" appears to have been common for Douglas at the time. Balloon Frame with very careful insertion of studs into perimeter beam notches (floor structure beams are "notched" at 2-foot intervals for vertical studs and at 2-foot intervals for joists). Lumber appears to be pre-cut in multiples of 4, thus allowing for efficient use of material and minimal cutting on-site. "Notching" reduced the use of expensive nails. Some structural damage had to be repaired during restoration due largely to cuts into the framework since the 1930s and for heating and electrical improvements.

BAYOU HOUSE
1940s *(reconstruction, 2005)*
Water & Center Streets | Douglas
Vander Muelen Builders, *builders*

Keeping with the village scale and style, an older harbor front home becomes an 11 room reidence.

DOUD–SAX HOUSE
pre-1863
34 Wall Street | Douglas
Before and after 1996 renovation.

162

the neighborhood—and finish up with a very fine contemporary home. Nearby at 40 Spring is another example of creative re-cycling, a 1920s Ford Garage turned into an office-design studio space, and the Italianate residence at 36 Spring has been given back much of its appropriate face.

COMPATIBILITY OF SCALE AND SIZE—AND THE NEW ELECTRONIC HOME | In decades past, "leisure time" was something thought of occurring in outdoor spaces. Today, leisure is more and more centered on indoor spaces: shops, health clubs, galleries, museums, movie theaters, restaurants, and most of all, because of the world of television, the i-Pod, video games and the internet, the home itself has become the main leisure universe for modern America. Besides, this electronic revolution has also made it possible for many people to work at home. We have become "interior beings." As a result, by the 1980s many American homebuyers, most house plan magazines, and many developers were swept away by the "McMansion Syndrome": bigger houses with bigger rooms on bigger lots—and even home theaters. In most cases the McMansion is located next door to another McMansion, which is across the street (but very often without a sidewalk) from McMansion number three and so on, so that the overall effect is of bigness—and, of course, enormous comfort. Unfortunately, in traditional settings such as Saugatuck and Douglas, the intrusion of "bigness" can be disastrous for the surrounding property and, overall, the townscape. Big home lots also means the privatization of green space. Occasionally, a sensitive design, appropriate materials, and good landscaping can yield a picturesque scene—even when the building is uncharacteristic in either style or scale but for the most part, bigness only devalues the traditional scale of things.

BACK TO BASICS | Size isn't everything. Happily an impressive assortment of new Saugatuck-Douglas area construction suggests that neither suburbanization nor the McMansion is the only answer. The villages today have plenty of proof that new houses, cottages, and commercial structures can be of considerable size but at the same time keep to traditional scale and form. Nothing says "traditional" more a number of contemporary Craftsman type bungalow houses that have appeared on the local scene. And while waterfront land values and the modern demand for year-round second homes may be makiung the old-fashioned cottage a thing of the past, a pair of urban dwellers has done just that on a large wooded tract called Fern Hollow near Pier Cove, and we can find the Bird Cottage—a similar example of "small is beautiful" cottage plunked down right in the middle of Douglas.

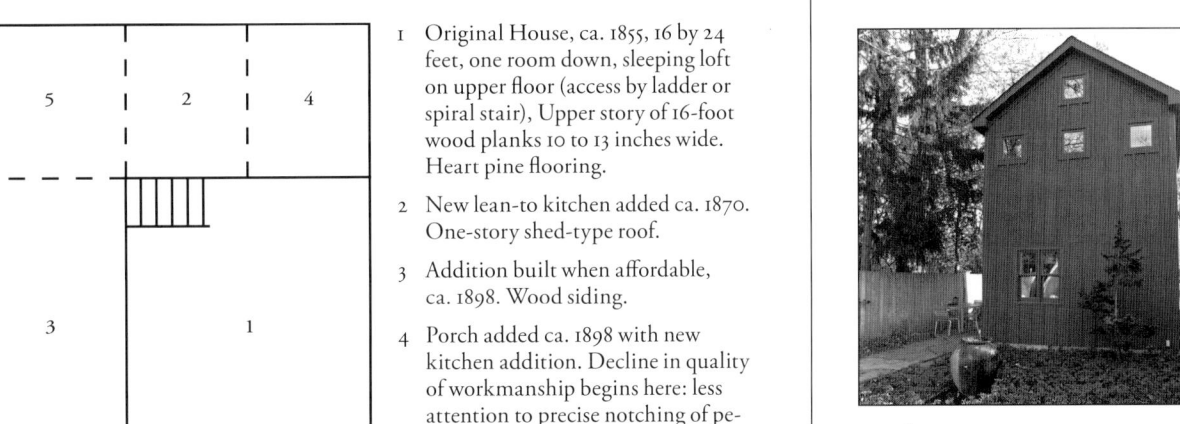

DOUD–SAX HOUSE

EVOLUTION OF THE FLOOR PLAN

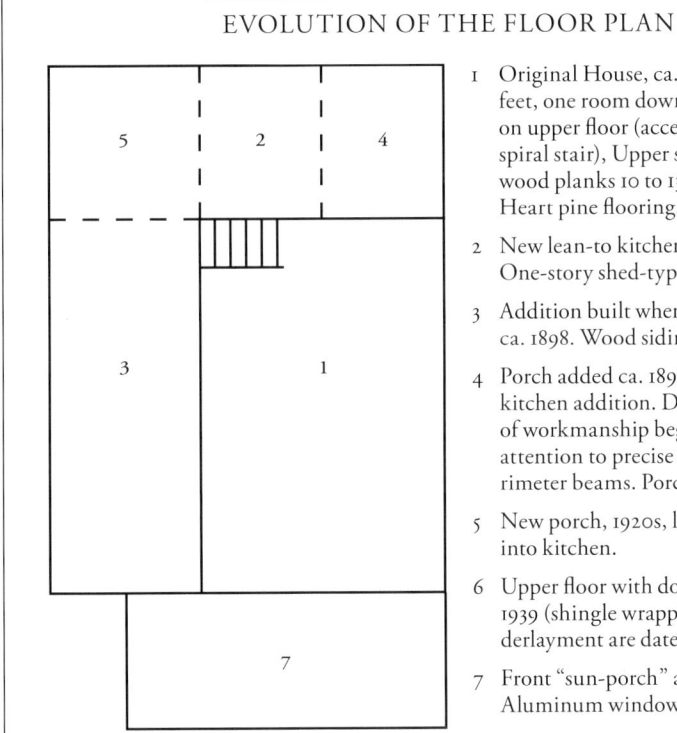

1. Original House, ca. 1855, 16 by 24 feet, one room down, sleeping loft on upper floor (access by ladder or spiral stair), Upper story of 16-foot wood planks 10 to 13 inches wide. Heart pine flooring.
2. New lean-to kitchen added ca. 1870. One-story shed-type roof.
3. Addition built when affordable, ca. 1898. Wood siding.
4. Porch added ca. 1898 with new kitchen addition. Decline in quality of workmanship begins here: less attention to precise notching of perimeter beams. Porch later enclosed.
5. New porch, 1920s, later incorporated into kitchen.
6. Upper floor with dormer added ca. 1939 (shingle wrappings used as underlayment are dated "1939").
7. Front "sun-porch" added ca. 1952. Aluminum windows.

THE BIRD HOUSE
31 ½ Spring Street
Douglas
Mark Neidlinger, *designer*
Jason Dedic, *builder*

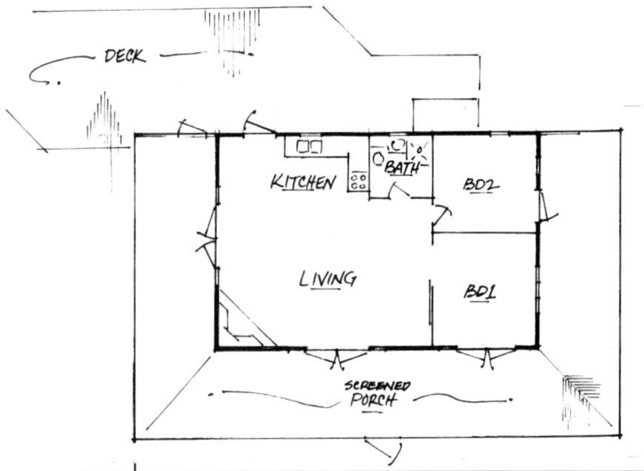

FERN HOLLOW COTTAGE PLAN

1989
Lakeshore Drive
Ganges Township
Kevin Martin & Duane Brown, *designers*

This traditional Michigan style cottage is buried deep within a 12-acre fern-filled wood approximately 1000 feet from Lake Michigan. Its wrap-around screened porch and four sets of French doors allow the warm summer breezes off the lake to cool the house. Built from traditional materials, including cove siding, split-face field stone, and pine floors, the cottage is utilized from the first spring days of April through October.

COMPATIBILITY & STYLE

WEAVING NEW THREADS INTO THE OLD FABRIC

On this page, three new houses and three very different design formulas, but each respects local architectural traditions, scale, and materials—one in the 1920s Colonial Revival manner, one in that of a folk-farmhouse, and the third a mirror of
the village barn tradition. Each is moderate in size and uses variation, articulation, and relief of the façade, exterior dimension, and material to reduce visual scale.

THE RED HOUSE
2000
325 Water Street | Douglas
Jeff Scherer, Scherer, Meyer, & Rockcastle, *architect*
Jarzembowski Builders, *builders*

BOWMAN HOUSE
2003
135 S. Washington Street | Douglas
Lake Home Builders, *designers & builders*

WERME HOUSE
1997
671 Spear Street | Saugatuck
Lake Home Builders, *designers & builders*

A History of the Buildings and Architecture in the Saugatuck and Douglas Area

RECENT CONSTRUCTION

From small to large, these houses represent the vast variety in new home design in the Saugatuck-Douglas area. While style and size vary, most of these projects have rejected imitation materials, avoid placing the garage at the street side and, generally, complement the traditional character of the villages and surrounding countryside.

(from upper left to lower right)

WATER STREET HOUSE
2005
78 Water Street | Douglas
Looman Construction, *reconstruction*

GREGERSEN HOUSE
2006
5 Park Street
Saugatuck
David Gregersen, *designer*
Richard Meckley, *construction*

CANNARSA/PHILLIPS HOUSE
2005
3464 Riverside Drive | Saugatuck
Charles Kenneth Carlson, *architect*

RIEKSE HOUSE
2000
727 Pleasant Street
Saugatuck
John Rotonda, *designer*

SCHIPPER/SEROS HOUSE
2004
3438 Riverside Drive | Saugatuck
Rick Haver, *designer*
Jim Lucky, *architect*

MOLENAAR/MC COMB HOUSE
1997
730 Golfview
Douglas
Barry Wood, Keystone Design Group, *architect*

all photos: Bill Werme

RAISING THE ROOF

(from upper left to lower right)

LYON HOUSE
1997
2979 Lakeshore Drive | Saugatuck Township

WINSTON HOUSE
2003
2982 Lakeshore Drive | Saugatuck Township
Thatcher & Thompson, *architects*

BATY/MATTESON HOUSE
2006
Washington Street | Douglas
Bud Baty & Max Matteson, *designers*

TEICH HOUSE
2006
860 Simonson Drive | Saugatuck
Steve Teich, *designer*

SPANGLER HOUSE
1999
18 Park Street | Saugatuck
Lake Home Builders, *designers & builders*

BELLA/DARK HOUSE
2001
751 Simonson Drive
Saugatuck

VINCENT HOUSE
1999
99 Ferry Street | Douglas
Lake Home Builders, *designers & builders*

PEANUT BUTTER, & JELLY HOUSE
2005
80 Water Street | Douglas
Amy Cook, *designer*
Looman Construction, *builder*

BAUER HOUSE
2000
560 Mill Street | Saugatuck
Steve Teich, *designer*
Lake Home Builders, *builders*

all photos: Bill Werne

166

ON BECOMING A THEME PARK? | Successful commingling of the historic with the new can breathe new vitality into neighborhoods and can contribute the visual fabric of a place. But it can also devalue the authentic and confuse the collective memory that is so important to establishing "place" and a sustainable future. The difficulty is in finding the right balance between satisfying the need for growth and renewal and that of maintaining stability and identity.

Building "historic" has been popular for a long time. For example, the "new" (present) Saugatuck Chain Ferry bears little resemblance to the original, nor does the charming "Old Mill" on Holland Street have much to do with real working lumber and tanning mills that dotted the 19th century waterfront and gave meaning to the lives and livelihoods of the villagers of that era. Despite their inauthenticy, most would agree that these picturesque modern interpretations contribute a certain "charm" to the villages and because of their modest scale and number against the backdrop of an otherwise "real" landscape, they have little serious consequence on the historic presence.

But a little goes a long way. What happens when real history is not deemed picturesque enough to grab the public eye? Is a fake waterfall on the Blue Star Highway—where old pine groves have stood for decades—an asset? Is the honesty of local vernacular building types and materials eroded when "Wisconsin stone" appears too frequently on Douglas's Center Street? How long before the "synthetic" overtakes the "real" and we can no longer "read" the stories the historic environment has long told us about who and where we are? Theme parks are picture-perfect illusions, imaginary simulations of real life—stage sets for enacting whimsical fantasies. Who lives at Disneyland? Historic environments are about people—and are embedded with layers of memory and meaning about their lives and deeds.

As we build, we might as a community ask, "Is what we are building better—or even as good as—what our forebears left us?" "Are we taking our stewardship responsibility seriously, building upon a valuable foundation to create a legacy worthy of the next generation?" "What will our buildings say about us?"

The truth of the matter is that whether we preserve the past, create "faux history," or invent the next phase of cutting edge modernism, we should expect no less of each other than to respect the scale, proportion, and character of the townscape/landscape to maintain the unique small-town attitude of this special place—mixing the old with the new in a way that honors both the oddities and the masterpieces of our past. The long-term issue is really one of sustainability. Theme park simulations are disincentives to real preservation and put authentic historic structures at risk. Real history is perhaps our best investment, rich in the elusive return called "sustainability."

AND THEN CAME CONDOMINIUMS | Saugatuck and Douglas felt the blast of condominium building beginning in 1970 with the construction of a large complex on the riverfront between Griffith and Butler Streets that closed visual access to the waterfront—the most radical alteration in the waterfront since the Big Pavilion actually opened considerable public access to the waterfront in 1909. Part of the initial demand for condominiums was from summer boat owners who desired weekend housing near dockside facilities. Public objection to such structures centered on the fact that the height of riverside condos obstructed the visual access that has been part of the community's history. Condominium building continued along the Culver-Lake Street riverside in Saugatuck into the 1980s when it was banned from the waterfront, but is still underway in Douglas—with unfortunate results on Douglas's Ferry Street where a dense 2004 complex now obscures the once splendid view on descending on Campbell Road. The City of Saugatuck blocked the half of the Ferry Street project that was to lie within its boundaries; consequently, the development arose only on the Douglas side of the boundary. Also in Douglas, an equally dense and visually demanding condominium and new retail corridor development at the Blue Star and Center Street, Douglas (the old Tara Restaurant property) was begun in 2004, encouraged when the Douglas Council sold a key parcel of village-owned property to the developer.

While on the one hand condos are viewed by some as an unwelcome invasion, on the other hand it may be argued that the urge to reside at the waterside is a century-old phenomenon and that from a practical standpoint stacking people floor-above-floor and side-by-side in condo buildings is not only cost-effective but also is preferable to cluttering the precious woods and remaining open green spaces with more dwellings, or replacing existing small cottages with over-scaled mansions. Some of the newer small-scale condo projects actually fit into the townscape quite well. The problem, of course, lies in deciding "how big" and how much "traditional" or "historic" space should be given over to development profits—and ultimately, how much obligation do local governments have to protect what is left of the historic and natural environment.

OBSTRUCTED VISTA
2004
Campbell Road & Ferry Street
Douglas

Condominiums and a wall of garages replace former pedestrian-vehicular view of Lake Kalamazoo from Campbell Road.

GATHERING PLACES: HISTORIC IDENTITY AS A PUBLIC ASSET | Three significant building rehabilitation projects—those of the Saugatuck Pump House, the Douglas Village Hall-Dutcher Lodge, and the Saugatuck Center for the Arts (SCA)—were citizen initiated and centered on returning life to buildings that had been important in the history of the community.

The Pump House stands along the Kalamazoo River at Mt. Baldhead Park. It was built in two sections (1904 and 1910 respectively) to house Saugatuck's first municipal water system and first municipal electric power generating station. As an historical message it tells the story of modernity and civic improvement, of when and how the age of dirty and dangerous oil lamps and inadequate water supply came to a close. By the 1950s the structure was no longer used and had fallen into disrepair. It was rescued in 1972 when Dr. and Mrs. William Shorey, of Chicago, contracted with the Village to restore the building in exchange for a twenty year lease for its use as a cottage. The Shoreys were one of the first of the Douglas lakeshore cottage families—and Mrs. Shorey was an artist with connections with the nearby Ox-Bow School. Expending vast energy and resources on its rehabilitation, the structure was brought back to life. In 1993 it was leased by the City to the Saugatuck-Douglas Historical Society, which undertook further restoration in adapting the building for public use as the community's first historical museum. Today the award-winning museum has a new streetside entrance, the Wilson Memorial pavilion, designed in the same Craftsman style as the Pump House itself and an enlarged walkway-garden that acts as an outdoor museum.

THE PUMP HOUSE

This was Saugatuck's first municipal water system facility. It was designed by Douglas summer resident John Alvord who was a well-known Chicago engineer (locally, he drew plans for the Shorewood cottage community). Another summer resident, Harry Bird, designed the water delivery system. Water was drawn from several large wells at the foot of Mt. Baldhead and pumped by large gasoline engines in the Pump House to a 100,000-gallon reservoir at the top of Lone Pine dune (north of Mt. Baldhead). The water then flowed by gravity back down the dune, under the river, and was delivered by pipe to street hydrants and buildings in the village. The new hydrant system greatly diminished the omnipresent fear of fire in a village built primarily of wood. An addition was made to the building in 1910, and for a time the Pump House generated electricity.

By 1970 the building had fallen into disrepair. The heavy slate roof had pushed out the walls and broken the building's interior tie rods. A portion of the west wall had fallen in and exposed the building to the elements, while the east wall footings needed replacement. Windows and door needed extensive restoration, and much of the brickwork needed attention. Subsequently, a rescue operation was carried out by the William Shorey family with local builder Bob Koberink. Shoreys had arranged with the Village in 1974 to undertake major restoration in exchange for a 10-year (then renewed) lease to use the building as a summer cottage. In 1993 the City of Saugatuck leased the building to the Saugatuck-Douglas Historical Society, which, in turn, carried out a $110,000 project to convert it for use as a museum while preserving the original character of the building.

† THE PUMP HOUSE &
HISTORICAL MUSEUM
1904-10 (restored 1974, 1993-5)
(upper left to lower right)
East Façade (photo, ca. 1910)
East Façade (photo, ca. 1960)
West Façade (photo, ca. 1975)
East Façade (photo, 1999)
735 Park Street at Mt. Baldhead
Saugatuck

Adaptive use at its best. Thanks to the efforts of the William Shorey family who rescued the badly deteriorating Pump House in the 1970s, the waterfront jewel lives on today housing the award-winning Saugatuck-Douglas Historical Museum and garden-walkway, operated by the Saugatuck-Douglas Historical Society. The Stan Wilson memorial entrance pavilion was added in 2001.

† WILSON ENTRY PAVILION
2001
735 Park Street at Mt. Baldhead
Saugatuck

Gateway to the Saugatuck-Douglas Historical Museum, riverfront garden, and outdoor learning center.

In 1990 a group of Douglas citizens formed the Douglas Historic Preservation Committee (DHPC) with the goal of rehabilitating the Village Hall-Dutcher Lodge building that had long been the principal gathering place for the people of the Douglas. The building (see chapter 1 for a discussion of its history) had been deemed structurally unsound. With widespread support from the community and from the Douglas Village Council, the Committee subsequently raised over $100,000 to restore the building. The restoration was completed in 2002, and the Village (now City) government has returned to its historic home.

A third major restoration project occurred in the Saugatuck village center. The Saugatuck Center for the Arts project is an ambitious venture to recycle the abandoned Lloyd J. Harriss (later Rich's) pie factory on Culver Street into an arts and culture venue—"creating and arts center for an arts community." Spaces inside the SCA include The Shannon O'Donnell Art Studio; a conference room/classroom; a flexible performance space; an exhibition gallery; and the centerpiece, The Bertha Krueger Reid Theatre, which houses the Mason Street Warehouse theatre company—as well as support spaces such as offices, dressing rooms, catering kitchen, etc. Outside, the steel skin from building's south wing was stripped away, exposing the signature red arches and making way for an environmentally friendly "rain garden" to filter run-off water from the building and surrounding areas and to accommodate outdoor events such as the seasonal Green Market. Like the Historical Museum project, the SCA is the beneficiary of considerable community funding and volunteer support. The SCA was designated as a 2004 Catalyst Project of the Michigan "Cool City" program, and subsequently received additional grants from Michigan Council for the Arts and Cultural Affairs and the Department of Environmental Quality. Housed in one of the most important spaces of the old agricultural economy, the "new" SCA space symbolizes the importance of the Saugatuck area's new culture-based economy of the 21st century.

† LLOYD J. HARRISS PIE COMPANY
1950s *(photo ca. 1970)*
400 Culver Street
Saugatuck

When Lloyd J. Harriss brought post-World War II mass-production food technology to Saugatuck-Douglas, he created the home of America's first frozen pies and extended the local fruit growing industry to the world. Pie factory workers processed thousands of tons of fresh fruit annually. The factory doors closed and production ceased in 1998.

† SAUGATUCK CENTER FOR THE ARTS
2005
400 Culver Street
Saugatuck

After extensive renovation, the SCA provides a new arts and culture focal point in a town that prides itself on its long, rich history in the arts. The SCA's mission is "to enhance the performing, cinematic, and visual arts; arts education; and cultural experiences available to children and adults in Saugatuck, Douglas, and the greater lakeshore community."

RAISING THE ROOF

In 2006 the Saugatuck-Douglas Historical Society initiated a project to preserve one of Michigan's historic and architectural gems, the Old School House on Center Street Douglas (chapter 2), as a new space for the teaching and enjoyment of area history.

THE OLD SCHOOLHOUSE
1866
130 Center Street | Douglas

"Public spaces" are those spaces where people meet other people, can see and be seen by them, and very often carry on discourse or physical interaction, much of which encourages a sense of community, civic culture and a connection to nature and history.[3]

ALLEGIANCE TO LOCALITY: THE BED & BREAKFAST REVOLUTION | Since the days of loggers, mill workers and sailors, Saugatuck and Douglas have been places where people lived in other people's houses. Bed & Breakfast houses provide urban and suburban guests exactly what they are seeking: "local" and "real" with modern (and sometimes luxurious) amenities. Among the earliest modern-age bed & breakfasts in the area were the revived Rosemont Inn, and the Kirby House, the former home of Sarah Kirby and later the old Douglas Hospital, opened in 1984. By 2005 there are nearly 40 other bed & breakfast houses in the Saugatuck and Douglas area, including a number of old residences brought back to life: the Douglas House, Newnham Inn, the Park House, the Ivy Inn, the Victorian Inn, Twin Oaks Inn, Marywood Manor, Sherwood Forest, Moore's Creek Inn, and the Wickwood Inn. Beechwood Manor, for example, is the restored 1874 home of former American diplomat Warner Sutton. Meanwhile, several larger hotel-resorts have been restored and even extended, including the Maplewood Hotel and the Belvedere. These thriving enterprises, many of them shown in chapter 4, demonstrate that restoring and recycling buildings is good business sense—because visitors to the area prefer staying in places which have an ambiance of authenticity and a link to the past. It's what they come for!

NEW HOMES FOR ART | As public interest in the local arts scene revived and even surpassed its heyday of the 1920s and 1930s so did the number of area art galleries—a number of which have converted old buildings as inventive venues for new art. The Vesuvius Gallery (Blue Star Highway south of Glenn) was established in a carefully restored Greek Revival farmhouse. On Saugatuck's Butler Street the James Brandess Gallery occupies the old Saugatuck Post Office, the Water Street Gallery occupies Jean Goldsmith's former house, the Santa Fe Gallery is in the old Wilson Ice Cream factory and shop, and the Saugatuck Art Gallery occupies the lower floor of the famous old Singapore Bank building. In Douglas, the River Guild houses two long-established galleries, the Joyce Petter and Button galleries, and nearby on Center Street are a handful of galleries. On the outskirts, the former Peach Belt School house on highway M-89 has been converted into an artist studio. Joining this arts explosion is a parade of sculpture called "Art Round Town"—an ever-changing exhibition that literally uses street space throughout Saugatuck as its exhibition space.

THE NEW BLUE | Despite overbuilt and pedestrian unfriendly street intersections, strip malls, a truck-stop invasion and substantial cutting of its wooded streetscape, a number of new structures along the Blue Star highway suggest that this pathway into the villages is not fully doomed to suburban-like sprawl. Indeed, the Blue Star has been the recipient of a number interesting commercial building projects, some new and some reconstruction—proving that that an earlier trend toward homogeneous strip mall, chain motels and fast food outlets may not be what the buyer (or seller) wants. The Keller Building is an excellent example of how to reuse an old gas station and the barn-like Pump House Gym and the Woodland Realty office building are interesting contemporary reflections of the area's rural roots.

GREEN SPACE, PUBLIC SPACE AND SUSTAINABILITY | The idea of compatibility between humankind and nature is a time-honored tradition in the Saugatuck and Douglas area. As we have seen earlier (Chapter 4), the

KELLER BUILDING
Reconstruction of the Johnson Gas Station
2000
105 Blue Star Highway
Douglas
John Hurst & Bonnie Keller, *design*
Zomerlie Construction, *contractor*

LIGHTHOUSE REALTY
2005
29 Blue Star Highway | Douglas
Judy Hillman, *design*
Larry Basil, *architect*

DUNES RESORT, MOTEL ADDITION
2004
333 Blue Star Highway
Douglas
John Hurst, *architect*

170

A History of the Buildings and Architecture in the Saugatuck and Douglas Area

woods, dunes, waterways and beaches that we regard as our natural landscape are very much human constructions that began in the 1890s. This story of constructing both the physical form and the distinctive soul we call "Saugatuck" is about the reversal of a half-century of clear-cutting and environmental punishment that had begun in the 1830s. The turning point appears to be just before and just after 1900 when the landscape gardener O. C. Simonds sought to reconcile the natural with the manmade world at his experimental Pier Cove nature sanctuary. And in a more simple gesture, it was in 1900 that Mr. Fred Wade began to plant Washington State beach grass and Oregon blue grass along the Lake Michigan shore to hold back dune erosion.[4] Both actions were directed to mend the damage done to the landscape by several generations of irresponsible lumbering. This was also the very time that we begin to see a remarkable succession of private and public land acquisition that allowed for greater public access to the woods, dunes, and waterfront. Former industrial plots, abandoned dunes and clear-cut forest were redesigned and replanted. The actors in this process were the village fathers and civic-minded individuals—and some entrepreneurs. The beneficiaries in the process were a new and diverse "public"—poor children from the inner city, artists and writers, boating and fishing enthusiasts, cottagers, and so on. The outcomes were, in effect, a new form of architecture of leisure layered onto great forests, harbor fronts and beaches: a grand park at the great dune "Baldhead" and other wood and dune preserves; a great dance pavilion, a number of schools for the arts, a chapel in the woods, cottages and resorts, a string of public beaches, nature preserves, an arboretum and landscape restoration movement, a range of camps and camp grounds, dune buggy rides, harbor side boardwalks and, as a bonus, a marvelous way to navigate nature: a chain ferry. Views of nature were important and the area developed a reputation for fine private gardens. There was much planting of trees. Even the bridge connecting the villages became a green space. Public access to nature was a form of civic virtue.

Most of this access was "public" space of some sort. It was a remarkable turnaround that conserved hundreds of acres of what we would now call "developable land" and makes up an important connective tissue or "common ground" that came to define community life. Some of this was fully public in that it was initiated by local government for the people. It was without a master plan but reflected a shared vision and a respect for the environment. And much of it had to do with the cultural demands of those armies of urban folks who piled into the backward little villages because they were ideal places to play, pray and map out new lives connected to nature. A camp here, an art school and a place for cottages and an arboretum there. Spectacular bathing beaches and hiking trails. In a sense, the Saugatuck area became an urban outpost. With regard to the "sustainability factor"[5] our turn of the century Saugatuck ancestors gave current society the greatest asset imaginable: a much celebrated natural environment.

WOODLAND REALTY BUILDING
New Construction
2004
2987 Blue Star Highway
Douglas
Charles Kenneth Carlson, *architect*

PUMP HOUSE GYM
New Construction
2003
Blue Star Highway
Saugatuck Township
Darienzo, D'Arienzo and Eickhoff, *designers*
Looman Construction, *builder*

CAPTAIN'S QUARTERS MOTEL
Reconstruction
2004-6
3242 Blue Star Highway
Saugatuck Township

171

S. S. KEEWATIN & RED DOCK AREA
Lake Kalamazoo
Blue Star Highway looking west to Mt. Baldhead

An important public sightline, public space, and an icon. The S. S. Keewatin passenger ship of the Canadian Pacific Railway line was built in Glasgow's Goven shipyard in 1886 and was given a berth in the Douglas harbor in 1967 by R. J. Peterson. It is presently a ship museum. The compound includes a lighthouse replica and a summertime outdoor café and bar—and terrific water views. The site is the area of the Red Dock—where much of the fruit from local orchards was loaded and shipped across the Great Lakes.

A History of the Buildings and Architecture in the Saugatuck and Douglas Area

RECONSTRUCTING THE NATURAL ENVIRONMENT

TWO LAKES & A RIVER

The natural history of the Saugatuck area centers on a century long legacy of maintaining and expanding public access to the natural landscape. Here we understand the natural environment as something that is actually shaped by the human hand—allowing for preservation as well as public access to vast stretches of beach, dunes, wooded trails and waterfront vistas. Within this area are sites which hold historical and archeological interest, such as the old lumber town of "lost" Singapore, the fishing village of Fishtown, old shipwrecks sites—as well as man-made woodland and dune trails.

(from upper left to lower right)

1. Early "Public" Beach *(now Denison beach) (1930s)*
2. Oval Beach, Lake Michigan *(est. 1936)*
3. Big Pavilion, Lake Kalamazoo *(constr. 1909)*
4. New Harbor Cut *(1906)*
5. Michigan's Longest Boardwalk, Saugatuck *(1950s)*
6. Historical Museum, Mt. Baldhead Park, 1993
7. The Stairs, Mt. Baldhead Park *(1880s)*
8. Douglas Beach House, Lake Michigan *(1908)*
9. Mt. Baldhead Park with observation tower *(est. 1883)*
10. Presbyterian Camps, Lake Michigan *(est. 1896)*
11. Coghlin Park *(est. 2002)*

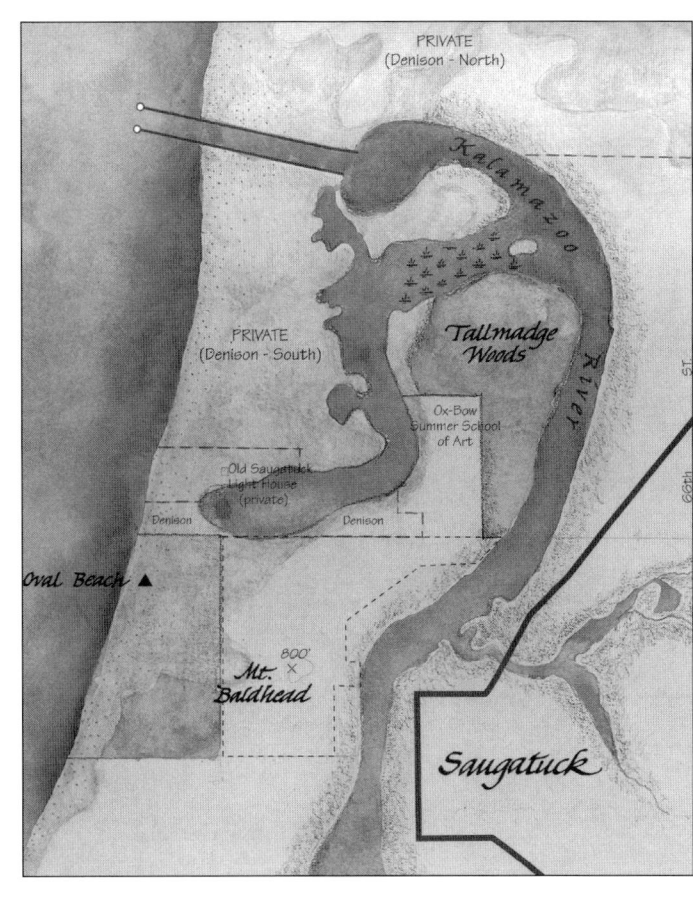

PRESERVING PUBLIC ACCESS

THE DENISON BEACH–DUNES PROJECT

The south Denison beach has been open to public use for nearly a century—with access only by way of Oval Beach or by boat. Under the leadership of the Save Our Shoreline (S.O.S.) citizen's action group, the City of Saugatuck has succeeded in the first step of negotiations to save this important property from development and guarantee public access to future generations. The S.O.S. partnership includes The Conservation Fund, The Nature Conservancy and the Land Conservancy of West Michigan. The $24 million campaign began in 1996 with the financial support from a large individual pledge, a public campaign, and a grant from the Michigan Natural Resources Fund. The north Denison beach property (north of the Kalamazoo River channel entrance to the Saugatuck-Douglas harbor) remains vulnerable to development.

THE BLUE STAR HIGHWAY AS A VISUAL ASSET | From the north I-196 Interstate entrance to M-89, the Blue Star Highway is a pathway to information and a thousand destinations. It is also a visual pathway that has offered a number of pleasant natural vistas—stretches of white pine forest, a blueberry farm here and there, as well as commercial, bridge and water scenes. The Keewatin entrance to Saugatuck and Douglas demonstrates the value (and potential) of preserving the Blue Star as a visual entrance to the villages. Encouraging interesting (and sometimes quirky) new and old commercial architecture—along with tree preservation—is a way to counteract the tree destruction and strip mall syndrome that has taken over much of the Blue Star's northern stretch. Continued attention to tree protection and various forms of basic design guidelines as set forth in 2006 by the Saugatuck Township may result in preservation of visual spaces and lines of sight that complement the area's natural landscape and as well as attention to the preservation of one of the icons of our Great Lakes history—the steamship S.S. Keewatin. Only the future will tell.

THE END OF GREEN? | Now in the early 21st century we see a persistent eating away at these big pieces of nature. Some of this has been gradual nibbling; driven by our reluctance to live without certain urban-like amenities and an insistence that we must live with bigger houses, bigger automobiles and more widgets and gadgets. But most of the damage has come from big and small "development" bites at the hands of property developers, combined with a surge in demand on the part of many Americans to acquire al little piece of heaven on earth. The addition of hundreds of new houses on the periphery of the villages has staggering long-term infrastructure implications: wider streets, more traffic controls, more pressure for public sanitation and road repair, more classrooms and, of course, a greater need for increased city management.

In a sense, some of what we witness is a return to the days of the lumber barons who stayed around for a short time and then took their profits and moved on. Whereas some damage from the lumber years could be corrected by reforestation and ending water pollution, much of today's damage is arguably more serious. A biologically diverse ecosystem may be at its end.

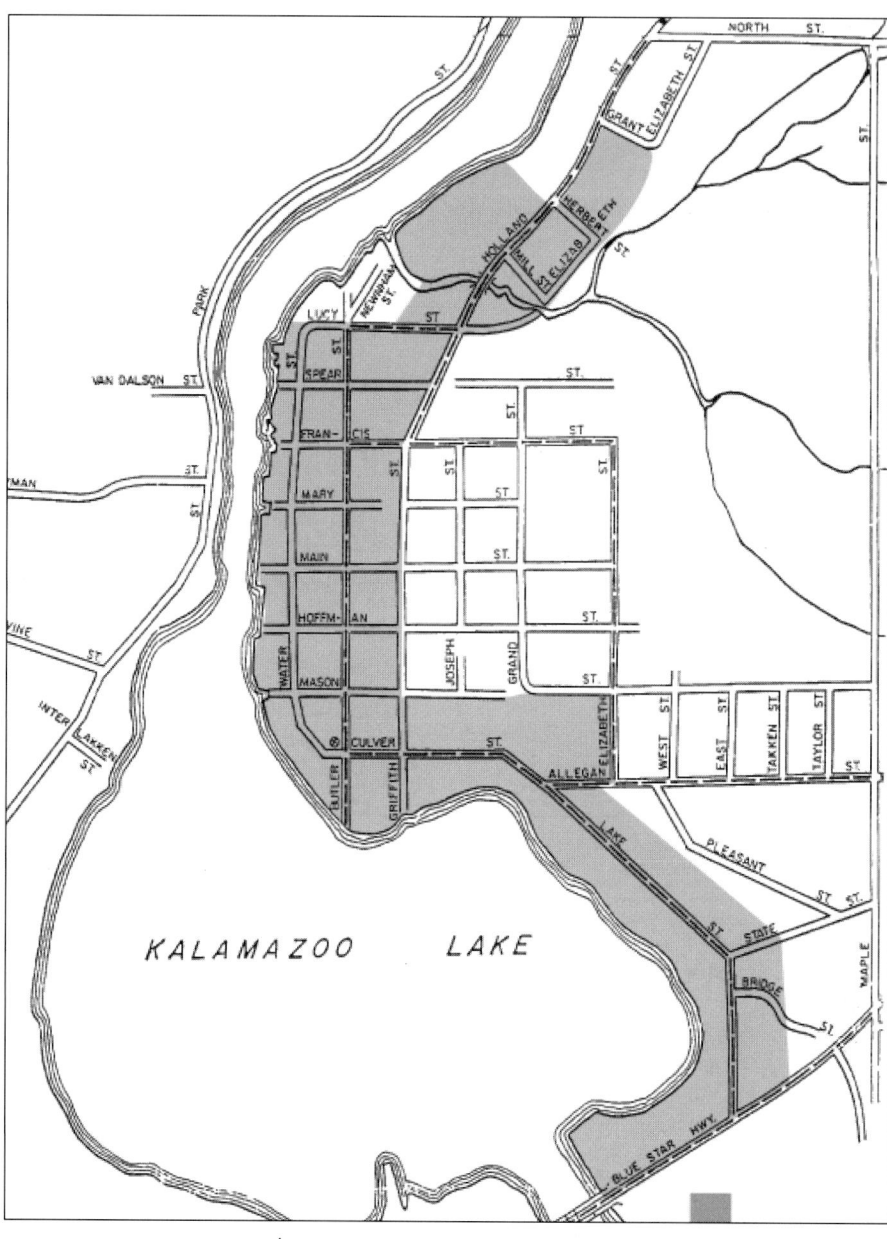

HISTORIC DISTRICT
City of Saugatuck

"Happy is such a town as Saugatuck, which is equipped with all modern amusements and yet has preserved many historical places of its past to give the summer guests"

—MAY FRANCIS HEATH
Saugatuck, June 14, 1936

HISTORIC DISTRICTS? | The commercial centers of the "villagescape" –both Douglas and Saugatuck—have been highly contested spaces in the battles over changes to the historic fabric. In Saugatuck the appointed referee in these battles is the Historic District Commission—a group of citizens appointed by the City Council to uphold (and interpret) certain building and design standards mandated by city ordinance. The Commission has jurisdiction over such issues as scale, size, overall appropriateness of design and the like and has an advisory responsibility as well. The picture of the Historic District Commission working in collaboration with property owners in the district to preserve Saugatuck's sense of place has often been overshadowed by a public perception that the commissioners are nit-pickers who do nothing but worry about paint color. Some of this criticism comes from ill-informed individuals who see "property rights" as something that does not extend to the property values of the person next door—or to the long-term economic and cultural sustainability of the community. The fact of the matter is that on balance the Historic District Commission can point to a rather striking record of achievement—halting some construction projects that would have disfigured Saugatuck's traditional village façade and providing historical context and design advice and encouragement.

SHORT-TERM PROFIT OR LONG-TERM SUSTAINABILITY? | The picture is clear. Saugatuck has always invested in history because it is good business. The traditional rural-village townscape and streetscape has value—real measurable economic value. As the thing that draws people here, it is perhaps its greatest capital asset. The remodeling and re-styling of the villages in the 1920s (see Chapter 5) is a testimony to this fact. The renovation and rehabilitation projects sketched out above are examples of a recent wave of private and citizen accomplishments. The benefits are community-wide.

Since about 2000, however, the overall pull is in the opposite direction. Large and small scale suburban-like housing and strip-mall retailing developments with all their related infrastructure (water, health and emergency services, municipal administration, streets, fire protection, schools) demands. How do we make decisions about building scale, size, style, and function that mirror and complement the traditional townscape—particularly in an age in which vast amounts of development dollars are flooding in from the outside? How does the community encourage suitable and sensitive development that welcomes growth without destroying the existing social-aesthetic fabric?

While "zoning" and "planning" by government bodies are some of the best ways to do this, Saugatuck and Douglas area zoning and planning mechanisms are generally weak and often work in favor of new development at the expense of existing property owners and long-term sustainability. Environmental and villagescape proposals must conform to what are, for the most part, fairly charitable local zoning and planning requirements. The "Historic District" designation in the village center area (the "flats") of the City of Saugatuck is an exception. Equally important, the Tri-Community Plan (of 2005) for Douglas, Saugatuck and Saugatuck Township, requires each governmental unit to attend to the preservation of the area's historic character and its natural setting (with particular emphasis on preservation of green space, area farmland and keeping visual access to area waterfronts).[6] The Tri-Community Plan also asks for further identification of historic properties and implementation of historic preservation ordinances.

The history of historic preservation in America is a huge success story—one that demonstrates that the most favorable cultural and economic results are gained when property owners, architects/builders, local historic commissions, city councils and cultural and civic organizations work together to build a community plan and then work together toward mutually acceptable outcomes. The people of Michigan are blessed with a number of "smart growth" networks and a state government which cares about its amazing history.[7] What is missing in the Saugatuck area story is a comprehensive historic resources survey[8] which would center on documentation of human-built and natural structures. This is one of the building blocks of a good community "sense of place." Since 1998 the Saugatuck-Douglas Historical Society has gone partway toward this goal by beginning a community-wide building survey, with the goal of documenting every building in the Saugatuck area villages. This book is one of the outcomes of this on-going survey.

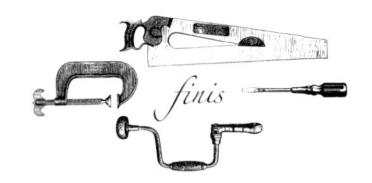

finis

ENDNOTES

CHAPTER ONE

1 William Cronon, *Nature's Metropolis: Chicago and the Great West* (1999).

2 Cited in SDHS Building Survey File: 888 Holland Street, Park House, p. 29, "Mr. and Mrs. Horace D. Moore."

3 *Allegan Journal,* August 2, 1858.

4 May Heath, *Early Memories of Saugatuck*, p.146.

CHAPTER TWO

1 Brick was an uncommon building material for most of the first century of Saugatuck area building — despite the existence of several local brick works, one along Wiley Road and another near the present junction of Old Allegan Road and the Blue Star Highway. Brick making depended on access to clay pits, which appear to have been in short supply. In contrast, nearby Holland – Zeeland area saw the development of a major brickmaking industry. See Michael J. Douma, *Veneklasen Brick* (2005).

2 *The Commercial Record,* July 16, 1870; *Atlas of Allegan County Michigan* (C.O. Titus, 1873); Gerber tannery is noted in *The Commercial Record,* November 21, 1868.

3 *Allegan Journal,* January 29, 1866.

4 Saugatuck's earliest schools were, first, the Ward School, located on the trail between Singapore and Saugatuck —and eventually superceded by the Pine Grove School in the village, on Mary Street. Ward School was eventually moved to Saugatuck in 1915 to be used for additional classroom space adjacent to the new school on the hill. When it was destroyed by fire in 1950 it was being used for high school shop and home economics classes.

5 *Allegan Journal,* January 29, 1866.

6 The union school system was formed by the State of Michigan in 1847 whereby it was intended that the schools be places to train teachers for the common one-room schools. One of the first was in Grand Rapids in 1848.

7 *The Commercial Record,* November 30, 1877, September 6, 1878.

8 The comment on the Congregational Church is found in *The Allegan Journal,* August 8, 1866; For the "Dutch" Reformed Church (another reference names it the German Reformed Church —see Titus's *Atlas of Allegan County Michigan,* 1873); see *The Commercial Record,* August 16, 1868.]

9 *Allegan Journal,* February 20, 1886. It is believed that one of the village's founding families, the Morrisons, were Universalists.

10 A considerable amount of male drinking was connected to work. Saugatuck shipbuilders, for example, celebrated the completion of certain parts of the ship with set-ups at a local saloon. Commercial Record. February 25, 1887.

11 Henry H. Hutchins, *Recollections of the Pioneers of Western Allegan County.* (1919-25, reprinted, 1977)

12 *The Commercial Record,* December 5, 1884.

13 Cited in *Seventieth Anniversary of First Congregational Church* (booklet, 1930).

14 *The Commercial Record,* January 23, 1880.

15 The only account of this I have see is a letter by Wm. A. Taylor which is included in *Seventieth Anniversary of First Congregational Church* (1930) p.7.

16 As cited in James Schmiechen, "The Victorians, the Historians, and the Idea of Modernism in *The American Historical Review,* April, 1988, p. 312.

17 Gwendolyn Wright, *Moralism and the Modern Home: Domestic Architecture and Cultural Conflict in Chicago* (1980) p. 23.

18 George E. Dunn worked in the shipbuilding trade and, as well, had a small woodworking factory on the village square where he could furnish his clients with doors, windows, blinds, scroll work, moldings, and so on. He was a member of the Congregational Church choir and a member of I. O. G. I. branch n. 835.

19 *The Commercial Record,* February 18, 1878.

20 *The Commercial Record,* December 24, 1871; The Lakeshore Commercial, January 28, 1871.

21 Orson Fowler, *The Octagon House: A Home For All* (1853, reprint, 1973) p.65

CHAPTER THREE

1 William A. Taylor, letter written in 1930 and included in "The Seventieth Anniversary of the First Congregational Church of Saugatuck, Michigan," 1930, p.7.

2 *The Commercial Record,* September 9, 1887; for figures on local fruit production, see Henry S. Clubb, *The Saugatuck and Ganges Fruit Region, for Lake Shore Agricultural and Pomological Society* (1875; reprinted 1991, Pavilion Press); *The Commercial Record,* February 5, 1886. This was 170,311 baskets of peaches; 15,102 barrels of apples, and 9,905 crates of berries.

3 *The Commercial Record,* October 1, 1886.

4 *The Commercial Record,* December 16, 1887.

5 *The Commercial Record,* August 20, 1970.

6 H. L. House and H. E. Graham, Contract, Dec'd. for Record, November 8, 1867, 3 o'clock P.M., Ralph Pratt, Registrar. Saugatuck-Douglas Historical Society Archives.

7 "An Old Apple Tree," handwritten essay by May Francis Heath, Saugatuck-Douglas Historical Society archives. N.d. She notes that it was one of seven seedlings brought at the same time. Seymour's farm is also known as Lake Ridge Farm. It is told that the first peach orchard came to Allegan County with the discarded peach seeds picked up in front a hotel in Buffalo N.Y. by a little girl traveling west with her family in 1833. The girl was the daughter of Silas Durham. *Record Book of the Pioneers of Allegan County.* "Reminiscences of the Early Settlement" (1878) p.17.

8 Gwendlyn Wright, *Building the Dream: A Social History of Housing in America* (1981), p. 109.

CHAPTER FOUR

1 Schribner's Magazine, as cited in Ronald Pisano, *Idle Houses. Americans At Leisure,* 1865-1914. 1988. pp. 86-91.

2 Why this happened is an important question and is perhaps related somewhat to the construction of a new swing-bridge which, in effect, blocked the possibilities of its continuing as a riverside economy.

3 Daniel Burnham and E. Bennett, *Plan of Chicago.* 1909. pp. 43-44.

4 Excerpts from "American Plan" by Cella Gamble House" in Saugatuck-Douglas Historical Society Newsletter [insert], p. 41. The Gambles came to Saugatuck in 1901, building a cottage of their own in 1909.

5 Plan of Chicago, p. 50. For a discussion of this moral reinterpretation of domestic building and architecture see Gwendolyn Wright, *Moralism and the Modern Home,* p. 124.

6 For example, "Free Reading Rooms" were established in Saugatuck along with classes in music, bookkeeping, shorthand, and typewriting—under the leadership of Professor Latta and a group of local women. See *Allegan Journal,* 11-23-1900; 1-11-1901; 3-22-1901;4-12-1901.

7 *The Commercial Record,* August 24, 1900.

8 *The Commercial Record,* 8-1-1927

9 *The Commercial Record,* September 1, 1899; December 22, 1899; the Maplewood example is found in the vacation promotion brochure sometime between 1923 and the mid 1930s titled "Saugatuck. Michigan's Greatest Summer Resort," no date. SDHS archives.

10 *The Commercial Record,* March 20, 1903. It appears to have adopted the name "Maplewood" in 1898.

11 It has been argued that this Anti-Semitism was in reality due to local businessmen reacting to a perceived Jewish domination of the nearby South Haven resort scene. This author has not been able to verify this claim.

12 *The Commercial Record,* August 20, 1909; See Kit Lane, *Saugatuck's Big Pavilion* (1977) and taped interviews, Saugatuck-Douglas Historical Society Oral Interview Project, m.s., July 1994.

13 For a discussion of George W. Maher in the Saugatuck area, see Kit Lane, *The Popcorn Millionaire and Other Tales of Saugatuck,* 1991.

14 Conversations with Virginia Lane, September 1998; see also, *The Commercial Record,* August 24, 1900. Tent Cottages were very much in vogue in the 1890s–1910s —being part of an American "back-to-nature" craze. Most tents had wood platform floors like this one appears to have had, and some had conventional doors, carpets, and ordinary furniture.

15 Excerpts from Cella Gamble House, "American Plan," in Saugatuck-Douglas Historical Society Newsletter, Local History Insert, p. 41.

16 The Commercial Record, February 12, 1896.

17 Frederick Gutheim, ed., *Frank Lloyd Wright On Architecture* (1941), p. 24.

18 Gustav Stickley, *Craftsman Homes,* "Introduction to the Dover Edition," by Alan Weissman, (Dover Reprint, 1988). p. vi.]

19 The story of this cottage is taken from "The Gage Cottage," *Saugatuck-Douglas Historical Society Newsletter* (Insert), p. 71.

20 Virginia and Lee McAlester, *A Field Guide to American Houses* (1984), p.440.

21 Nancy Budd, *Lake Shore Chapel* (1972), p. 27.

22 Gustav Stickley, *Craftsman Homes. Architecture and Furnishings of the American Arts and Crafts Movement.* (1908), p.185.

23 Gustav Stickley, *Craftsman Homes,* "Briarwood: A Hillside Home Among the Trees," (Dover Reprint, 1988) p.134.

24 *The Commercial Record,* March 28, 1924.

CHAPTER FIVE

1 Peter Schmitt, *Back To Nature: The Arcadian Myth In Urban America* (1969/1990) pp. 183-85

2 *The Commercial Record,* July 19, 1930.

3 *The Commercial Record,* March 28, 1918.

4 These are the words of Dr. W. B. House, president of the Saugatuck Chamber of Commerce in 1924; *The Commercial Record,* October 23, 1924, and reprinted in *Saugatuck-Douglas Historical Society Newsletter* (Insert), p. 47. An earlier letter in *The Commercial Record* made reference to the "troubles" of the summer of 1923 brought on by "tough elements from Chicago"; *The Commercial Record,* February 15, 1924; the "Saugatuck The Beautiful" reference is from a Fruit Growers State Bank "Saugatuck, The Beautiful" promotional calendar with a Herman C. Simonson photo, ca. 1925. The reference to Maher's proposals with regard to village planning is found in "George W. Maher, Prairie on the Lakeshore," in Kit Lane, The Popcorn Millionaire and Other Tales of Saugatuck (1991).

5 Early Colonial Revival tended to be picked up by the east-coast elites. Its principal early promoters were Charles F. McKim, Wm. R. Mead, and Stanford White, and interior designer Candace Wheeler. For Candace Wheeler see, Jean Dunbar, "One House at a Time," *Preservation,* September/October, 1998.

6 Many architectural historians have viewed the period between the two wars as twenty years of "missed opportunities" —meaning that instead of looking to the building styles of the past we should have been moving with modernism into the future. See, for example, John Burchard and Albert Bush-Brown, *The Architecture of America, A Social and Cultural History* (1966) Part IV.a

7 *The Milwaukee Journal,* July 28, 1940, Section 7, p. 5 (Saugatuck-Douglas Historical Society Archives, Fursman File).

8 Marker, National Register of Historic Places, 1985.

9 Kit Lane, *Painting the Town. A History of Art in Saugatuck and Douglas* (Saugatuck-Douglas Historical Society, 1997) p. 33.

10 One of Maher's most noted houses, "Pleasant Home" at 217 S. Home Avenue, Oak Park, Chicago, is open to the public. Some of the furniture designed by Maher is included in the design collection of the Art Institute of Chicago. For a discussion of Maher in Saugatuck, see "George W. Maher, Prairie on the Lakeshore," in Kit Lane, *The Popcorn Millionaire and Other Tales of Saugatuck* (1991).

11 "Furnishing the Small House," *Chicago Sunday Tribune,* [n. d. Typed manuscript, Florence Hunn Collection].

CHAPTER SIX

1 This was one of the responses to a survey of community life in "Middletown" (Muncie, Indiana) in the 1920s by the sociologists Robert and Helen Lynd. Cited in James A. Henretta, Et. Al., *American History* (second edition, 1993), p. 736.

2 Ibid, p. 737.

3 Ibid, p. 737.

4 See Daniel Vieyra, *Fill 'Er Up": An Architectural History of America's Gas Stations* (1979). For a brief history of Gus Reiser and his station see Kit Lane, ed., *Heroes, Rogues, and Just Plain Folks. A History of the Saugatuck Area* (1998), p. 55-56.

5 The Harding Hotel on Park Street advertised a weekend package for party-seekers: a room, two meals, and round-trip bus transportation from Chicago. Radios blared and the place was in "an almost constant uproar." "Harding's Hotel," by Helen Gage Desoto, *SDHS Newsletter,* n.d., 137. For more on this see James Schmiechen and Jack Sheridan, *Off the Record A Pictorial History of Saugatuck in the '40s and '50s* (2002) pp. 22-23.

6 See "Dear Vacationer" map and letter, Saugatuck Chamber of Commerce, ca. 1952. Saugatuck-Douglas Historical Society Archives.

7 The second Harding Hotel, known as the "Harbor Club," was even shorter lived. It was a gigantic Quonset-hut-like structure at Ferry and Center Streets, built in 1948 with a large bar and was fully paneled in knotty pine. It was never fully opened because of failure to obtain a liquor license, partly because of objections from nearby cottagers.

8 The history of the ferry is told in Kit Lane, "The Dustless Road to Happyland," in *Chicago-Saugatuck Passenger Boats,* 1859-1929 (1995).

9 Kit Lane, ed., *Allegan County Historical Atlas and Gazetteer* (1998) p. 7. The greatest part of this growth was in Douglas, from a population of 447 in 1950 to 813 in 1970.

10 As one historian generalized for the nation as a whole, "a massive, uniform, banal and horribly ugly highway culture…" John Burchard and Albert Bush-Brown, *The Architecture of America: A Social and Cultural History* (1961, 1966) p. 254.

CHAPTER SEVEN

1 Twin "Saugatuck" signs originally hung by pole and cable over the street, one on Lake Street near the Blue Star entrance to the village and the other at the north entrance at Holland & Washington Streets. The signs were of porcelain on metal with neon and colored incandescent lights; they were most likely designed and financed as a WPA project. The sign that remains is the one that originally hung at the north entrance. It was rescued by Henry Van Singel minutes before it was to be hauled away to a junk metal yard. The Johnson Sign Company of North Muskegon handled the reconstruction, and the sign was installed at the corner of Lake Street & Blue Star Highway in 1994.

2 It held off for many years in allowing further business development in the "shopping plaza" area at Center and the Blue Star and for some years after World War II there was no place in Saugatuck to purchase groceries.

3 I am indebted in this chapter to the wealth of analytical guidance found in Gerald A. Danzer, Public Places. Exploring Their History. 1987

4 *Allegan County Journal,* May 3, 1901: "Fred Wade received this week from Washington two bags of seed, one common beach grass, and the other blue grass from Oregon. The seed will be planted at different places near the harbor and a close record kept of its growth." In this same spirit Saugatuck citizens planted willow trees along the causeway bridge connecting Saugatuck and Douglas in the 1870s, and later used a 1930s WPA program to plant the trees on the Saugatuck hill and along the Oval Beach Road, and more recently, a community effort was undertaken to plant trees along the Douglas portion of the Blue Star highway, and the Saugatuck Township Board has acted to slow the destruction of the Townships green-corridors.

5 I use as a definition of "sustainable" development that of Stephen Wheeler: development that improves the long-term health of human and ecological systems. As cited in R. LeGates and F. Stout, *The City Reader* (2nd ed. 2000) p.434.

6 Specifically, the Tri-Community Plan sets a goal "to preserve and maintain sites and structures that serve as significant visible reminders of the community's social and architectural history and that contribute to the economic and cultural development of the community." "Tri-Community Comprehensive Plan" [of Saugatuck, Douglas, and the Saugatuck Township], 2005.

7 See, for example, Michigan Land Use Institute pamphlet, "A Civic Gift. Making Smart Growth a Reality in Michigan," October, 2003, and the Michigan Historic Preservation Network report, "Investing in Michigan's Future: the Economic Benefits of Historic Preservation," 2005. The Michigan Department of History, Arts and Libraries has taken a number of innovative approaches to the preservation and promotion of the state's history and historic landscape. See www.michiganhistory.org

8 "Historic resources are districts, buildings, sites, structures or objects that exemplify a period of history. Their historical value may be achieved either through association with significant historical events; through association with the lives of persons significant in our past; by embodying a particular style, type or method of construction; by possessing high artistic values; or by yielding, or being likely to yield, information important to history or prehistory. Historic resources are typically fifty years of age or older, but resources of lesser age may qualify if they have extraordinary significance." [cited in "Michigan's Historic Resources Survey Program" release, October 21, 2004, www.michigan.gov]

IMAGE CREDITS

All credits read clockwise from bottom left.

All images in this book are protected by copyright and may not be reproduced in any form or by any means without express permission (in writing) from the Saugatuck-Douglas Historical Society.

KEY TO ABBREVIATIONS:

SDHS Archive | *Saugatuck-Douglas Historical Society Archive (sdhistory.com)*

Stull | *photographer Vicky Stull (vickystull@earthlink.net)*

and

Werme | *photographer Bill Werme (Bill@Werme.com).*

COVER | The Big Pavilion, SDHS Archive.

CHAPTER ONE | Page x.: SDHS Archive. Page 1: Harpers Weekly, October 20, p. 188. Page 2: Map, letter by Wm. Butler to his father, April 1834, SDHS Archive; map, Pier Cove, Atlas of Allegan County, C. O. Titus, 1873, p. 79. Page 3: Author's drawing; mill photo, SDHS Archive; Morrison photo, SDHS Archive; log houses, Henry Hudson Hutchins, Western Allegan County Pioneer Days (reprint, 1997). Page 4: map, "Mouth of Kalamazoo River, Michigan" Map G. N. No. 51, U.S. Top. Engineers, 1857; photo, SDHS Archive; Page 5: floor plan, Richard Smith, Port Washington [WI] Historical Society; handwritten letter, SDHS Archive; photos, Deam family collection. Page 6: SDHS Archive; SDHS Archive. Page7: SDHS Archive; Stull. Page 8: Stull. Page 9: Stull. Page 10: Werme; Page 11: SDHS Archive; Werme; Werme; Werme; drawing by Carolyn R. Stich; Page 12: SDHS Archive; Werme. Page 13: drawing, Margaret McDermott. Page 14: photo, Betty Mulder; SDHS Archive; map, Atlas of Allegan County, C. O. Titus, 1873, p. 77. Page 15: Drawing, Sylvia Randolph; SDHS Archive.

CHAPTER TWO | Page 16: SDHS Archive. Page 17: SDHS Archive; SDHS Archive. Page 18: Werme. Page 19: Johnson Fox; SDHS Archive; SDHS Archive; Werme. Page 20: Stull. Page 21: Werme; SDHS Archive. Page 22: SDHS Archive; SDHS Archive; courtesy of Don dan Reken. Page 23: SDHS Archive; SDHS Archive/Simmons Collection; SDHS Archive/Simmons Collection; SDHS Archive; SDHS Archive. Page 24: Stull. Page 25: Stull; Andrew Jackson Downing, Cottage Residences (1873); same. Page 26: Stull; SDHS Archive. Page 28: Werme; Werme; Werme; Jack Sheridan; SDHS Archive; SDHS Archive. Page 29: SDHS Archive; Werme. Page 30: Stull. Page 31: Stull; Stull; Werme; SDHS Archive; SDHS Archive. Page 32: Stull; drawing by Carolyn R. Stich. Page 33: Werme; Werme. Page 34: Stull; Stull. Page 35: Werme. Page 36: Mulliner Box and Planing Co. Catalogue [for 1893], Chicago, p.122; SDHS Archive. Page 37: SDHS Archive; SDHS Archive; SDHS Archive; SDHS Archive; Werme; drawing by Bill Kemperman. Page 38: SDHS Archive; SDHS Archive. Page 39: Page 40: SDHS Archive, Simmons Collection; SDHS Archive, Simmons Collection. Page 41: SDHS Archive. Simmons Collection.

CHAPTER THREE | Page 42: Stull. Page 43: SDHS Archive. Page 44: Stull. Page 45: Stull. Page 46: SDHS Archive; Werme. Page 47: Map, author; SDHS Archive. Page 48: Werme. Page 49: Werme. Page 50: SDHS Archive; SDHS Archive. Page 51: SDHS Archive; SDHS Archive. Page 52: Werme. Page 53: Werme; Werme; Werme; SDHS Archive. Page 54: Werme; Werme; Werme; Werme. Page 55: Werme. Page 56: SDHS Archive; SDHS Archive. Page 57: SDHS Archive; Werme. Page 58: drawing by Carolyn R. Stich; drawing by Carolyn R. Stich; SDHS Archive; SDHS Archive. Page 59: SDHS Archive; Carolyn R. Stich; author drawing. Page 60: SDHS Archive; SDHS Archive. Page 61: Stull. Page 62: SDHS Archive; SDHS Archive. Page 63: SDHS Archive; SDHS Archive; Werme; Stull; SDHS Archive.

CHAPTER FOUR / Page 64: SDHS Archive; Werme; SDHS Archive; SDHS Archive; SDHS Archive. Page 65: SDHS Archive. Page 66: SDHS Archive; SDHS Archive. Page 67: SDHS Archive; Stull. Page 68: SDHS Archive; SDHS Archive; Werme; SDHS Archive; SDHS Archive; SDHS Archive SDHS Archive; SDHS Archive. Page 69: SDHS Archive; drawing, author. Page 70: SDHS Archive; SDHS Archive; Peterson Collection; SDHS Archive; SDHS Archive. Page 71: SDHS Archive; SDHS Archive. Page 72: Stull. Page 73: SDHS Archive; drawing, author. Page 74: SDHS Archive; SDHS Archive; SDHS Archive; SDHS Archive. Page 75: SDHS Archive. Page 76: SDHS Archive. Page 77: SDHS Archive, Simmons Collection. Page 78: SDHS Archive; SDHS Archive; drawing by author. Page 79: SDHS Archive. Page 80: SDHS Archive. Page 81: Stull. Page 82: Stull. Page 83: SDHS Archive; Dick Haight; Dick Haight. Page 84: Werme. Page 85: Werme. Page 86: Werme; watercolor by Judy Anthrop; photo by author. Page 87: Werme. Page 88: Werme; Werme; Ann Renaldi; Ken Carls; Werme; Werme; SDHS Archive. Page 89: SDHS Archive; SDHS Archive; SDHS Archive; SDHS Archive; Werme. Page 90: Werme. Page 91: drawing by George Clark; SDHS Archive; SDHS Archive. Page 92: Werme. Page 93: Simonds Family Collection; Jack Sheridan. Page 94: SDHS Archive. Page 95: Katherine Wilcox; Carolyn R. Stich. Page 96: Stull. Page 97: SDHS Archive; SDHS Archive. Page 98: Shay Collection; Shay Collection. Page 99: Werme. Page 100: Gerry Millar; SDHS Archive; Shay Collection. Page 101: Werme. Page 102: Werme. 103: Werme; SDHS Archive. Page 104: Werme; SDHS Archive; Werme. Page 105: Werme. Page 106: Werme. Page 107: SDHS Archive. Page 108: SDHS Archive; SDHS Archive.

CHAPTER FIVE | Page 110: SHHS Archive; SDHS Archive. Page 111: SDHS Archive, Simmons Collection; SDHS Archive, Simmons Collection. Page 112: Werme. Page 113: entire page courtesy of Felt Estate Restoration Project; Page 114: SDHS Archive; Peterson Collection. Page 115: Werme. Page 116: Werme; SDHS Archive. Page 117: Werme. Page 118: Stull. Page 119: SDHS Archive; drawing, Carolyn R. Stich. Page 120: Stull; Stull. Page 121: Stull; drawing, Margaret McDermott; Sull. Page 122: Stull. Page 123: drawings, Ken Carls; portrait, Eddy family. Page 124: Werme; Werme; Stull; Stull. Page 125: Stull. Page 126: Stull. Page 127: SDHS Archive; SDHS Archive; SDHS Archive. Page 128: Sears, Roebuck, and Company, Catalogue, 1926. Page 129: Stull; SDHS Archive. Page 130: Drawing "Fish Town," from May Heath, Early Memories of Saugatuck, 1830-1930 (1953) p. 73. Page 131: SDHS Archive, Hunn Collection.

CHAPTER SIX | Page 132: SDHS Archive, Simmons Collection. Page 133: Ken Carls. Page 134: SDHS Archive; SDHS Archive; SDHS Archive. Page 135: SDHS Archive; SDHS Archive; SDHS Archive; SDHS Archive; SDHS Archive; SDHS Archive; SDHS Archive. Page 136: Kit Lane Collection. Page 137: SDHS Archive, Simmons Collection; SDHS Archive. Page 138: Werme. Page 139: SDHS Archive; SDHS Archive; SDHS Archive; Werme. Page 140: SDHS Archive; SDHS Archive; SDHS Archive; Stan Kaftan Collection. Page 141: SDHS Archive; SDHS Archive; SDHS Archive; SDHS Archive .Page 143: Ted Kimball; Stull. Page 144: SDHS Archive; SDHS Archive. Page 145: all four, SDHS Archive, Simmons Collection. Page 146: SDHS Archive; SDHS Archive. Page 147: Gerry Millar Collection; SDHS Archive, Simmons Collection; SDHS Archive; Werme.

CHAPTER SEVEN / Page 148: SDHS Archive; Page 149: Werme; Page 150: SDHS Archive; SDHS Arcive. Page 151: SDHS Arcive; Ken Carls; Jim Schmiechen; Jim Gowran. Page 152: Werme. Page 153: Werme ; Werme; Werme Werme; Werme. Page 154: Werme . Page 155: Werme. Page 157: Werme; Werme; Werme; Werme; Werme; Werme; Werme; Werme. Page 158: Werme; Dawn Stafford. Page 159: Werme; Werme; Werme; Werme; Werme; Werme; Werme; Werme. Page 160: Werme; Stull; Stull. Page 161: SDHS Archive; Stull; Stull; Stull. Page 162: Werme; Stull; SDHS Archvie. Page 163: drawing, Ken Carls; Werme; drawing, Duane Brown. Page 164: Werme; Werme. Page 165: SDHS Archive; Werme; Werme; Werme; Werme; Werme. Page 166: Werme; Werme; Stull; Werme; Werme; Werme; Werme; Werme; Werme. Page 167: Werme. Page 168: SDHS Archive; SDHS Archive; SDHS Archive; Werme. Page 169: SCA; Ken Carls. Page 170: Werme; Werme; Werme; Werme.

Page 171: Werme; Werme; Werme. Page 172: Werme. Page 173: SDHS Archive; SDHS Archive; SDHS Archive, Simmons Collection; SDHS Archive; SDHS Archive, Simmons Collection; Werme; SDHS Archive; SDHS Archive; SDHS Archive, Oleson Collection; Mark Cook, artist, Concerned Citizens for Saugatuck Dunes; Map, Ken Carls.

A History of the Buildings and Architecture in the Saugatuck and Douglas Area

INDEX

Note: for specific listings of cottages by owner or name, see "Cottages;" for churches, see "Churches;" for hotels, boarding houses, B&Bs, see "Hotels…;" for motels, see "Motels."

A
Adams, A. T., 11
—house, 11
Addams, Jane, 66
Aladdin Homes Company, Bay City, Michigan, 58
Alcohol, Taverns, drink issue, 4, 9, 12, 13, 21, 26-27, 78, 114, 136, 137
—Union Ale, 69
All Saint's Episcopal Church, 24, 25, 29, 114, 130
—Parish Hall, 115
—Retreat House, 121
Allahee Lodge, 83, 89
Allen, F. P. and Sons
—architect, 112
Allen, William, 97
Alvord Bridge, 91
Alvord, John, 107
—architect, 100, 168
—bridge, 91
—cottage (see cottage)
American Institute of Interior Design, 131
Ames, Captain Richard, 28, 48
—house, 28
Amity Motel (see motel)
Anthony, Susan B., 12, 26, 34
Anthrop, Judy, 86, —house, 124
Anti-Semitism, 72
Applecrest Inn, 67
Architecture, defined, 6
Architectural styles, see Art Moderne, Bungalow, Carpenter Gothic, Country Gothic, Folk Victorian, Colonial Revival, Arts & Crafts, Stick Style
Arrowhead Resort Motel, 140
Art Moderne, 135
Art 'Round Town, 170
Artist Guild, 124
Arts & Crafts, 23, 94-107, 124, 127, 130, 131, 139
—inscriptions, 101
Astor House, 12
Auction House Restaurant, 39
Auburn Station and Garage (see service station)
Automobile/automobile culture, 132-138, 141, 147
Avalon Cottage, 83

B
B&Bs, see Hotels
Back-to-nature movement, 118, 138
Baker, Wallin-Smith House, 29
Ball, Mead-Nyson House, 32
Ball, John, Restaurant, 63
Balloon frame, 29, 33, 48, 50
Bandle, James H., 70
Barns, 29
—Art, 56
—Bird, 54
—Douglas Livery, 135
—Erlandson's, 54
—Gerber, 54
—Keller, 53
—New, 156-157
—Till, 52, 153-155
—Tillstrom, 53
—Walker-Borough, 54
Barnett, George D.
—architect, 125
Barr, Henry and Olga, 48
—house, 31
Barto, D. O., 83, 93, 160
Basil, Larry, architect, 170
Basket factory, 25, 111
—Douglas, 50, 51, 54, today, 160
—Saugatuck, 48, 51
Batavia Resort, 70
—Halverson Farm, 70
Baty, Bud & Max Matteson
—designers, 15
Bauer House, 165
Bay Building, 152
Bayou House, 162
Beach grass, 171
Beach House, Oval Beach, 145
—Douglas. 144
—Till, 52, 153-155
—Beach culture, 131, 145
Beachmont, 69 (see Hotels, Boarding Houses, Inns)
Beachway Hotel, 69 (see Hotels, Boarding Houses, Inns)
Bed & Breakfast houses, 170 (see also Hotels, Boarding Houses, Inns)
Beech-Hurst Farmhouse, 122
Beechwood Manor (see Hotels, Boarding Houses, Inns)
Bekken, Herman, blacksmith-shop, 17
Bella/Dark House, 166
Belvedere Farm and House Inn, 120, 145
Bendixon, Lillian, 124
Bennett Mansion, 17
Bennett, David A., 117
Benton, Thomas, 71
Berrien County, 43
Beyster, H. E. and Associates, architects, 144
Big Pavilion, 74, 75, 77, 78, 119, 136, 137, 141
—Fire, 137
Big Pool, 127
Bird Center Resort, 71, 138
Bird, Carrie and Elsie, 37, 67
—Charles, E., 43
—Deziah and Henry, Jr., 28
—Drug Store, 37
—H. M., 97
—house, 28-29
Blackie the Hobo, 131
Blacksmith shop, 17, 69
Bleeker House, 49
Bliss 83, 89
Blue Star Memorial Highway, 133, 174
Blue Tempo Bar, 142 (see also Gay History)
Boarding houses, 13, 66 (see Hotels, Boarding Houses, Inns)
Boat building and ship yards, 43, 65
Boating, 137
Bonnie Meadows, 30
Bowman House, 164
Braced frame construction, 7
Bradley House, 11
Brandess Gallery, 170

Breuckman, Minnie, 121
Brewery, 69
Brittain, Captain R. C., 33, 47, 49
—house, 14, map, 47
—Leonard, 47
Brown, Duane, 161
Browning Path, 93
Bryan, Ellen, 69
—Rosemont Inn, 67
Buffalo House, 150
Bungalow style houses, 94-96
Burn's IGA grocery, 143
Burnham Residence, 64
Burnham, Daniel, 30, 66, 107
Burns, Ed and Marge, 127
Burns, Johanna, 48
Burns-Yaksic House, 32
Busy Bee Café, 97
Butler, William and Mary,1, 3, 93
—William G., 2
Byrd, Duncan, and house, 96

C
C. Whitney and Company, 50
Cabin Bar, The, 37
Camp Gray, 93
Camp Uneeda Rest, 80
Campbell, Alex, 87
Campbell, Captain John B., 48
Campbell, Captain John, 32
Campbell, John, 71
Cannarsa-Phillips House, 165
Cappelletti House, 31
Captain Phelps, 57
Captains houses, see Ship Captains
Carlson, Charles Kenneth, architect, 139, 171
Carpenter Gothic, 22, 24, 29
Casablanca Hotel, 70, 136
Central Michigan University, 81
Century of Progress Exhibition (1933), 119, 130
Chain Ferry, 47, 127, 146, 171
Chalet Studio, 97, 130
Chambers, Col. B. C., 70
Chaps Restaurant, 39
Charlie's Ice Cream Shop, 64, 142
Chataqua (for the poor), 108
Cheney, Howard, architect, 120-121
Chestnut House, 161
Chicago, Art Institute, 131
—Economic and cultural influences, 1, 17, 43, 46, 62-69, 72-78, 81, 84, 93-94, 103-108, 1118-21, 130-131
—Urban Poor (see Forward Movement)
—Society of Artists, 72
Chicken-As-You-Like-It Restaurant, 142, 143
Churches, 21-25
—All Saints Episcopal, 22, 24, 26, 113, 115, 130, 152
—Children's Chapel of Lakeshore Chapel, 130l
—Christian Science Society, 60, 121
—Community Church of Douglas, 144
—Congregational (Douglas) United Church of Christ, 23, 26
—Congregational

(Saugatuck), 21-22
—Lakeshore Chapel, 130, 106, 108
—Methodist (Douglas), 23
—Methodist (Saugatuck), 23
—Pillar Church, Holland, 11
—Reformed, 21-22
—St. Peter's Catholic, 23, 25, 144, 161
Ciolek, David & Dave Scholten, 153
Clarke, George, 91
Clearbrook, 1
Clipson Brewery & Twin Gables Inn, 69
—Samuel, 69
Clute, Walter M., 72
Coates, Captain Charles, 47
—Captain L. B., 34
—Timothy, House, xii
Coburn, Walter and Betty, 141
Coghlin Park, 50, 173
Colonial Inn, 67
Colonial Revival, 118, 119, 120, 121, 122, 124, 125, 127, 128, 130, 131, 140
—defined, 116
—Village, 130
—Williamsburg, 119, 120, 130
Columbia Hotel, 69
Commercial fishing structures, 40
Community, defining of, 17-21, 113-115, 168-169
Comstock, A. J., 103, 110,
—House, 103
—Comstock, H. H., 4
Condominiums, 167
Congregational Church (United Church of Christ), 26
Congregational Church (see Churches)
Cook, 109
—Amy, designer, 165
—David C., 108, 117-118
—Mansion, 117
—Paul, designer, 171
Cool Cities, 149
Cooper, James Fenimore, 15, 28
Coral Gables, 64, 69, 136
Cottage Home, 156
Cottages, 84-94, 158, 168
—Alibi, 89, 102
—Alvord, 100
—Avalon, 83
—Barto, D. O., 83, 159-160
—Baty/Matteson, 166
—Beech-Hurt, 123
—Belle Rive, 158-159
—Benoist, 159
—Bird, 163
—Bliss 83, 89
—Delaney, 107, 125
—Duex Goose, 92
—Elam, 89
—Fern Hollow, 163
—Gage, 103
—Grand Street, 159
—Gray/Zerate, 89
—Hellmuth, 126
—High Camp, 89
—Hillside, 94
—Huff, 159
—Ibsen, 159
—Kamman, 99, 131
—Kemah, 104, 105

—Knollenberg/Jones, 131
—Lodge, 131
—Mack, 159-160
—McCormick, 89
—Mellander/Deem, 158-159
—Merrill, 98
—Moore, 85
—Nelson, 85
—Norton, 83
—Orchard House, 81
—Pike, 159
—Porter, 102
—Renaldi, 89
—Rose, 89
—Sandrift, 84
—Shafroth/Elam, 89
—Simmons, 81
—Smulski, 85
—Springer, 104, 105
—Stutzman, 131
—Swift, 108, 109
—Tallmadge, 86
—Thiele, 107, 125
—Thieda/Masters, 89
—Timber Bluff
—Tonawanda, 102
—Tree Tops, 86, 158
—Upton, 89, 90, 91
—Van Raalte, 89
—W. H. Simpson, 100
—Worthington, 87
—Yellow, 89
Cottagers, 93, new type, 149
Country Gothic, 22
Cozy Kitchen, 142
Craftsman style, 94, 168
Cranbrook, Bloomfield Hills, 81
Crawford, Captain George, 48, 49, 92
—House, 94
—Louise, 92
Cronon, William, 1
Crouse, Jonas S., 18, 49
—House, 44
Crow Bar, 136
Crow Hotel, 69
Cummings House, 147
Curtis House, 11
Curtis, 2
Curtis, Adams, 3
Curtis, William and Hope, 11
Curtis, William, 11

D
Dancing, 7, 8, 13, 20, 34, 74-79, 136-138, 141-142
Darienzo, D'Arienzo and Eickhoff
—designers 171
Dark, Bella/ House, 166
Dates, Albertine, 71
Daverman, J. and G., 120
Daverman, J. H. & Son
—architect, 59, 60
Davis Restaurant, 62
Davis, Alexander Jackson, 29
—Captain Benjamin W., 48
—Donald "Toad", 142
—James, 62
DDA, see Douglas
Deam, Arthur F., 4, 5, 75
Dedic, Jason, builder, 163
Deer Creek Inn, 28
Delaney, Mrs. and Mrs. John O'Fallon, 91, 107, 124-125, 131
Delaney-Theile Cottage, 125

Demerest, Demi, 138
Demeter, Ed and Marie, 142
Demond Supermarket (SuperValu), 143
Dengler, C. H., 56, 57
Denison Beach-Dunes Project, 173
Department Store, see Leland
Dew Drop Inn, 135
Dibble, Elias, 6
Dienhart, Walter A. and Miriam, 124
Dingleville, see Wallinville, 29
Dock Bar, 78, 137
Dole, James, 67
—Thomas, 12
Doucette House, 58, 60, 152
Doud/Sax House, history 162-163
Douglas, (see also, churches, schools, hotels)19, 23, 25, 26, 143
—Athletic Club, 23
—Basket Factory, 50, 51, 64, 160
—Beach House, 114
—Boats, 43
—Dinette
—Everyday People Café, 38
—Community Church, 144
—Council, 167
—DDA (Downtown Development), 162
—Dunes Resort, 140, 141
—Elementary School, 144
—Heritage Preservation Committee, 162
—Historic building renaissance, 161
—Hospital, 59
—House, 2, 7, 12
—Methodist Sunday School, 30
—Soda Bar and Grill, 38
—Union School, 18, 19
—Village Hall, 20
Douglas Dunes Resort, 140-41, 170
Downing, Andrew Jackson, 22, 25, 27, 29
Dock Bar, 78, 136-137
Duck Pin bowling alley, 63
Dudleyville, 2, 7
Dunes Resort, see Douglas Dunes Resort
Dunes View Cabins, 139
Dunn, George E., 2
Dunning, William, 24
Durham, Gordon, 19
Dutch Colonial, 127
Dutcher, 1, 9
—George N., 31, 33
—House, 11-12
—Lodge (Masonic), 20
—Thomas Benton, 20
—William F., 12
Dutcher-Mark House, 33, reconstruction, 162
Dvorak, Miss Mildred, 140

E
E. E. Weed & Company, 50, 51
Eagle House Hotel, 2, 7, 12
Eckdahl Twins, 19
Eddy, Benjamin, 123

—Lillian and Scott 39, 122-123
—Raymond, 123
—Scott, 123
Edgcomb House, 128
Ed-Mar, 142
Edwards Ltd. Store, 161
Edwin House, 108
El Tovar Lodge, 100
Elliott, Captain James, 43, 46, 47
Ellis House, 32
Elms Hotel, 67, 136
Emerson, Ralph Waldo, 80
Everyday People Café, 38, 161

F
Family life, 57, 109
Farm, Bandle, 130
—Dengler, 56
—Halverson, 70
—J. F. Taylor's Lake Ridge, 43
—Lake Ridge, 49
—Orchard, 122
—Riverside, 43, 56
—Shorewood, 49
—Streamland-Quiet Creek, 56
—Terrace Park, 65
—Till, 153
—Walbrecht, 28
—Weed 28
—West Fruit, 46
—Windover, 30
Farmhouse, Barr, 48
—Beech-Hurst, 122-123
—Belvedere, 110
—Cappelletti, 48
—Graham, 30
—Harvey L. House, 46
—Sorensen, 46
—Spencer, 50
—Wallbrecht-Dugan, 28
—Whitney, 48
—Weed, 45
—Williams, 46
Fast Food, 142
Faucett, Rachel and Emily, 120
Felt, Dorr E., 112
—Mansion, 112, 113
Fernwood, 45
Field, Howard Associates, 144
Fifties Modern, 143
Finley, John and Elenora, 123
—William, 142
Fire, 137, 142
—Fighting, 27
—Fire House, 21, 63
Fires of 1871, 43
Fishing, commercial, shanties,,4, 40, 138
Fishtown, 4, 40, 130
Flats, the, 16, 22
Flint, company,, 21, house, 31, family, 31
Flour (grist) mill, 111
Folk Gothic, 124
Folk Victorian, folk-farmhouse, 28, 29, 80, 89
Ford Garage, 40
Forward Movement, 80
—Association Camp/Park, 72, 91, 108
—Park, 91
Fowler, Orson, 34, 35
Fox, Johnson, 19
—House, 152

Francis, John, 67
Freeman and Newnham's Garage, 133
Frolic Inn, 31, 67
Fruit Exchange in Saugatuck, 111
Fruit Growers-farming, 43-44, 50-51
Fruit Growers State Bank, 50, 62
Fursman, Frederick, 72, 73, 118, 119, 120
—House, 118

G

Gage, Jean Richardson, 102
Gallas, George and Joann, 151
Galligan House, 146
Gamble, William, 109
Gammons, Jennings- House, 57
Ganges, 1, 3
Garage, various, 133-136 (see Service Station)
Garage, Freeman and Newnham, 133
Garesché, Marie, 131
Garlinghouse Plan Service, 147
Gas station (see service station)
Gay and lesbian history, 37, 67, 140, 141, 161
—Bar/Resorts, 140-142, 170
Gerber family, 1, 31, 37
—Center Street building restoration, 161
—Daniel, 17, 63, 151
—Tannery, 28
Glasow's Goven shipyard, 172
Globe, Tavern, 26
Goldsmith, Jean, house, 116
Good Goods (see White House), 32, 67
Goodrich, Dr. Asa House, 32-33
Gordon Spencer's country store, 37
Goshorn, 1, creek, 29, lake, 27
Gotham, Lou, 138
Gothic Revival, 24, 26, 28, 29, 34, 100, 124
Grace Hotel, 70
Graham, Hugh F., 26, 31, 46, 49
Ganges Post Office, 30
Ganges's first Post Office, 39
Gray, Reverend George, 72, 108-109
—Thomas, 32
Great Bonanza Merchant, 32
Greek Revival, ?,9, 10, 11, 12, 27, 28, 34, 45, 49, 123
—How to Identify, 11
Green Space, 170-173, see also Public Space
Gregersen, David, house, design, 166
Greyhound Bus Depot, 39
Griffin & Henry mill, 17
Guild, Mr., 103)

H

H. B. (Harry) Moore House, 34
Hackley, Charles, 33
Haile, James, 12,
—Tavern, 8, 9
Hamburg-New York Steamship Line, 60
Hames, George, 24, 42

Hamilton Hotel (Saugatuck House)
Hampstead, New Hampshire, 5
Hans, Mary, 19
Harbart, W. S-family, cottage, 83, 108-109
Harding Hotel, 136
Harris pie factory, 169
Hatfield, R. G., architect, 25
Haver, Rick, 162, contractor, 158
Heath, Block Building, 37, 62, 63
—D. A. "Doc", 62, 63
—May Francis, 128, 130, 175
—George P., 17
—George P., steamboat, 47
—House, 127, 128
—Judson 8, 12
—Judson, House, 7
Hedgerow Villa, 671
Hellmuth, George, 127, 131
—Harry and George, architects, 107, 126
—Harry, 131
—(HOK) Obata and Kasabaum, 131
Helmer, Robert, 123
Henry Schnobel's Hardware, 41
Henry, John and Isabel, 67
Hewett, Erwin and Abigail, 123
High Camp, 89
Hilaire, 131
Hillman, Judy, designer, 170
Hoerman, Carl, architect, 97, 98, 99104, 114-115, 120, 127, 130, 150
HOK, Hellmuth,Obata, Kassabaum, architects, 126
Holabard, Roche, Simonds, architects, 81, 93
Holiday Hill-Marina resort, 141
Holland, Dorothy Garesché, 134
Hoogterp, Reverend William J., 144
Hooker, Mary, 100
Hotels, Boarding Houses, Inns, B&Bs (see also, Motels)
—Batavia Resort, 70
—Beachmont 67, 69
—Beachway Hotel 69
—Belvedere Inn, 120
—Butler Hotel, 64, 71, 119-120, 136
—Casablanca, 70, 136
—Coral Gables 67, 69, 136
—Colonial Inn, 67
—Deer Creek Inn, 28
—Douglas House, 170
—Eagle House 2, 7, 2
—Elms 67, 136
—Grace Hotel, 70
—Hamilton Hotel, 6
—Hedgerow Villa, 76
—Howard's Inn 70
—Idlease Hotel, 69, 71
—Idler's Rest, 67
—Ivy Inn, 170
—Kalamazoo Hotel 69
—Kirby House 59-60
—Lake Kalamazoo House, 69
—Leindecker Hotel 67, 69, 136
—Maplewood 71, 72, 120-121, 131, 136
—Moore's Creek, 170
—Mt. Baldhead, 16

—New England Home, 67
—Newark House Hotel, 35
—Newnham Inn, 67
—Park House, 12, 34, 67
—Pokagon Hotel, 67, 69, 71
—Riverside Inn 72-73
—Riverside Rest 70
—Roamer's Inn, 70
—Rosemont Resort 69
—Saugatuck House Hotel
—Sherwood Forest Inn 58
—Shriver's Inn 73
—Sprucewood Cabins, 71
—Timber Bluff Cottages, 158
—Tourist Home Hotel 51, 64, 69, 71, 75, 136, 141
—Twin Gables Inn 69, 71
—Twin Oakes Inn 67
—Union Hotel 12
—Union House Hotel 26
—Utopia, 67
—Valentine Lodge 69, 71
—Victorian Inn 61
—Wickwood Inn, 170
—White House Hotel, 32, 67
House, Dr. W. B., 114
—Edwin, 56
—Harvey, 56
—Roadside Market, 56
Houtcamp, "Ellie", 19
Howard, Lillian, 70
Howard's Inn, 70
Huff, Captain H. John, 48
Hull House, 94
Hunn, Florence Ely "Danny", architect, 42, 102, 131
Hurst, John & Bonnie Keller, design, 170
—John, architect, 86

I

Idlease Hotel, 69, 71
Idler's Rest, 67
IGA Store, 127
IGA Grocery, 127 (see Van Syckel)
Illinois Athletic Club, 125
Indians, Native Americans, 3, 7, 15, 51, 75, 15, 110
—Chief Blue Sky, 67
—Corn Field, 2
—Burial ground, 120
—Ojibwa, 6
—Ottawa, 6
—Papooses, 5
—Pewabic Pottery, 94
—Property righst, 2
Interurban train station, 119
International Style Art Deco, 118, 141
Iron-Clad Basket Factory, 48, 51
Italianate architecture, 29-37, 45, 48

J

Johnson and Stockbridge Sawmill, 14
Jarzembowski Builders, 53, 164
Jefferson, Thomas, 9, 10
Jenkins, A. E., 14
—House, 14, 15
Jennings/Gammons House, 57
Jewish visitors, see anti-semitism
Job, Frederick W., 28-29, 121
Johansen, John C., 72

John Ball Restaurant, 63
Johnson, Elwin, 63
Johnson, John Butler, 80
—Elwin, 135
—House, 28
—O. R., 33, 47
—O. R. sawmill, 17
—Robert Butler, 82
—Samuel, 67
Jordan family, 102
Jousma, Mr. and Mrs., 139
Judson, Elnathan, 7

K

Kalamazoo Hotel, 69
Kalamont, 32, 33
Keewatin, steamship, 172
Keller Building, 170
Keltner, Cordelia, 19
Kemah, 104-105, 130 (see also, Springer, Hoerman)
Kerr Building, 38
Kilwin's Confectionery, 21, 152
Kimball, Ted, 143
Kirby House, 59, 60, restoration, 161
—Sarah Gill, 59, 60
Kirkland, Wallace, 72
Kleeman, T. F., 12,
—Residence, 9
Koberink, Bob, 168
Koning Hardware Store, 60
—House, 60, 120
—House-Victorian Inn, 61
—Ira
—house, 120
—John, 60
Kraemer's Feed Mill & Store, 111
Kreager, Dr., 63
Kreager, Herman, 60
Kunstler, James Howard, 149
Kurz, George, builder, 58, 59, 107, 118, 124-125, 131

L

Lake Home Builders, 164
Lake House, 26
Lake Kalamazoo, 167
—House, 59, 71
Lakeshore Agricultural Society, 18
Lakeshore Chapel, 100, 106, 107
Laketown Township, 111, 112
Lakeview Lanes, 143
Land Conservancy of West Michigan, 173
Landis Lodge, 100, 101
Landmark Building, 20, 21, 36
Leather Tanning (Factory), 17
Leet Walk (Helen), 91
Leindecker Hotel, 67, 69, 136
Leland, Department Store, 62-63
—Alley, 63
—Captain Thornton W., 49, 63
—Lee Leland, Leland Lodge, 6
Lighthouse Realty, 170
Lighthouse, 4, 5, 11
Limbert, Charles, 94
Lion House, 124
Lloyd, Gordon W., architect, 22, 24, 29
Log Cabins, 6, 64, 142

Log House, 3
Looman Construction, 33, 166
Loomis House, 3
Lucky, Jim, architect, 165
Ludwig, Keith, 28
Lundberg's Dew-Drop Inn, 133
Lumber trade, 1-2, 17,43, 61
Lyon House, 165

M

M&M's, 142
M-11, 133
MacDonald's Central Store, 38
Maher, George W., 80, 100, 114, 120, 130
—architect, 101, 150, 212
Maplewood Hotel, 71, 72, 120, 121, 131, 136
Marinas, 146
Mark House, 33, reconstruction, 162
Market, House's Roadside, 56
Marriott, Robert, 127
Marsh, Hollister F., 12
Marsh's General Store, 12
Marshall Field's, Chicago, 107
Marshall House, 5
Martel, John Baptiste, 31, 43
—House, 131, restoration, 152
Martin, Kevin & Duane Brown, designers, 163
Mason, Michael and Alice, 72
Mason Street Warehouse theatre, 145
Masterson/Spooner House, 158
McComb, Molenaar/ House, 166
McCormick, James, 3
McDonald Corporation, local opposition to, 142
McDonald, Crawford, 17
—L. W., "People's" Store, 63
McGraff, Mr., 135
McVea, Bill and Gertrude, 134
—Elizabeth, Homestead, 67
—Grocery, 133
—Rachel, 37
—Store & Gas Station, 134
Meckley, Richard, construction, 166
Megis, Joseph P., 140
Merrill, Peterson, 131
Methodist Church, 2, 23, 143
—Parsonage, Pier Cove, 2
Meyer, Scherer, & Rockcastle, 164
Michigan Council for the Arts and Cultural Affairs, 169
Michigan Natural Resources Fund, 173
Michigan's Cool Cities, 149
Millar Brothers Station, 133, 134
—House, 146, 147
—Orville and Stephen, 134
—Orville, 147
Millinery Shop, 38
Miser, Captain and Mrs., 34
Mixer Addition, 35
—Captain Charles, 35, 46
Molenaar/McComb House, 166
Moore, Harry B., 34
—H. D., 12, 34, 39
Mooreville, 34
Morrison, 1, 3, 9
—Hall, 21

—Home, 7
—House, 6, 28
—Julia E., 3
—Stephen A., 2, 20, 28
Motels, 138
—Amity Motel-Dunes Resort, 140, 141
—Arrowhead Resort Motel, 140
—Captain's Quarters, 171
—Douglas Dunes, 140-141, 170
—Miro, 140
—Pines, 139
—Pine Crest Tourist Inn, 140
—Saugatuck Lodges/Tin Cricket, 139
—Ship 'n shore Motel-Boatel, 141
—Timberline, 141
Mt. Baldhead, 16
—Hotel, 51, 69, 71, 136
Mulder House, 14, 15
Music, Big Band, 78

N

National Houses, 146
Nature Conservancy of Michigan, 173
Neidlinger, Mark, designer, 163
Neiman, LeRoy, 72
Nelson House, 28
New England Home, 67
New Richmond, 51
Newark, 1, 35
Newark House Hotel, 35
Newnham, Harry, 67
—Inn, 67
—Richard's Post Card Shop, 64
Nichols, Moses, 4
—farmstead, 70
—Stephen D., 4, 5
Nicolas Building, 37
Nies-Koning's Hardware Store, 60
Night clubs, 136
Nikols House, 2
Norton, John Warner, 39, 72, 73
Nysson, Albert, and house, 31-32

O

Oak Manor, 11
Oak Openings, 28
Octagon House, 34, 35, restoration, 162
Odd Fellows Lodge, 20
Oldenburg, Claes, 72
Olendorf, Bill, 72
Olmstead, Frederick Law, 107
Oosting Home Store, 147
Opera house, 21
Orchard House, 2
Orchards, 43, 51
Orville Oval Beach, 127, 132, 173
—Beach house, 144
Ox-Bow, 114
—Inn, 73
—Studios removed,150
—Summer School of Painting, see Schools

P

Paderewski, Ignace Jan, 85
Papageorge, George, architect, 166
Park Addition, 138
Park House, see Hotels
Parks, Emily, 136
Parsonage, Pier Cove, 11
Paschke, Ed, 72
Peach Belt School, 156, 158
—Store, 37
Peaches, 43
Peanut Butter & Jelly House, 165
Peoples Store, 143
Perkins, Fellows, & Hamilton, architects, 110
Perryman, E. S., 67
Peterson, R. E., 146
Petter Gallery, 145, 161
Phelps, W. G., 71, House, 95
Pier Cove, 1, 2, 131, map, 2
—Forest, 156
—Ravine, 93
Pine Crest Tourist Court, 138, 140
Pine Grove School, 119
Plank house, construction, 3
Plaza Tourist Court, 139
Pluim family, 144
Plummer, 1
—Captain George, 46, 57
—House, 57
—Jennings/Gammon House, 57
Point Pleasant Garden House, 160
Pokagon Inn, 67, 69, 71
Pond House, 122
Porches, 80, 82
Port Washington, Wisconsin, Lighthouse, 5
Port-O-Call, 143
Post-and-girt system, 7
Prairie Style, 81, 84, 100, 103, 130, 131
Prentice, Joseph W., 50, 111
—Mrs., 111
—Willard, 50
Presbyterian Camp, 80, 132 (see Forward Movement)
Preserve America, 150
Public spaces,17, 20-21, 170, 174, see also Green Space
—bathing beaches, 171
—camp, 171
—hiking trail, 171
Pump House Gym, 170, 171
Pumpernickels Restaurant, 12
Putnam's General Store and Post Office, 36-37

Q

Queen Anne architecture, 57, 59, 60, 61, 62
—how to identify, 58
Queen Victoria, 27

R

Ranch style houses, 146, 147
Randolph House, 15, 29
Recycling of buildings, 156
Red Barn Theater, 145
Red Dock, 172
Red House, The, 164
Red Ribbon Club, The, 26
Redebaugh, Charles, 71

A History of the Buildings and Architecture in the Saugatuck and Douglas Area

Reed, Samuel, 67
—Roger Feed and Livery Store, 62
—Livery, Transfer Line & Feed Store, 63
Reformed Church, 21, 22
Reiser, Gus and Pauline, 134
Reid Theater, Saugatuck Center for the Arts, 169
Renaldi, Ann, 80, 88
Respite Coffee house, 161
Retail trade, decline of, 143
Rich's Pie Factory, 169
Richards, Charles, 3
—Jacob, 28
Rieske House, 166
Riley-Slack-Ellis House, 32
River Guild, 97, restoration, 161
Riverfront, 69
Riverside Inn, 72, 73
Riverside Rest, 70
Roadside Architecture, 133
Roamers' Inn, 70
Roaring Twenties, 111
Robinson, Miller, 37
Rockefeller, John D., 119, 121
Rogers, Reuben, 43
—Robert J., 140
Root Beer Barrel, 142
Rosemont Resort, 69
Rotonda, John, designer, 166
Rupprecht, Edgar and Isabel, 72
Russell, Robert, 69

S
Saloons, see Taverns
Samuel Johnson House, 31
Sante Fe Gallery, 170
Saugatuck, 23 (see also, churches, schools, hotels)
—Art Association, 120
—Art Gallery, 170
—Center for the Arts (SCA), 145, 168
—Chamber of Commerce, 127
—Congregational Church, 21, 130
—Drug Store, 6
—Entrance sign restored, 149, 151
—Fruit Exchange, 50
—Harbor, 4
—Historic District, 158-160, 174-175
—Lighthouse, 75
—Municipal water system, 168
—Service Station, 133
—Township Offices, 63
—Union School, 19
—Village Hall, 110, 120-121, 130
—Woman's Club, 120, 121, 130
—Woods, 156
—Yacht Club, 146
Saugatuck-Douglas District Library, 23
Saugatuck-Douglas Historical Society, 168-169, 175
Save Our Shoreline group, 174
Sax House, 162
SCA (see Saugatuck Center for the Arts)

Schaberg, John, 49
Schipper/Seros House, 165
Schools, Saugatuck/Douglas, 17-19, 144
—Ox-Box Summer School of Painting, 5, 79-71, 120-121, 130
—Peach Belt, 156, 158t
—Pine Grove, 118, 120
—Taylor Art School, 73
Schnobel, Adolph, 41,
—Henry, 36
Schoeneich House, 32
Schuitema House, 33
Schultz, Christopher, 7
Sears, Roebuck and Company, houses, 58, 128
Seros, Schipper/ House, 165
Seven Gables, House of, 25
Service Station/gas stations, 133-136
—Auburn, 135
—Force, Ed, Snug Harbor, 135
—Freeman & Newnham, 135
—Lundberg, 135
—McVea's Store & Gas Station, 134
—Millar Brothers, 133-134
—Rasmussen, Ray, Lighthouse, 135
—Reiser's, 133-134
—Saugatuck, 133, 135
—Van Syckel's Station, 133, 127
—Wright's, 135
Sewers, George, 138
Seymour, Herschel, 51
Shafer House, 53
Shafroth-Elam Cottage, 89
Sherwood Forest Inn, 58
Shingle mills, 43
Ship Captains, 43- 47
—Houses, listing, 46-47, map 4746
Shorewood, 107
Shorey, Dr. and Mrs. William, 168
Shriver, docks, 40
—Charles and Henry, 73
—Charles family, 73
—Shriver's Inn, 73
Shumann, Olga H., 153
Silverstein, Shel, 72
Simonds, 2, 81
—O. C., 81, 93, 94
—Orchard House, 12, 80
Simonson, Herman, and studio, 66,
Singapore, 2, 13, 14
—Bank building, 170
—lumber mills, 15, 33, 43
—Yacht Club, 146
Slack House, 32
Smart growth, 175
Smith-Wallin House
Snout houses, 156
Soda Lounge, 62
Spangler House, 165
Spencer, Michael and Matilda, 18
—Michael B., 50
—Robert C. Jr., 103
—Robert Jr.
—architect, 103
Spooner, Masterson/ House, 158
Springer, William and Alys, 104
St. Augustine Seminary, 112

St. Peter's Catholic Church, 23, 25, 144
—School, 65, 143, 160
Stafford, Dawn, 158
Stage Coach Stop, 8
Stanton, Solomon, blacksmith, 69
Steamboat, George P. Heath, 47
Stearns, Fred, 111, 141
Stick Style, 100
Stickley Brothers, 94
Stimson, Dr., and building, 36
Stockbridge, 34
—Francis B., 29, 33
—sawmill, 14
Streamland Farm-Quiet Creek, 55, 152
Streamlining, 118
Street, history of, 39
Strip-Malls, 149
Suburban living, suburbanization, 111,156
SuperValu supermarket, 143
Sutton, Warner P., 22

T
Tallmadge, Thomas Eddy, 66, 72, 73, 118, 119, 120, 121, 130
—architect, 104, 121, 150
Tanning factories, 1, 29
Tara Restaurant, 50, 131, 136
Tastee Freeze, 142
Taverns (see also alcohol)
—Blue Tempo, 142
—Cabin Bar, 37
—Dock, 78, 137
—Globe
—Hailes, 9, 12
—Kleeman, 9
—Lake House, 26
Taylor, Cora Bliss, 75, 128
—A. B., 95
—Art School, 73
—J. F., 49
—Residence, 73
—Reverend J. Rice, 22, 24, 25, 29
—Studio, 73
—Wilcox House, 95
Teich, Steve, designer, house, 166
Television, impact of 138
Tents, 66
Terrace Park, 65, 66
Thatcher & Thompson, architects, 165
Theater, 145 (see also, Red Barn, Mason Street)
Thew House, 152
Thompson, Fred, 104
Thoreau, Henry David, 80
Thornton Leland's Department Store, 62
Till, 29
—Henry, 49, 57
—Barn restoration, 152-155
Tillingbast, Clark, 50
Timber Bluff cottages, 158
Tisdale, George, 28
—House, Deer Creek Inn, 28
—William Graham, 28
Tolstoy Road, 93
Tonawanda, 131
Tornado of 1956, 5
Toulouse Restaurant, 63

Tourism, 64, 65
Tourist Home, 51, 64, 69, 136
—Home Hotel, 71, 75, 141
Treaty Tree, 93
Trees, 49
Tri-Community Plan, 175
Truman, President Harry, 117
Trumbull, Captain, 58
Trumbull, Emma, Hedgerow Villa, 67
Tumble Inn Café & Recreation, 108
Turnbull, Captain, 58
Twin Gables Inn, 69, 71
Twin Oaks, 67

U
U. S. 31, 133
Ulbricht, Elsa, 120
Uncommon Grounds coffee house, 60, 142
Union Hotel, 12
Union House, 26
Union Schools (see Schools)
United Church of Christ (see Congregational Church, Douglas)
Upham, Captain Sherman, 21
Upton Cottage, 90-91
Urban sprawl, 149
Utopia, 67
Utton Family, 15,
—House, 15

V
Valentine Lodge, 69, 71
Van Dalson, Mrs., 83
Vander Muelen, builders, 156
Van Dyke, Martin & Sons, contractors, 144
Van Leeuwen House, 15, 29
Van Syckel Grocery, 127, 133
—Fire, 151
Veneration of Trees, 93
Vesuvius Gallery, 170
Victorian Architecture, 25, 27
Victorians, 27
Village Hall (see Saugatuck, Douglas)
Vincent House, 165

W
Wade, 12
—Fred, 171
—Jonathan, 2, 10
—House, 10, 11
—Nathan, 11
—Tavern, 2, 7
Walker, Dr. R. J. House, 28, 51
—Walker, Harry L. architect, 106, 108
Wallbrecht, Henry, 28, 43
Wallin, Alfred, 29
—Franklin B. and Orcelia, 29
—Franklin family, 29
—House, 29
—Tannery, 29
Wallinville, 1, 29
Walz, Edith, 50
—Fritz, 28
—Walker House, 28
Walz's Butcher Shop, 36, 37
War of 1812, 9, 12
Warren, Mabel ("Jim"), 131

Washington Market, 12
Water Street Gallery, 116, 170
Water Street House, 166
Watson and Tallmadge (see Tallmadge, Thomas Eddy)
Webster, Jim, 53
Weed, Elmer E., 45
—Joshua, House, 45
Weigert's Douglas Café, 39
Werme House, 164
Werme, Lesa, 153
West Winds Camp Grounds, 134
Wheeler House, 31
White House (Inn), 32, 67
—House, 31
Whitman, Walt, 80
Whitney, Calvin, 48, 51
—Basket Factory, 51
—House, 51
Wicks, Frank and Carrie, 120, 131
—Mrs. F. H., 72
—Park, 47
Wickwood, 128, 129
Wilcox House, 95
Wild Cat Mill-Town, 14
Wiley House, 120
Wilkin's Hardware, 60
Williams, B. S., 46, 49
—James and Caroline, 123
—Minnie, 50
Williamsburg, Virginia, 121
Williamson, John D., 110, 111
Wilson Ice Cream Shop, 143, 170
Wilson Memorial Pavilion, 168
Wilson, Captain W. P., 48, 49
Winslow House, 122
Winston House, 165
Wolbrink, A.O. Department Store, 39
Woman's Club, 120
Wood, Barry, architect, 166
Woodbury, Connecticut, 7
Woodland Realty, 170
—Building, 171
World Columbian Exhibition (1983), 46
Wright House, 29
Wright, Frank Lloyd, 34, 58, 66, 101, 106
Wright's Pavilion, 64

Y
Yaksic House, 32
Youth culture, 136

Z
Zomerlie Construction, 170
Zoning, 167, 175

SELECT BIBLIOGRAPHY

Budd, Nancy, *History of Lake Shore Chapel*, (1974)

Douma, Michael J. *Veneklasen Brick: A Family Company and A Unique 19th Century Dutch Architectural Movement in Michigan*.(2005)

Dunbar, Willis F., *Michigan: A History of the Wolverine State* (1971)

Fowler, Orson S., *The Octagon House: A Home for All* (Dover, 1973)

Handlin, David P., *The American Home: Architecture and Society, 1815-1915*, Boston and Toronto, (1979)

Heath, May Francis, *Early Memories of Saugatuck* (1930, 1953 edition)

Hutchins, Henry Hudson, *Recollections of the Pioners of Western Allegan County* (1919-25, reprinted 1977)

Hutchins, Henry Hudson, *Western Allegan County Pioneer Days* (1919-25, reprinted 1995)

Kemperman, William, and James Schmiechen, "A Walk Down Center Street [Douglas]" (1997)

Kemperman, William, Photo and Illustration Archive

Lane, Kit, "The Dustless Road to Happyland," *Chicago-Saugatuck Passenger Boats, 1859-1929* (1995)

Lane, Kit, *Douglas: Village of Friendliness* (1987)

Lane, Kit, ed., *Western Allegan County Michigan* (1988)

Lane, Kit, ed., *Allegan County Historical Atlas and Gazetteer* (1998)

Lane, Kit, *Painting the Town: A History of Art in Saugatuck and Douglas* (1997)

Lane, Kit, *Saugatuck, A Brief History, Illustrated* (1973)

Lane, Kit, *Saugatuck's Big Pavilion, The Briughtest Spot on the Great Lakes"* (1977)

Lane, Kit, *The Letters of William G. Butler and Other Saugatuck Tales* (1994)

Lane, Kit, *The Wreck of the Hippocampus and Other Tales of Saugatuck* (1992)

Lorenz, Charles J. *The Early History of Saugatuck and Singapore, Michigan 1830-1840* (1983)

McAlester, Virginia and Lee, *A Field Gujide to American Houses* (1993)

Oleson, Todd, Photo and Illustration Archive

Newsletter, "Inserts," Saugatuck-Douglas Historical Society, 1997-2006

Saugatuck-Douglas Historical Society Archives

Saugatuck and Douglas Township Assessment Rolls, 1848, 1863, 1867, 1869, 1899, 1920

Schmiechen, James, *Off the Record: A Pictorial History of Saugatuck in the '40s and '50s*. (with Jack Sheridan and Kit Lane) (2001).

Schmiechen, James, and William Kemperman, *Snapshots: A Saugatuck Album* (2003)

Schmitt, Peter, *Back to Nature: The Arcadian Myth in URban America* (1969, 1990)

Sheridan, James E., *Saugatuck Through the Years* (1982)

Wagenaar, Larry J., "Douglas: A Unique History of Community," unpublished m.s., (1987)

Wright, G., *Moralism and the Model Home: Domestic Architecture and Cultural Conflict in Chicago, 1873-1913* (1980)

Zimmerman, Cindy and Bob, *Ninety-five Years Young: The Story of the S. S. Keewatin, 1907-present* (2002)

COLOPHON

*This book was designed and composed by Ken Carls
for the Saugatuck-Douglas Historical Society and Museum.
The text is set in Adobe Garamond types.
One thousand five hundred copies were printed and bound with
soft covers at Crouse Printing in Champaign, Illinois.
A special numbered edition has been bound in cloth over board
at Lincoln Bookbindery in Urbana, Illinois
by Christopher Hohn and Tedra Ashley.*

APRIL 2006